AFRO-ASIA
AND
CONTEMPORARY POLITICS

AFRO-ASIA AND CONTEMPORARY POLITICS

Jagdish P. Sharma

ANAMIKA PUBLISHERS & DISTRIBUTORS (P) LTD.
4697/3, 21A, Ansari Road, Daryaganj
New Delhi 110002
Phones: 3201531, 3281655

First Published 2003

ISBN 81-7975-035-3

PRINTED IN INDIA

Published by Anamika Publishers & Distributors (P) Ltd., 4697/3, 21A, Ansari Road, Daryaganj, New Delhi 110002. Typeset by VGA, MU-61D, Pitampura, Delhi 110088 and Printed at Nagri Printers, Delhi.

Preface

The position that the Afro-Arab and Asian nations occupy in history is a unique one. India's relations with the Afro-Arab and Asian World constitute a vast and intricate tapestry woven from many strands. India has long been a consistent supporter of Afro-Arab-Asian causes. The fight against imperialism gave birth to freedom movements in both the regions and spawned nationalist leaders who gave new hope and direction to their people. The similarity of the plight of their countries and the common goal of independence from foreign rule brought together the nationalist leaders from the Afro-Arab and Asian region. A lot of social, political, economic, strategic and military changes and realignments have taken place in the last fifty years which have affected both India and the Afro-Arab-Asian world.

The post-cold war era has witnessed a profound transformation in the international environment, throwing up fresh challenges to the foreign policies of India and Afro-Arab-Asian World. India has sought to respond optimally to the dynamic, emerging situation, and to safeguard and promote the national interest in relation to the outside world. A major focus in India's Arab-Islamic and African foreign policy since the 1990s was to create an atmosphere of mutual trust and economic cooperation. In neighbouring Afghanistan the situation continues to be fluid and politically and economically unstable. India's policy remains firm in its support of the unity, sovereignty, territorial integrity and independence of Afghanistan. India kept in close touch with different parties and actors and continues to play a role in regional and international efforts to bring peace and stability in Afghanistan. India's positive and constructive interaction continued with Iran during the Presidency of President Rafsanjani and continues with his successor, President Khatami. India is keenly watching the democratic transition in Iran under the reformist agenda of President Khatami. In the economic and commercial field, the two sides took follow-up action on the decisions taken during the

Ninth India-Iran joint commission held at Tehran in February 1997. Agreements were signed pertaining to the inter-institutional cooperation between the two countries in areas like scientific research, training, technical cooperation etc. The trilateral agreement on international transit of goods between India, Iran and Turkmenistan came into force. This would greatly facilitate trade and reduce transit time in transport of goods between India and Central Asian Republics using Iranian ports and railways. Indo-Iranian cooperation was particularly fruitful during the anti-Taliban operations of US-led coalition in Afghanistan.

India continued to have very close and warm relations with the Central Asian states. The Central Asian region is of strategic, social, economic and political importance to India since it is situated practically in our neighbourhood. Over the centuries, India and the Central Asian states have had intensive interactions, both commercial and people-to-people, and shared many common values and perceptions. It is of significance that in the contemporary context, India and these republics share similar views on the dangers of religious fundamentalism, extremism and political and military intervention. Relations between India and the Central Asian states were marked by significant high-level visits. The Central Asian states are keen on increased levels of trade and greater economic cooperation with India. At the same time they were becoming increasingly concerned over the threat to peace in their region emanating from the Afghanistan-Pakistan axis. As Uzbek President Islam Karimov said, India is a natural ally of Uzbekistan in the fight against terrorism.

Indo-Turkish relations saw a high level of interaction through bilateral exchanges in political, economic, commercial and cultural fields. The rise of Taliban in Afghanistan had drawn India, Iran and Turkey closer together in their assessment of the new threats to regional security and stability. Both were deeply concerned over the forces of extremism and destabilisation.

The Gulf region, which is an area that adjoins our immediate neighbourbood, is of considerable importance to India's political, economic and strategic concerns. Traditionally, India has had close and cordial relations with the Gulf countries as history and geography have laid a stable foundation for an enduring affinity. In the case of Iraq, despite its traditional friendship. India has scrupulously adhered to the United Nations Security Council resolutions but would like the UN sanctions to be lifted in tandem with Iraqi compliance with the UNSC resolutions. Conscious of the hardships the Iraqi people are facing due to the economic sanctions, India has extended humanitarian relief to Iraq, including supply of milk powder and baby food, wheat, tea, medicines, medical equipment and stationary items.

India's relations with countries of West Asia and North Africa are multifaceted and are marked by mutual goodwill and warmth. Functional cooperation agreements with many countries in these regions were concluded. India extended steadfast support to the Arab and Palestine causes as well as the West Asia Peace process. India is deeply concerned at the current lack of progress in the Arab-Israeli Peace process, which has vitiated the atmosphere and threatened the implementation of the interim Oslo accords and the resumption of the final settlement negotiations. India called for speedy redeployment from the West Bank by the Israeli forces and eschewing of all unilateral acts particularly expansion and construction of new Jewish settlements. India maintained its steadfast support for the Palestinian cause. India's friendly relations with Palestine were given a new momentum by the state visit of President Yasser Arafat to India from 20-22 November 1997. During the visit, a Memorandum of Understanding on cooperation was signed between the Government of India and the Palestine Liberation Organisation, on behalf of the Palestine National Authority. The MOU provided for a structural framework for bilateral cooperation in diverse areas.

The union home minister L.K. Advani, who was on a four-day visit to Israel and the Palestinian territories in June 2001, called on President Arafat. Mr. Advani's trip was followed by a visit of Mr. Jaswant Singh, India's External Affairs Minister. Mr. Singh visited Israel for the first time. He called on President Arafat at Ramallah. India is yet to begin a serious economic relationship with the Palestinian areas, including the West Bank and Gaza Strip. Allaying apprehensions that India was tilting towards Israel and moving away from its traditional Arab friends, Mr. Jaswant Singh told journalists at the end of his four-day visit to Israel that New Delhi's ties with Tel Aviv were not at the cost of its "consistent" support to the Palestinian cause and their right of an internationally-recognised homeland. Israel sent its foreign minister on a visit to India to strengthen the friendly ties.

India's multi-faceted relations with the countries of Arab and African continent were further strengthened through exchange of visits. Leading among them was the Prime Minister Atal Behari Vajpayee's visit to Morocco and the return visit of Morocco's Prime Minister Abderrahmane El Youssoufi to India. The King of Morocco made an important visit to India. There were ministerial and official level contacts with several other countries and a number of agreements were signed. India's gesture of humanitarian assistance to Sudan and its human resource development under the ITEC programme were manifestation of India's commitment to South-South cooperation. Relations with Algeria continued to be marked by warmth and closeness. On the heels of the G-15 Summit held in Cairo in May 1998, Vice-President Mr. Krishna Kant met president Mr. Liamine Zeroul of Algeria. The President of Algeria Mr. Abdel Aziz Boutiflika was the guest of honour at our Republic Day parade in 2001. Bilateral ties of friendship, mutual understanding and cooperation with Egypt were strengthened. India's relations with Libya continued to be marked by understanding and cooperation. India had consistently worked for a just solution to the Lockerbie issue. Bilateral relations with Tunisia continued to develop satisfactorily. India maintained cordial relations and cooperation with the regional organisations, namely the League of Arab states and the Arab Maghreb union. As in the past, the recent years saw continuation of the high-level of interaction with the countries of African continent. However in a reversal of fifty years of non-aligned foreign policy—India suddenly withdrew recognition of the struggling Saharwi Democratic Republic (SADR). This has come as a surprising move. This is the first time in Independent India's history that India has de-recognised a nation, however disputed it may be. The Rajiv Gandhi government had accorded SADR recognition in 1985 in pursuance of the Non-Aligned movement's policy of reversing the wrongs of colonisation. The 1985 recognition reflected New Delhi's support to the United Nations efforts to organise a referendum to ascertain the wishes of Saharawi people who are locked in struggle with Morocco. Some of the African governments described the move as a "total surprise" from the Vajpayee government which, they said had acted under pressure from Morocco.

Ascendancy of conservative religious elements in the Arab-

African region has had a negative bearing on India's concerns as evidenced by the growing sympathy being shown by the Organisation of Islamic Conference (OIC) including at the 27th meeting of its foreign ministers held in Kuala Lumpur in the first week of July 2000, towards Pakistan's stance on Kashmir. India has stopped issuing knee-jerk reactions to the resolutions on Jammu and Kashmir passed at the behest of Pakistan by the various OIC meetings.

This book is essentially a collection of articles and papers which I had contributed to newspapers and journals or presented at national and international seminars and conferences. Since the articles have been written keeping in view the requirements of the media there could be some overlapping in the expression of views on changing developments. I have taken care to incorporate the historical backgrounds and present the latest events in the context of the relevant regional developments. The main objective of this book is to provide a comprehensive survey and developments of the main issues of contemporary history, politics and international affairs. It is in the hope that this book would provide a useful research and background publication that I am presenting it to the academic community, students and the general public in the book form.

I am grateful to some leading intellectuals who inspired me in my academic and literary pursuits from time to time. Among them are Professors Late Ram Rahul and K.R. Singh of Jawaharlal Nehru University and Professors Harjinder Singh, K. Mathews, Dr. Dharmpal, Mr. Attar Chand, Mr. K.M. Singh and Mr. S.K. Sawhney of the University of Delhi. I would also like to thank Mr. T.V. Venkitachalam (Chief Editor) and Mr. Shekhar Mehra of *National Herald* newspaper, Mr. Bharat Bhushan and Mr. Arun Kumar formerly of *Press Trust of India*, my wife Suraksha for helping and encouraging me, my son Manas for his patience in bearing with my day-to-day tasks, and my students Anand, Manoj, Manojranjan and Ranjeet. I am equally grateful to the staff of the Indian Council of World Affairs library and my publisher who ensured that this volume was prepared as quickly and efficiently as possible.

JAGDISH P. SHARMA

Contents

Afghanistan: Past and Present

1. Focus on Afghanistan

It is unfortunate that Afghanistan was in turmoil for nearly two decades. No nation has been left more ravaged than Afghanistan and none has suffered as much from direct foreign intervention and fundamentalist violence as this single country. The Afghan people are in agony, caught up in a spiral of militant and fanatic violence that has practically brought the state to its knees.

The emergence and capture of power by Taliban, a politico-military, radical Islamic force, in the later half of (on 27 September) 1996, supported by Pakistan, has confused the already complicated struggle for power in Kabul. Since the Taliban took over, violence has ruled the roost in most parts of Afghanistan followed by fanaticism that imposes restrictions on women, banning them from going to work and forbidding them from appearing in public unless covered from head-to-toe and forcing men to grow beards and pray at mosques. Replacing communism with an Islamic ideology has not helped in healing the divisions.

Afghanistan has been the focus of worldwide attention for more than two decades now. It was the last staging post for the Cold War confrontation, and the withdrawal of the Soviet troops from this country signified the end of the Cold War. While the end of the Cold War brought relative peace at the global level, peace and stability have eluded Afghanistan like a mirage.

Of late signals from the US indicate that American policy-making is reverting to Cold War policies in South Asian region which it seemed to have abandoned after withdrawal of Soviet forces from Afghanistan. Pakistan is again being armed discreetly to play the role which it had played during Cold War years, this time aimed at the oil reserves of Central Asian States, adjacent to Afghanistan, and also for cornering the Iranian regime which has been Washington's *bete noir* since 1979 when the pro-US Raza Shah Pehlavi was overthrown. The US administration has not taken kindly to the efforts of Tehran to establish close regional trade linkage between the Central Asian Republics and India.

After Soviet troops were withdrawn from Afghanistan in February 1989, the Islamic Mujahiddin, who had waged a (nearly) decade-long war of resistance, turned their guns on the Soviet-installed regime of President Najibullah. But it was not until the fall of communists in Moscow in August 1991 and the end of Soviet aid that they were able to deal a decisive blow to the Najibullah regime in Kabul.

The interim Mujahiddin government under President Burhanuddin Rabbani was sworn in 1992. Many were hopeful that with the fall of Kabul work would begin on the reconstruction of Afghanistan, the repatriation of refugees, and the installation of an elected government. This proved a wishful thinking. With the fall of communist regime in Kabul the last thread that had united the Mujahiddin was gone and old political divisions that had been suppressed in the name of Jihad re-emerged. The war had dramatically shifted the balance of power among the different Afghan ethnic groups.

Meanwhile, a new force emerged in the south. In late 1994, a group of Pashtun Islamic radical students and their leaders, allegedly trained in Pakistan, began to seize power from local Afghan warlords. By March 1995 they were at the gates of Kabul. Since then, the fighting in Afghanistan has marginalised the country. Afghanistan no longer exists as a single country but is divided into separate areas controlled by different militias.

However, continuous conflict in Afghanistan affected regional stability in Russia, Central Asia, Iran and India. Russia has warned the Taliban that should they succeed in getting their conflict to northern Afghanistan bordering Russia's southern neighbouring states of Uzbekistan, Tajikistan and Turkmenistan, Russia's role in the region would become inevitable. The Taliban occupation of Kabul, made the leaders of Russia, Kazakisthan, Krighizia, Uzbekistan and Tajikistan come together in Alma Ata. However, the leaders of the CIS states "concerned" found it possible not to enter into war against fundamentalism immediately. The Russian advocates of a strong state see the execution of former Afghan President Najibullah and fall of Kabul to Taliban militia as a fresh geopolitical defeat for Moscow after the decision on NATO's expansion to the East and the withdrawal of Russian federal forces from Chechnya.

India is concerned about Pakistan's (growing) influence in the Afghan region which is seen as a threat to its national security. This is the reason which has brought India and Iran closer. Iran has an ancient rivalry with the Pashtun Afghanistan from which the Taliban is drawn and is concerned that Sunni Taliban may dilute Iranian Shia influence in the region.

The other reason for concern is oil, gas and mineral resources in the Central Asian states. Pakistan wants a route through Taliban-controlled Afghanistan to Turkmenistan and Central Asian states, which would be independent of Russia. Iran has a direct link to Turkmenistan, and Turkey has a planned one.

Incidentally, for Iran, one more consequence of the Taliban's victorious advance on Kabul apparently was upsetting the peace-making plans for Afghan settlement which were initiated at Iran's Foreign Ministry. The October 1996 Teheran conference criticised the recent flagrant violations of human rights in Afghanistan, particularly the rights of women. It called for an immediate end to such practices in conformity with the relevant provisions of the UN Charter. Iranian Foreign Minister Ali Akbar Velayati announced that Iran would continue to stress a regional initiative to resolve the Afghanistan dispute. But he also made it clear that it could not be an isolated effort.

Compared to other neighbouring nations, Iranians have great affinity with the Afghan people. Common religion, history, culture, and especially language tie these two nations together so that the slightest socio-cultural or even political development in either of these countries makes an inevitable impact on the other.

Iran denounced the Soviet invasion and occupation of the Afghan territory in 1979 and called for the unconditional withdrawal of the Russian forces. After Soviet withdrawal (1988-89), Iran was among the first countries to recognise the Mujahiddin government there. Along with Turkey, Iran, Pakistan and the six Central Asian States, Afghanistan was included in the Economic Cooperation Organisation in 1993. Drug trafficking is another major factor that has affected Iran as a result of Afghanistan's instability.

India and Iran need to intensify coordination to get the warring factions in Afghanistan to the negotiating table, the Speaker of the Iranian Parliament, Mr. Nateq Noori, opined in his last visit to India. The visiting leader praised India for its contribution and participation at last October's conference on Afghanistan held in Teheran. Both India and Iran were also present at the subsequent UN sponsored conference on Afghanistan in New York.

Mr. Noori, who held wide-ranging discussions with Indian Prime Minister, Mr. H.D. Deve Gowda, the External Affairs Minister, Mr. I.K. Gujral, and other leaders said, India and Iran are coordinating to bring the warring factions together in Afghanistan to end the hostilities which would help usher an era of peace in that country.

"Wherever there is crisis it does affect the neighbouring areas. Any unsettled condition in Afghanistan is bound to affect Iran, India, Pakistan and Central Asian Republics. If the crisis drags on, it will harm Pakistan, more than anything else in terms of political stability and economic development", says Nasser Safhafi-Ameri, Deputy Chief of Mission, Embassy of the Islamic Republic of Iran, Delhi.

In the opinion of Iranian Ambassador to India, Mr. Ali Resa Sheigh Attar, "Afghanistan is a sensitive and vital issue for both India and Iran. India is a major player in Asian affairs hence it has the potential to establish peace in Afghanistan."

Current developments of Afghanistan are of considerable long-term relevance to India. More fighting in Afghanistan would continue to pose a risk not only to Afghanistan but it has a potential of spreading out to the whole South-West Asian and Central Asian region. It is likely to affect India-Pakistan relations quite adversely.

Afghanistan was the focus of attention in India's External Affairs Minister, I.K. Gujral's recent talks with the Iranian leaders, especially the role of the Taliban militia. India has also told Iran that the elements backing the Taliban are the same which have been trying to destabilise Kashmir through terrorism.

According to Mrs. Gillane Allam, Egyptian Ambassador to India, there is fallout of the Afghan crisis on the Arab world, Iran, Pakistan and South Asia. Arab countries, Mrs. Allam feels, are basically supportive of President Rabbani's government. It is only the Pakistani government who has got direct links with the Taliban militia. The assessment in Cairo now is that both the Rabbani and Taliban factions are losers in grasping power in

Afghanistan. There is no winner and no loser in that country except that the innocent Afghan people are suffering. The crisis there led Afghanistan to become the centre for the export of terrorism and fanaticism directed towards India, Egypt, Algeria and neighbouring Gulf. This hurts Islam in terms of its image, in terms of Hindu, Christian and other world.

"All the fundamentalists have been trained in Afghanistan and Pakistan", says Mr. Abdelhamid J. Bereksi, former Algerian Ambassador to India. He adds, "they have a great network serving in the Arab world. The link of Afghanistan with what is happening in Europe and Arab world is direct. Many youths have been brain washed, trained, armed and financed. The implications of the Afghan crisis for Algeria are very direct. Our people were trained and used in Afghan drama. I see no difference between the Algerian GIA (armed Islamic group), Jamite Islami in Egypt or Taliban in Afghanistan. What is happening in the name of religion in Afghanistan will open the eyes of Muslim nations. Taliban is using the religion of Islam as a political and military weapon. In a Muslim country one must have the courage to say that this is religion and this is politics. Islamists represent only the past which is totally dead".

The financing of the Islamic militant movements has played a significant part in their success. In Egypt, Sudan and Afghanistan, large amounts of external money, especially from Saudi Arabia, contributed to the strength of these groups. Money has been regularly and broadly distributed by Saudi Arabia to Islamist movements worldwide for many decades, especially after 1980, in an effort to influence them and strengthen them against Iranian pretensions to the leadership of Islamism. Some 2,000 Algerians were recruited by the Saudi-based World Muslim League and went through Jeddah on their way to training camps in Pakistan before taking on Soviet occupation forces in Afghanistan. By 1992 most of them had been repatriated to Algeria.

Neither the OIC nor Syria recognised the Taliban militia in Kabul. It does not want the religious conservatives to take Afghanistan five hundred years back to history. "We are all for the peaceful settlement of the Afghan crisis. The only solution to the turmoil in Afghanistan is to have all factions come and sit together rationally and to think about a situation of peace. They are killing themselves and their brethren. There is no justification for such killing of brothers, children and women in the name of Islam," said Mr. Ali Mansour, former Syrian Representative in India.

Reacting to the response of the Arab world, Mr. Masood Khalili, Afghan Ambassador to India says "the Arab world helped us during the war against Soviet occupation. Now they have passively reacted to the emergence of Taliban militia. While the Arab world (52 countries) follows the policy of wait and watch, only one non-Arab Islamic neighbour Pakistan is behind them. Common people, especially the women in the Arab world, see the Taliban imposition as going back to pre-Islamic era".

"Our formula to the solution of Afghan crisis is very clear", Mr. Khalili reiterated. "Let us solve the problem politically, that is, one, Taliban must leave Kabul; we also withdraw from Kabul; two, to demilitarise Kabul; and three, we both work on a broad-based formula of ceasefire, elections and elected government. In this interim period a neutral hand or third force or the UN should take over the administration of Kabul. The peaceful political negotiations should include all ethnic groups in Afghanistan (Pushtun, Taziks, Hizarah, Uzbeks). Military conquest and destruction is no solution to the present crisis in Afghanistan", concluded Mr. Khalili.

The situation in Afghanistan turned for the better with the rout of the Taliban. The interim administration headed by Mr. Hamid Karzai has embarked on the daunting task of restoring peace and development with international aid.

2. Afghanistan: A Study

Peace has again eluded Afghanistan with the imposition of sanctions by the United Nations and suspension of the latest talks, aimed at ending two decades of war, continuing instability and socio-economic and political crisis. Ignoring last-minute pleas by the ruling Taliban militia for a temporary postponement of the imposition of sanctions, the United Nations went ahead (on November 14, 1999) to slap punitive sanctions on Afghanistan demanding the arrest and turning over the suspected Islamic terrorist Osama bin Laden for trial on charges of plotting the 1998 bombings of US embassies in Africa.

The UN Security Council did not formally meet to consider the request of the Islamist Taliban militia. Under the terms of the world body, all overseas assets of the Taliban are to be frozen and blanket ban imposed on flights owned, operated or leased by the Ariana Afghan Airlines. Humanitarian assistance and flights for the pilgrimage to Mecca would be exempted. In addition to demanding Bin Laden's handover, UN resolution 1267 also took the Taliban militia to task for abuse of human rights, mistreatment and slavery of women, use (by force) of child soldiers, opium production and last year's assault on the Iranian consulate in Mazar-i-Sharif.

The US initiated resolution received the votes of all 15 Council members, although Malaysia and Bahrain expressed concern about the effects on ordinary Afghans, and China also expressed some reservations. At least 225 people were killed and more than 4,000 wounded in the almost simultaneous bombings of the US embassies in Tanzania and Kenya on August 7, 1998. Shortly after the embassy attacks, the US launched missile strikes against bases in Afghanistan alleged to have been used by Bin Laden's Al-Qaeda group. The US already has imposed its own sanctions against the Taliban, including freezing the assets of Afghanistan's national Ariana Airline and banning US investment and trade with the area under Taliban control. The US State Department has also offered rewards of $5 million, each for information leading to the arrest or conviction of the culprits.

The US Federal Bureau of Investigation (FBI) chief said Bin Laden also faced charges in New York following alleged attempts to procure chemical and biological agents for "terrorist activities". He mentioned Bin Laden's alleged connection with Ramzi Ahmed Yousef, an Islamist guerilla convicted of the 1993 US World Trade Centre bombing, who was suspected of planning to blow up 11 US civilian airlines from his Manila base in 1994. The US, along with India, has faced the ravages of international terrorism. In the post-Kargil operations, India was seriously concerned about the militant Taliban and Osama bin Laden's involvement in Jammu and Kashmir.

Russia witnessed the Chechnya trouble spill over to the streets of Moscow. Even ardent Islamic sympathisers of the Taliban cannot condone the acts of militants like Osama bin Laden. To some in South and West Asia and elsewhere, his name may be popular and even children are named after him, but for those who have lost their kith and kin and property to terrorism, his name conjures up pain and agony. Very troubling to Washington and others is Osama lending his "services"—providing arms training and monetary assistance—to terrorist militant groups elsewhere plotting against the US.

Afghanistan's ruling Islamist Taliban militia warned the United States to end "hostility" towards it or face natural calamities such as earthquakes and storms. The warning was in a message by the militia's supreme leader, Mullah Mohammad Omar, issued from Taliban headquarters at the southern Afghan town of Kandhar, addressed to the American people urging them to pressurise their government to "cease hostility" against the Taliban's Islamic Emirate, otherwise the US would suffer earthquakes and storms. The Taliban chief rejected a UN demand to hand over Saudi dissident Osama bin-Laden currently believed to be hiding in Afghanistan and instead proposed that a group of Islamic scholars advise them on a "solution".

"Osama issue is an Islamic issue and the only way to resolve it is through a unanimous decision by Ulema (Islamic theologians) of three Islamic countries, including Afghanistan, Saudi Arabia and another third Islamic country (Pakistan)" a spokesman for the office of Taliban supreme leader Mullah Mohammad

Omar told the Pakistan-based Afghan Islamic press. He further said, "If the United States wants to impose sanctions upon us it must be known that God is on the side of the just and no one can challenge God". Wakil Ahmed Muttawakil, the new Talibanese foreign minister, is not hesitating to involve the 55-member Organisation of Islamic Conference (OIC) in the Osama affair by proclaiming the Taliban logic that "the Almighty is definitely on our side".

The Taliban chief also offered to hold talks with "anybody" to check terrorism, which it is accused of encouraging. He said in another statement that Afghanistan had never been a refuge for terrorists. "Neither are we terrorists, nor (do) we support terrorists", the Afghan Islamic Press (AIP) quoted the chief as saying. "It is far from justice that nowadays in the world no distinction is being made between Mujahaddin (Islamic holy warriors) and terrorists", AIP quoted Omar as saying. Omar said the whole world was happy when the Mujahiddin from the rest of the world came to Afghanistan to fight the so-called Soviet occupation in the 1980s.

"Most of these Mujahiddin returned to their countries after the collapse of the Soviet Union, only to face difficulties and torture there, and some stayed back in Afghanistan", he said. However, Libyan President Muhammer Gadhaffi in an interview alleged that suspected international terrorist leader Osama bin Laden is a renegade former employee of the US Central Intelligence Agency. "Osama bin Laden is one of those naive Moslems who were duped by the United States and were used to fight the former Soviet Union in Afghanistan", Gadhaffi told the *Al-Hayat* daily. Such people, who were "a fabrication of the American intelligence services, later turned against the United States and began attacking its interests, he said. Gadhaffi further added that armed Libyan Islamic radicals who returned to the country at the beginning of the 1990s from Afghanistan "were a small group which has been totally liquidated". "Some of them repented and helped the authorities to discover the hiding places of the others. This group was swiftly dismantled", he said.

Violent anti-American protests rocked Kabul as UN sanctions against the Taliban went into effect in mid-November. Columns of young men carrying the white flag of Taliban marched through Kabul and Karachi chanting slogans against the US and the UN. In Kabul common people expressed anger at the sanctions. The Taliban militia in power has sought to play down the impact of the sanctions, but Kabul residents, already facing years of social terror and economic hardships, are deeply demoralised. "It is hard enough here", said Amanullah Khan, a waiter in Kabul. "The ordinary people will suffer due to Osama's presence and it will make no difference to the ruling government".

Mullah Mohammad Omar is a close friend of Osama and has said that he would rather see the destruction of half of Afghanistan that survived the Soviet invasion untouched than hand over a "fellow Muslim in need" to the West.

For far too long has India been a passive onlooker of the deteriorating conditions in Afghanistan much after the withdrawal of Soviet troops from that country. Fratricidal religious warfare based on tribal loyalties had its own logic. But it was the capture of Kabul three years ago by the Taliban conservative militia, backed to the hilt by the Pakistan army and intelligence agency (ISI), which really threatened Asian stability while seeking to turn Afghanistan into a source of international terrorism. The reverberation of the fall of Kabul has been felt in the entire South-West Asian, Central Asian and Russian region by disturbing the regional peace, stability and security. India has been concerned on the 'alien' nature of atrocities and human rights abuses, of particularly women and children, being committed in the name of Islam in the Taliban-ruled parts of Afghanistan "with inspiration from outside source (Pakistan)".

India's permanent representative at UN, Mr. Kamlesh Sharma, said in his statement at the UN Security Council that "the territories in Afghanistan which Taliban have occupied through military force have become a breeding ground for international terrorism. International terrorist groups find a safe haven here and in the areas straddling Afghanistan's southern borders. There are numerous training camps for terrorists and from these camps and bases, extremists and terrorists go out into the region beyond to carry out acts which are the very anti-thesis of all civilised life".

India has been interacting closely with Iran, Turkey, Russia, Central Asian neighbours of Kabul and recently with the US on the Afghan situation. The Indian Prime Minister, Mr. Atal Behari Vajpayee, while paying homage to those who had made the supreme sacrifice while fighting invaders in Kargil and cross-border insurgents in Jammu and Kashmir, expressed his serious concern about the situation in Afghanistan where terrorism and religious extremism had affected the socio-economic and security environment. Outside interference in Afghanistan must stop, he stressed, concerned about the spread of international terrorism.

India and Turkey have initiated a regular dialogue on Afghanistan. Turkey's special envoy on Afghanistan, Mr. Aydemir Erman, was in New Delhi to hold intensive discussions with senior Indian officials on the recent developments there. Mr. Erman's visit coincided with India's conscious effort to highlight the negative regional and global implications of the fundamentalist entrenchment in Afghanistan. Both India and Turkey agreed that a political alternative to the present set-up in Afghanistan is required. For this, a new government which was broad-based and reflected the ethnic mosaic of Afghanistan was required. The United Nations, both sides agreed, needed to play a pivotal role in this exercise.

The Taliban and Bin Laden phenomena are the offshoot of the disastrous policies pursued by several countries in Afghanistan particularly the US, Saudi Arabia and Pakistan during the past two decades. Officials in Washington, Riyadh and Islamabad visualised Moscow's retreat as the first crucial step in the re-emergence of an Afghanistan ready to ally with the United States. The US-Saudi-Pakistani alliance had played the central role in training, arming and financing the Afghan Islamists to expel the Russians from Afghanistan. With the Soviet withdrawal accomplished—a severe blow to Moscow in the cold war—Washington put Afghanistan on the back burner. But the collapse of the Soviet Union in December 1991 gave a second wind to the Northern Alliance or Islamic coalition movement, which acquired a momentum of its own. It's seizure of power in Kabul in April 1991 following the fall of the secular leftist regime of Muhammad Najibullah, paved the way for the rise of the extremist Taliban Islamic movement two years later and its subsequent capture of Kabul.

The Taliban are the least concerned about the fate of the hapless and subjugated people of Afghanistan, which they have reduced to a huge concentration camp. Did the founders of US policy in Afghanistan during the Carter and Reagan administrations (1977 onwards) realise that in spawning Islamic militancy with the primary aim of defeating the Soviet Union they were risking sowing the seeds of a phenomena that was likely to acquire a life of its own, spread throughout Arab-Asian and African world and threaten US interests?

The Afghanistan problem thus is a creation of US cold war politics. And in considering any problem of strategic diplomacy, due consideration should be given not only to one's self-interest, but also to its future implications. Afghanistan problem is a source of concern to all in the region: China, Russia, Central Asia, India, Iran and Turkey.

This is so because of Afghanistan's strategic and economic importance to them. Therefore, an urgent understanding between them over Afghanistan is necessary. The establishment of a congenial national government which takes into account the national needs and interests of Afghan people can bring peace and stability to the hapless population and give peace a chance.

3. Destruction of Bamiyan Buddha

For the last few years Afghanistan has paid for turning its back on Buddha by symbolically blasting the historic Bamiyan statues. One is not superstitious to think that the destruction of the Buddha statue brought about the troubles for the country. It is the mental make up of the Taliban rulers whose political, social and cultural goals were diametrically opposed to what the Buddha stood for, that was responsible for the country's travails.

The spirit of Buddha, which is peace and non-violence, are now required more than ever as the country embarks on its reconstruction. I am not saying it in the religious sense. It's not that the people should embrace Buddhism but the humanitarian values of all the religions, including Islam, should be accepted in the functioning of the government and the interaction of different sections of the society. Since the predominant religion of Afghanistan is Islam, it would be interesting to have a look into its cultural attitudes in the past.

Since its inception, Islam as a great religion has preserved and even maintained all historic cultural expressions, including the Egyptian Sphinx, the Persian Persepolis, ancient houses of worship in Turkey belonging to other cultures and religions, and the pictures, images, artifacts and possessions they housed. In fact, had it not been for Islamic protection, these historic legacies or structures and artifacts may not have survived. Khalifah Umar provided an excellent example upon entering holy Jerusalem. He prohibited the destruction of any Christian images or places of worship. Muslim scholars and jurists also prohibited the destruction of places of worship and religious and cultural artifacts belonging to non-Muslims. It is worth-noting that the land now called Afghanistan was part of the Persian Empire which was conquered by Arab armies fourteen centuries ago.

Since then, many of the illustrious Muslim rulers have ruled over it, and yet none sought to destroy the giant historic Buddha statues of Bamiyan. This is precisely why these statues had survived. To destroy them in the name of Islam by the fundamentalist Taliban was to consider itself to be a superior Muslim than all their predecessors. This is truly ridiculous and totally contrary to the spirit of Islamic principles of humility, tolerance, freedom of thought, consultative democracy and preservation of peace and human prosperity.

Another instance of fundamentalist misdeamenour was the prescription of a dress code for minority Hindus. This evoked worldwide protests, bringing to mind the Naxi persecution of Jews and the Israeli persecution of Palestinians. The international outcry compelled the Taliban to prescribe separate identity cards instead.

The Taliban movement spread in the 90s rapidly throughout the Southwestern Provinces. They promised to end the fighting in Afghanistan and restore law and order under the Islamic Shari'at. They imposed strict Islamic code for women, demanding full veiling and barring them from work outside the home, and closing girls' schools. They also enforced the dreaded Islamic codes of criminal punishment.

The ferocity with which the Taliban sought to enforce the seclusion of women and girl child in Kabul and other captured parts of Afghanistan prompted the European Commissioner for Humanitarian Assistance, Emma Bonino (herself detained by the Taliban during a September 1997 visit to Kabul) to describe their regime as one of 'gender apartheid'.

The Malaysian Prime Minister, Dr Mahathir Mohammad said the Taliban was doing a disservice to Islam by preventing women from working—even as doctors to treat women patients. Addressing a student symposium at the Malay University in Kuala Lumpur, Dr Mahathir stated: "Do we want to be like that (Taliban)? These are not our models." Dr Mahathir has called for a World Conference against Terrorism in the name of religion.

Religious fundamentalists, such as the Taliban, have strenuously opposed the advancement of Afghan women. Not all Islamic groups shared the Talibans conservative and repressive approach. When Kabul university reopened its doors in April 1995, it did so as an avowedly co-educational institution with over 2,000 female students. However, one of the Taliban's first moves on occupying Kabul was to close the university, and when it reopened in 1997, female students were banned. The number of destitute female beggars in Kabul increased.

The Taliban social and cultural carnage in the vicinity of Kabul overshadowed the sharp fall in mortality elsewhere in Afghanistan. The human costs of the Talibanese occupation of Afghanistan are staggering. The conflict and the crisis in Afghanistan in the 1990s produced massive dislocation of the population forcing most of them to flee to neighbouring countries. Human development has been severely disrupted as the Afghan population now contains a substantial component of physically, mentally and economically disabled war victims and destitute widows and children.

The vandalism and the deliberate destruction of the Buddha statues carried out by the Taliban fanatics in Afghanistan was condemned by the world community. Its destruction by the Taliban in the name of religion shocked all civilised nations. The Arab-African and Islamic nations including Algeria, Egypt and Islamic Iran, also expressed their outrage at the destruction. Muslim scholars condemned this in no uncertain terms as also scholars belonging to other religions. Egypt sent its Chief Muslim cleric grand Mufti Nasr Farid Wasel all the way to Afghanistan to appeal to the Talibal to change their order. India had reason to be concerned about Pakistan's growing influence in the Afghan region as it was a threat to its national security. The Saudis largely treated the developments in Afghanistan and the emergence of Taliban as a religious issue and deferred to their own religious establishment, which was dominated by the conservative Islamists.

The jihadi agenda of Taliban and their Pakistani-Saudi supporters threatened the South West Asian region and its security. Given their domestic developments, Pakistan and Afghanistan are economically, politically and culturally dysfunctional. A major task of countries in South and South West Asia, particularly India, Algeria, Egypt, Iran, Turkey and Pakistan, should be to ensure that fundamentalism or religious extremism should not cast a shadow on the day-to-day socio-economic life of the people. The greatest damage is done by the militant jihadi groups with their extremist violence in Afghanistan, Pakistan and in the Indian state of Kashmir. The politics of both India and Pakistan have to contend with the fundamentalist factor. Fortunately, the fundamentalists are not allowed to have a major say in India's democratic politics.

In the sub-continental context the threat posed by the fundamentalist Taliban spread beyond Pakistan's border. Afghanistan under Taliban offered a safe heaven for the cultivation of the fundamentalist ideology. There were indications that Pakistan had started becoming wary of the Taliban's extremist ideology and the risk of its fundamentalist influence seeping across the borders into Pakistan's body politic and civil society.

Religious bigotry is not going to serve any religion. The real basis of every religion is enlightened ideas. Those who believe in fanaticism are harming their own religion. Jihad is a very outmoded concept, when man is living under modern states under the United Nations umbrella. The spirit of Bamiyan Buddha that has been destroyed needs to be revived.

4. Central Asia: Iranian and Turkish Perspective

Among the West Asian states, Turkey and Iran have a special relationship with Central Asian States. Both of them are located in the immediate neighbourhood and apart from geographical proximity, they have significant socio-cultural influence in the whole of Central Asia. Both have connections with Central Asia since very earlier times. Even despite almost a century of centralised Russian and Soviet rule, the Central Asian Republics we have today, since 1991, have looked upon both Iran and Turkey as role models for their socio-economic and political development in the recent years. This paper makes an attempt to study the relations of Iran and Turkey with the states of Central Asia since 1991.

With the disintegration of Soviet Union in mid-1991, a new chapter in the history of Central Asia opened with the emergence of the independent republics of Central Asia. At the end of 1991, five sovereign republics came into existence, namely Kazakhstan, Kyrghyzstan, Uzbekistan, Tajikistan and Turkmenistan. Stretching over a vast territory, the new Central Asian States are situated in a geo-strategically important region of Asia—a meeting point for South, West and East Asia. The States of Central Asia have geopolitical, strategic and economic importance for both Iran and Turkey, as well as for China, India and Russia. During the Soviet period, the Central Asian republics were extremely dependent upon the Soviet Union. Now they are seeking to diversify their economies to promote their trade. They are involved in the process of elaborating their own mechanisms for economic activities. One of the main directions of the foreign economic policy (FEP), which is being carried out by the Central Asian states, could be defined as follows—"Establishment of a new system of FEA based on market economy and search for new effective ways of cooperation based on the neutral status of these states". It (FEA) envisages establishment of new foreign economic relations (FER) between the Central Asian States, particularly Turkmenistan and the rest of the world on a new foundation; priority is given to bilateral relations and to closer bilateral integration in different fields of economy.[1] Moreover, they have had to cope with the onerous task of consolidating their newfound independence. They are in the process of consolidating their borders and developing their own currencies, customs posts, armies and embassies. In January 1993, the presidents of the Central Asian Republics held a summit meeting in Tashkent and announced that all necessary conditions had been met for the formation of a commonwealth of Central Asian Republics. Encouraged by the United States and Turkey, the governments of Central Asian states decided in January 1993 to establish an intergovernmental coalition to be known as the Central Asian Regional Union (CARU). The CARU was basically formed on the basis of their common Turkic ethnic roots. The founder also expressed a commitment to the concept of creating a greater Turkistan. The CARU rang alarm bells in Iran and also alerted the Kremlin in Moscow, China and, to an extent, India. And quite predictably, the CARU was applauded by the United States, Turkey, and Saudi Arabia.

Even before the official end of the Soviet Union the loosening of ties between Moscow and the Central Asian Muslim republics had brought down the "iron curtain" between them. After 70 years of separation from their ethnic and religious kinship, Soviet Muslims eagerly began to seek contact and re-acquaintance with them. The most dramatic manifestation came in January 1990, when large crowds from Soviet Azerbaijan tore down border posts and poured into Iranian Azerbaijan. Since then, official and non-official contacts between Soviet Muslim republics and other Muslim countries have multiplied. For obvious ethnic, cultural and historical reasons, Iran and Turkey have emerged as principal poles of attraction. But other Muslim countries, including such key Arab States as Saudi Arabia and Egypt, have not been absent from the scene. Saudi Arabia, in particular, has been extensively involved in Central Asia through encouraging Islamic education. Iran and Turkey have the advantage of geography. Landlocked Central Asian states also realise that their access to the sea can be attained mainly through Iran.

The Iranian Perspective

The Iranian leadership is aware of this geographic imperative. In fact, large areas of Central Asia fell within the orbit of the Iranian world for a long period. Iran gradually lost them to the Imperial Russian advances in sixteenth, seventeenth and eighteenth centuries. Iranians reacted swiftly as the Central Asian Republics started opening up[2] and proposed to Central Asian leaders "the revival of the silk route".

The Iranian proposal involves the building of road links and land routes of the Central Asian states to Iran. Agreements were reached initially to build a 200-kilometre rail-road line from Mashhad to Sarakhs linking Iran with Turkmenistan, and an additional 300 km of rail-road line in Kazakhstan connecting Iran to China and the Pacific. Mr. Ali Akbar Velayati, former foreign minister of Iran, in his January 1995 visit, made a strong appeal for Indo-Iranian cooperation for tapping economic opportunities arising out of the opening up of the Central Asian states. He specifically mentioned the areas of oil and gas, textiles, railways and light and heavy engineering where scope for such cooperation existed. He pointed out that Iran was building rail links with the CIS states, and India, with its expertise in the field, could help in achieving this. He also said that CIS states were known to have the second largest reserves of gas in the world and Iran was trying to tap this. India could take advantage of this by setting up joint fertiliser plants in Iran, which could supply the nutrient to India. He also said that CIS states had a good supply of cotton and both Indian and Iranian companies could think of buying the commodity and processing them on a contract basis.[3] Accordingly, in a path-breaking move, India, Iran and Turkmenistan signed a memorandum of understanding (MOU) in April 1995 that provided access to Indian goods to the Central Asian Republics through the Iranian land route. It is upgraded into a treaty status and would improve trade and economic cooperation between the three signatories besides increasing the flow of transit between Central Asia and India through Iran.[4]

In addition to establishing bilateral diplomatic relations with all Central Asian states Iran embarked on a number of regional initiatives, including, especially the ECO (Economic Cooperation Organisation) and organising the states bordering on the Caspian sea. The latter initiative brought together Iran, Azerbaijan, Turkmenistan Kazakhstan, and Russia. This opened up, for the Central Asian states, the facility of transferring exportable goods to international waters in the South, to Caspian Littoral states in the north, to the Arab world in the South West and to Turkey and Europe in the West. Iran's skilful diplomacy sprang into action at the sixth meeting of the organisation of the Islamic conference (OIC), which ended on December 11, 1991 at Dakar, the capital of Senegal. There, Iran itself determinedly set up as an alternative to Saudi Arabia as the world leader of Islam. Iran's president Hashemi Rafsanjani not only sponsored a proposal for admitting Central Asian states to the OIC, but also ensured the participation of Azerbaijan' delegates, Sheik-ul-Islam Allah Shakur Pashazade (Chairman of the Spiritual Administration of Caucasian Muslims) and Kazakhstan's deputy foreign minister, Sailau Batyrshaurly in the OIC meet. In January 1992, with president Niyazov and Velayati attending the show, Iran and Turkmenistan opened border crossing between them. The two dignitaries signed a memorandum of cooperation that provided for work to begin on the construction of a railway line to link Turkmenistan to Iran as well as on the construction of a railroad network connecting Iran to Turkey and the Mediterranean sea. In March 1992, the two states entered into an economic agreement. Valued at over $80 million, it provided for barter of Turkmen "goods and raw materials" for use in the Iranian industry. As in the case of Turkmenistan, relations between Teheran and Kazakhstan, too, developed rapidly after the establishment of diplomatic relations in early 1992. In February 1992, Foreign Minister of Tajikistan, Mr. Hakim Kayumov, met President Rafsanjani of Iran and expressed Dushanbe's desire for "cultural, political and economic cooperation" between the two states. During the Ashkabat summit meeting in May 1992, Iran established diplomatic relations with Kyrgyzstan and Uzbekistan. Both the states were interested in socio-cultural and economic cooperation with Iran. In early February 1992, an Uzbek trade delegation visited Iran, Turkey, and other West Asian countries. In addition to bilateral relations, the Islamic Republic of Iran also embarked upon a number of regional initiatives designed to promote its image as the leader of the Muslim world and as a major outside player in the political scene in the region.[5] Ignoring Washington's strong advice to avoid tightening economic links with Teheran, Turkmenistan's president Saparmurad Niyazov signed a memorandum of understanding with the leaders of Iran and Turkey at the summit of the Economic Conference Organisation (ECO) in Ashkabat on 14 May 1997 for a pipeline to carry an annual load of 30 bn cubic metres of natural gas originating in Turkmenistan. The $7 bn project—with Iran footing the bill for the pipeline in its territory, estimated at $3.5 bn—is expected to be finished by the year 2002. On 13 May 1996, President Rafsanjani of Iran inaugurated a rail link between Iran and Central Asia which was attended by 11 heads of state and dignitaries from over 50 countries. Former President Rafsanjani said the $210 m railway would benefit peace and stability in the region by moving two million tonnes of goods and half a million people between Iran and Turkmenistan.[6]

Turkish Perspectives

In the developing competition with Iran, Turkey has valuable assets of its own in Central Asia. Turkey, too, endeavoured to establish itself as a major outside participant in the affairs of the newly independent Muslim republics of the former Soviet Union. Located at the crossroads of three continents and three seas, Turkey serves as a bridge of friendship and cooperation between the East and the West, the North and the South. It promotes harmonious and mutually beneficial relations with all countries large or small, near or far; and contributes to the restoration of peace and stability in its periphery.[7] In addition to geography, Turkey has historic, ethnic, religious and linguistic affinity with the Turkish-speaking Central Asian states, except Tajikistan, which is a cultural continuation of Iran. However, while Turkish people in the region have many common ethnic and linguistic characteristics, there are also vast differences among them. For example, the various Turkik dialects are not mutually intelligible. Nor is there a classical Turkish language—unlike Arabic—which could be used as a common language among them. In spite of such linguistic differences, the cultural and ethnic ties endear Turkey to the Central Asian Republics and Turkey is quite an important player in the politics of this region. Though none of the countries involved (Iran, Pakistan, China, Afghanistan and Turkey) in the politics of the region has so far managed to overshadow Russian influence, the economic initiatives from many of them, and especially from Turkey, has helped these Republics to lessen their dependence on Russia. Turkey has given large credits to Uzbekistan ($500 million), Kazakhstan ($200 million), Turkmenistan ($75 million), and Kyrgyzstan ($75 million), in addition to establishing television links, cultural exchanges and Turkish language training programmes. The Turkish president in his February 1995 visit to India laid considerable stress on the possibility of Indo-Turkish joint ventures in third countries, identifying in particular the Central Asian countries. The Central Asian region is an area where the potential for cooperation is immense because of the ties both countries have in this region. India, along with Iran, is a familiar friend while Turkey, with its secular and democratic polity, is seen as a model, which the Central Asian Republics would like to emulate.[8]

Turkey moved on to establish its presence in the Central Asian Republics even prior to the dissolution of the former Soviet Union. In 1990, Ankara reacted favourably to Azeri and Kazakh requests for cooperation in telecommunications and signed an economic and cultural cooperation agreement with Turkmenistan. In November 1991, Turkey was the first foreign country to recognise the independence of Azerbaijan and, in December, it extended recognition to and expressed an interest in developing closer relations with all the other republics of the former Soviet Union. In addition, the presidents of Turkmenistan, Uzbekistan and Kirgyzstan visited Ankara and emphasised on the ethnic ties binding their people with Turkey. Relations between Uzbekistan and Turkey had entered a new stage with the signing of the agreements on cooperation in the spheres of economy, trade, transport, communication, culture, education, science, the media, tourism and sports in mid-December 1991.

However, relations between Kazakhstan and Turkey remained limited because Ankara proved reluctant initially to invest money in the Kazakh economy. But things started improving with the then Prime Minister Demirel's visit to Alma Ata on April 29, 1992. During that visit, he offered $200 million in credit as well as help in a number of major projects. Turkish firms took lead in assisting Kazakhstan in oil exploration, as well as in the construction of oil refineries and of an electric power station, the laying of a pipeline to Turkey later extended to Persian Gulf, the reconstruction of the port of Aktau, the transport of Kazakh goods from the Caspian to the Baltic and Black seas and the distribution of Kazakh goods in Turkey. It is, thus, Demirel's visit to Kazakhstan provided an important stimulus to the development of Kazakh-Turkish relations. In addition to Uzbekistan and Kazakhstan, Turkmenistan and Kyrgyzstan were the other Central Asian Republics with which Turkey attempted to establish close relations.[9]

The emergence of independent states in Central Asia has generated great interest in this part of the world that has not yet been properly understood. The interest has only grown with the discovery of enormous oil and gas reserves. As far as the role of Iran and Turkey is concerned both have brought a measure of stability to the region through their economic initiatives in the region. Both see Central Asia as a large and profitable market with great potential. Both the governments have taken active part in encouraging their respective business communities to expand their dealings with the CARs. They have also opened credit lines to export their products to the Central Asian States, though, in this respect, Ankara, with Western backing, has been much more active than Teheran. Nevertheless, both Iran and Turkey, because of their geographic location and the economic opportunities that they can offer, still remain significant regional players in Central Asia. Both are keen that political, economic and cultural stability should be strengthened there. The true significance of their relationship is that taken together they have so far formed a very good model of regional coexistence.

REFERENCES

1. M.B. Orazov and G.O. Khalova, "The Foreign Economic Policy of Turkmenistan" in *Contemporary Central Asia* (New Delhi), Vol. 1, No. 1, 1997, p. 25.
2. Gulshan Dietl, "Regional Transformation in Central Asia and its Impact on India" in Selim, Mohammad El-Sayed; *Egypt and India in the Post Cold War Would: Comparative Paradigms* (ed.) Cairo University: Centre for Asian Studies, 1996, p. 304.
3. *The Economic Times* and *The Times of India* (Delhi) January 5, 1995.
4. *The Hindustan Times* (Delhi) April 19, 1995.
5. Oles M. Smolansky, "Turkish and Iranian policies in Central Asia" in

Central Asia: Its Strategic Importance and Future Prospects (ed.), Hound Mills, Basing stoke, Hampshire and London: The Macmillan Press, 1994, pp. 285-290.
6. *Middle East International*, May 24, 1996, p. 14.
7. Suleyman Demirel, President of the Republic of Turkey quoted in *Middle East Journal*, Vol. 51, No. 1, Winter 1997, p. 11.
8. *The Pioneer* (Delhi), February 2, 1995.
9. Oles M. Smolansky, "Turkish and Iranian policies in Central Asia" in *Central Asia: Its Strategic and Future Prospects* (ed.) 1994, pp. 292-296.

5. India and Central Asia

Central Asia is one of the most important crossroads of the world. It is the central part of the continent of Asia between China proper in the East, India, Bhutan, Nepal and Afghanistan in the South. Iran and the Caspian Sea in the West and Russia in the North.

Central Asia is and has been the crucial part of Asia and has been the home of human cultural evolution. Owing to its immense mountain ranges, this centre of Asia has been called "High Asia". Being the cradle of human history it is unique in the world. It has the largest oil and gas reserves in the world. These have begun to attract attention internationally. There has been a tremendous change in the Central Asian society as a result of the spread of education and the rise in literacy in communications has spread mutual awareness between the region and the rest of the world.

Besides, the enormous reserves combining with its strategic location in the Eurasian heartland have created a fresh arena of competition among the major powers. Control of oil has been one of main objectives of American foreign policy as it has helped to establish its hegemony in the Gulf and Central Asia. The available evidence suggests that their rivalry would have important repercussions at the regional and global levels.

Central Asia continues to be a vital strategic region for India though former Soviet Union has crumbled. It holds a great deal of importance for us. India's history, be it of ancient or medieval period or later, shows that whatever happens in that region has its lasting influence on us.

"The geo-political situation around the region is such that New Delhi cannot ignore the developments there", said former Prime Minister I.K. Gujral recently. The present coalition Government led by Atal Behari Vajpayee also considers the countries of West and Central Asia as important partners. The visit of the President of Tajikistan in January 1999 to India was a useful opportunity to renew our links and share perceptions on regional development in Central Asia.

Scholars and researchers from eight Central Asian and South Asian countries who had converged in New Delhi for a four-day seminar on "Culture, Society and Politics in Central Asia", recently, dispersed with a resolve to work together to open up "free and secure lines of communication" between the two regions.

The group focused on the future cultural evolution of the Central Asian society and politics with more attention on past and present cultural links with India. The role of India was found to be particularly important because Indian cultural contracts spread through Afghanistan and Iran into Central Asia and from there into East Asia contributing to the cultural and philosophical framework of China, Japan and Korea. Merchants and settlers, missionaries and scholars were identified as the groups which helped in transmitting Indian culture to different parts of Asia.

A fervent appeal was made to revive folk arts and handicrafts, recreate traditional music and dance, give a new opportunity to drama and literature of the past in order to enable civilisational and national identities to cope with the cultural complexities of the modern world.

During the British colonial period, India and Central Asia became pawns in the Great Power game between the British and Russian empires. During the post-Independence period, India had thriving trade and cultural relations with Central Asia under the broad Indo-Soviet agreements. The Indian goods continued to be transacted and the flow of trade increased. Following the disintegration of the Soviet Union at the end of 1991, five Central Asian Republics have become independent. From a stereotyped, rigid Soviet system, these new states of Central Asia—Kazakhstan, Kirghyzstan, Tajikistan, Turkmenistan and Uzbekistan—have appeared in the world arena as independent actors. India recognised the need to strengthen its ties with the newly established Central Asian republics.

However, the Indian economic policy towards the region suffers from two serious limitations. One, overland routes are absent or unsafe. The lack of direct road or rail link puts India into a disadvantageous situation. Two, Indian economic scenario prohibits any large-scale aid, credit or investment in the region. India does appreciate the economic potential of the region and would like to gain access to its resources. The means at its disposal are, however, limited.

The Caspian oil reserve is estimated to be the largest in the world after the Gulf. With India importing increasingly large quantities of oil, this region should be of immense interest to us for economic reasons, if not only for its strategic location and historical and cultural ties with India.

India has a lot to offer to this area in terms of products and expertise because these countries are still emerging from the former Soviet Union. Indian technology is appropriate for the markets there. India can offer them use of its military training facilities as the terrain in the region and military equipment used is similar to that of India. The Indian Army has its Staff College and numerous schools dealing with subjects like tactics, mountain warfare and counter insurgency which are of concern to governments in the region.

In fact, there is a remarkable convergence of interests of India and Central Asia in the question of threat of Islamic radicalism. The Central Asian states are conscious of the attempts to bring in religious fundamentalism to undermine the people's confidence in their leaders, to destroy socio-political stability and national, civil and inter-ethnic harmony. Radical Islamists target to discredit democracy, the secular state, and multi-religious society. They provoke confrontation and conflict among social groups. Terrorists, fanatics and armed militants in the guise of fighters of faith are eager to impose their monstrous ideas on people.

Both Central Asia and India are victims of externally sponsored terrorism. Terrorist violence in Tajikistan, Uzbekistan and Jammu and Kashmir are believed to be an extension of terrorist activities of Pakistan-sponsored Taliban regime and other Islamic militant groups. It is learnt that the terrorist outfits in Afghanistan and Pakistan, which are involved in training mercenaries from many Afro-Arab-Asian countries for terrorist activities in Jammu and Kashmir are now finding it easy to spread their activities to Central Asia.

The US has been patronising some fundamentalist regimes in the region, and it should cause no surprise if it strikes a deal with Taliban also in the near future. American multinationals desperately want to establish a pipeline through Afghanistan for transport of Central Asia's precious oil and energy resources, besides a road which avoids Iran. Iran is sought to be isolated and bullied because with a defiant Iran and Iraq, the US would not have the grip over the Persian Gulf out of which flows the overwhelming bulk of West Asian oil for Japan and Western Europe, both major trade competitors for the US. The reactivating of the US policy in the Central Asian region with Pakistan as the spearhead, demands close watch by India.

In this background, former Prime Minister Narasimha Rao's two visits to Central Asian Republics of Turkmenistan and Kirghyzstan have a significance of international nature. Mr. Rao's visit focused on both the political and economic aspects of the relationship. During this visit the Prime Minister of India had signed as many as eight treaties, five with Turkmenistan and three with Kirghyzstan. These were major agreements aimed at promoting bilateral relations in the socio-economic sectors.

Both in Ashgabat and Bishkek, while addressing the parliamentarians, Mr. Rao made it a point to drive home India's new economic environment urging both countries to take advantage of the investment-friendly atmosphere by enlarging trade and commercial relations with his country. The bilateral agreements cover such areas as culture, arts, education, mass media, sports, science and technology, environment and tourism and setting up of a Joint Commission on trade and economy.

India offered a five million dollars credit to the Kirghyz Republic to finance joint adventures modernising industrial enterprises and establishing new small and medium scale units. The Indo-Kirghyz joint commission is being activated and steps are being taken to implement the agreements on inter-banking cooperation to facilitate trade in convertible currencies and also for training of personnel in Indian institutions.

Besides the banking agreement, the other areas of cooperation include a protocol between the Departments of Science and Technology of the two countries and establishing working groups for tourism and science. The discussion on specific projects in both republics showed that bilateral economic cooperation could be enhanced greatly with the development of regional cooperation. Turkmenistan invited India to take advantage of a multi-billion dollar oil and gas pipeline which was to link Iran, Afghanistan and Pakistan.

An Iranian delegation was also present at Ashgabat and had

extensive discussions with the officials accompanying Mr. Rao. By then, India was making use of the road link from Bandar Abbas in Iran to Turkmenistan but it was realised that movement by rail would be faster and cheaper. India had shown interest in upgrading the railway system in Iran to cut the distance between Bandar Abbas and Turkmenistan.

Similarly, Kirghyzstan showed keen interest in opening a surface transport route from India to the Central Asian Republics. On the security aspect, Mr. Rao's characterisation of "terrorism as a common challenge" was well received in both Capitals.

The new boost to bilateral relations was earlier given during the official visit of the President of Turkmenistan, Mr. Saparamurad Niyazov, to India in April 1992. That visit was one of the first official trips of Mr. Niyazov as the President of an independent Turkmenistan. During that visit the leaders of two countries signed six protocols and agreements, which established the legal base of bilateral cooperation in trade and economic field, in culture, education, arts, sports and tourism. The protocols on establishment of diplomatic and consular relations between the two countries were also signed during that visit.

Today, as a result of these agreements, trade and economic relations between India and Turkmenistan are being developed actively. Many Indian companies are working successfully in Turkmenistan in the field of commerce as well as in the production field. A number of joint ventures have been launched. Such firms and companies as Premier International Ltd., Lakshmi Machine Works, Ajanta Pharma Ltd. and many others are working with their counterparts for the sake of mutual benefits of the people of the two countries.

On the issue of Kashmir, "Turkmenistan made it clear that it is a bilateral issue to be discussed and resolved mutually between India and Pakistan and there is no international dimension to it. India appreciated Turkmenistan for its commitment to the secular and democratic path.

The former Indian Prime Minister, Mr. Narasimha Rao's visit to Uzbekistan and Tajikistan in July 1993 also laid a solid foundation of Indo-Central Asian friendship, with Indian signing the most-favoured nation treaty with Uzbekistan. To facilitate smooth entry of Indian goods in Uzbekistan and enhance economic relations between the two countries a transit agreement with Iran had been signed in November 1994 and Indo-Uzbek joint bank is in the offing. The two way trade between the two countries has increased tremendously. It grew from Rs.90 million in 1993-94 to Rs.480 million in the first 10 months of 1995-96. Indian films also play an important role in bringing these two countries culturally close. Films of Raj Kapoor specially, are very popular.

The President of Kazakhstan, Nursultan Nazarbaev, during his 1997 visit called upon the Indian industrialists and businessmen to set up joint venture businesses in Kazakhstan which is opening up its economy and industry for foreign investment. After months of hectic consultations, Indian ONGC Videsh Ltd. has clinched two major oil exploration projects in Kazakhstan. The company has also bagged rights to develop another oil field, besides the Pavla Door oil field, that is at the Ali Beg Molla oil field near the Kenkaya adjacent to the Caspian.

An expansion and consolidation of Indo-Central Asian relations is in the interest of both in terms of their regional as well as global concerns. It meets the vital interests of the two regions, developed on the principles of peaceful coexistence, equality and mutual respect. There is a voluminous increase in the pattern of our trade ties during this decade. Both take identical views and similar stands on major issues like terrorism and economic and social progress, and are loyal to the cause of international peace, security and development. The true significance of their friendship is that it forms a model of regional coexistence.

Iran

6. India-Iran Ties

The visit of the Iranian foreign minister, Mr. Ali Akbar Velayati to India in the 1990s reaffirmed the age-old ties between India and Iran which suffered a setback when Iranian President Hashemi Rafsanjani suddenly cancelled his October 1994 visit to India citing plague as the reason. Indo-Iranian friendship has stood the test of time. Both have been friends since the beginning of history. The people of India and Iran are inextricably interwoven with each other, as both have shared the same common cultural background and heritage.

In fact, beginnings of contact between Iran and India goes back to the Indo-Aryan civilisation period. Some historical findings claim that Iranians and Indian belonged to one single family and lived together for many centuries in the pasture lands of Central Asia. It is said that first Iranian and Indian Aryans lived in the plateau's of Central Asia prior to 6000 B.C. On account of certain common characteristics, the Indo-Aryan and Indo-Iranian languages are included in the family of Indo-European languages. In this context, the hypothesis has gained ground that European was the source from which the Aryans and their languages, whether in Iran or in India, emanated. Historical excavations, further, shed light on the traces of merchandise traffic by boat between India and Iran along the coast of Southern Iran through the Arabian Sea and the Persian Gulf. Iran supplied silver, gold, lead, zinc, turquoise and lapis Lazuli. Ivory was exported from India to Iran. Indo-Aryans went from western India to the countries like Afghanistan, Iran, etc. in course of trade or other purposes. The existence of some common gods and similarities in ritual practices among the Iranians as well as the affinities in the Iranian languages could have been due to contact with the vedic Indians from India going to Iran and the neighbouring countries.

During the Maurya period, Persian nobels were employed

by Mauryan Kings. The Kharosthi script was introduced by the Persian officials in the North Western Frontier and this continued to be in use till the 4th century A.D. The most important influence of culture, art and style of architecture of Achamenians on those of India. Emperor Ashoka made his epigraphy similar to that of King Darius of Persia. During the Islamic period, India became a meeting ground of two great old civilisations i.e. Indian and Persian through Islam. During this period, Persian language was propagated and influenced the Indian language culture. Persian came to be cultivated in a spirit of competition, even by non-Persian Muslims and Hindu whose mother-tongue was not Persian. Several rulers at Delhi and elsewhere, were themselves distinguished scholars and writers in Persian or its patrons. Sikander Lodi, himself a poet, was liberal patron of Persian language and literature. Emperor Akbar took positive steps in attracting learned scholars and liberal men from Iran and other places. Akbar's court was a resort of scholars, philosophers and poets, and of all that was best in Persian literature. Abul Fazl calculated that there were 50 reputed Persian poets in Akbar's court, headed by Abdul Faizi, well versed in Arabic, Turkish, Sanskrit and Persian. During the reigns of Jehangir, Shahjahan and Aurangzeb the tradition continued, though the momentum declined.

During the British era, there was not much sign of healthy cultural and social contact between these two states. British interests in Iran determined the relations between Iran and India. Years preceding the First World War (1914-18) were fraught with revolutionary movements in India. During the Pahlavi regime in Iran, cultural delegations were exchanged between India and Iran. In 1932 when the Satyagraha movement of Mahatma Gandhi was in full swing, King Reza Shah Pahlavi of Iran, invited the great Indian poet Rabindranath Tagore to Iran to suggest to him the educational methods by adopting which, Iran could inculcate the spirit of Patriotism in her people. Rabindranath was accorded a right royal welcome and on his 70th birthday, he was awarded the Pahlavi Monarch's Gold Medal. In pursuance of this programme, professor Poure Davond was sent on deputation to the Viswabharati University to teach Persian and Iranian culture there.

After the war, when India gained independence and became free to have international relations with the countries of her choice, it lost no time in consolidating contacts with the Asian countries and Iran happened to be one of them. The sagacious Indian Prime Minister Jawaharlal Nehru, first convened an Asian Conference and then the Bandung Conference which brought all Asian countries together. The effect was that Gandhi, Tagore and Nehru became the household figures in Iran and plenty of books about them appeared there. The autobiographies of Gandhi and Nehru were the first to be translated into Persian. The Indian Council for Cultural Relations brought out a Persian translation of the Bhagavad Gita by Dara Sikoh edited by Maulana Ajmal Khan and Kamgar Parsi and Vikram Urvashi by Dr. Syed Abidi.

Independent India's ties with Iran remained in a state of flux for many years. The resurgence of nationalism in India was largely triumphant. The resurgence of nationalism in Iran was aborted and thwarted with the help of outside agencies. The winds of nationalism blew in both countries. In Iran Mossadeq nationalised the foreign oil companies for which he was overthrown with the connivance of the CIA and the Shah was installed in full authority. The Shah had no interest in non-alignment. He joined the western military bloc system and his policy was antithesis of all that India stood for. Besides, during this period most Muslim states were carried away by the religious rhetoric of Pakistan, partly because of this and partly owing to the pro-western leanings of some Muslim regimes India encountered some problems in cultivating bilateral relations with individual countries. As Pakistan was a member of western military bloc system, the Islamic bond with Pakistan was emphasised in Iran. The new state of Pakistan, ever since its creation in 1947 has carried out anti-India propaganda and sought to post itself as the Champion of the interests of Muslim nation. This fact considerably influenced India's approach to the West Asian region. Pakistan's anti-India propaganda designs to fore an Islamic bloc against India also posed a serious challenge to Indo-Iranian relations.

It is only in the 1970s that the Indo-Iranian relationship has assumed significance. This has occurred due to a number of reasons such as changes in the regional environments of both India and Iran and the Super Power detente which has allowed policy-makers in both the capitals, but particularly in Teheran to delink, at least to some extent, the bilateral relationship between India and Iran from the global politics of the cold war. Relations had begun to develop earlier in March 1965 with the signing of Indo-Iranian economic agreement on the establishment of an oil refinery in Madras with an annual capacity of 2.5 million tons. It should be remembered that the agreement came through by Iran during and after the Indo-Pakistan war of 1965. It was, however, during Mrs. Gandhi's tenure that the inhibitions were overcome and relations changed qualitatively. India and Iran both realised the advantages of a closer relationship. Besides, it would help India in diluting Iran's tilt towards Pakistan. The process started gathering stream from 1968. This time, Morarji Desai, then Deputy Prime Minister of India, led an economic delegation to Iran. During this visit, Desai started negotiations for a Rs.2,060 million Indo-Iranian chemical and industrial complex to be set up in Gujarat, India. This was followed by the Shah of Iran's 12-day visit to India on 3 January 1969. The visit marked the rapid expansion of economic cooperation. A ministerial level joint machinery was formed to work out measures for economic, commercial and technological cooperation.

This was followed by a trade protocol signed in New Delhi on 15 February 1970, which laid the foundation for long-term trade, joint industrial ventures and for deeper economic cooperation. The ground was thus laid for a rapid development of Indo-Iranian economic ties. The Iranian Foreign Minister's visit to India in December 1973 provided an opportunity for yet another impetus to the expansion of ties. Both New Delhi and Teheran decided to reactivate the work of the Indo-Iranian Joint Commission on economic, trade and technical cooperation. Prime Minister Mrs. Indira Gandhi's visit to Iran in April 1974 and the Shah's visit to India in October of that year wear other high points in this developing relationship. The Joint Commission issued at the end of Mrs. Gandhi's visit indicated that Iran would provide India credit exceeding one billion dollars to help augment the capacity of her export-oriented industries, establish a joint shipping line with an initial capacity of 500,000 tonnes and triple the capacity of the Kudremukh iron-ore project to 7 million tonnes. The Shah's follow-up three-day visit beginning 2 October was a measure of the fast evolving relationship. These directions produced another trade protocol signed on 23 April 1975, under which production of select Indian export items would be financed by Iran.

The abrupt change of regime in Iran in 1979 did have some short-term adverse effect. Still, there are reasons for greater stability in their bilateralism. Ever since the outbreak of hostilities between Iraq and Iran in September 1980, Mrs. Gandhi remained in close touch with the leaders of several Non-aligned countries and had sought their suggestions and good offices in the search for a solution to the tragic war. In March 1985 when attacks on civilian targets were resumed by the two countries, Prime Minister Rajiv Gandhi as Chairman of NAM sent messages to the President of Iran and Iraq urging an end to attacks on civilian population as provided for in the UN sponsored agreements on June 12, 1984. He said, "the tragic conflict between Iran and Iraq two members in the Non-aligned Movement, has led to untold suffering to their peoples and caused us deep anguish. We are in close contact with the leaders of both countries and our efforts to restore peace are complimentary to the initiatives being taken by others to the same end. A de-escalation and cessation of hostilities is our common objective. We must persevere".

The Minister of State for Petroleum and Natural Gas, Mr. Satish Sharma visited Iran with a high level delegation in early July 1993. A memorandum of understanding signed on the occasion provided for immediate studies on the possibilities of laying a gas pipeline between the two countries and setting up a joint venture fertilisers plant on Qesh island. Iran, which has one of the largest reserves of natural gas in the world, is no doubt convinced that tie-ups with proven Indian expertise in the field of petroleum and natural gas development will be of mutual benefit. Besides, this, the unscheduled meeting between the Indian President, Dr. Shankar Dayal Sharma and his Iranian counterpart Mr. Hashemi Rafsanjani, which took place in the wake of fruitful discussions which the former Foreign Secretary Mr. J.N. Dixit, had with Iranian leaders testifies to the desire of two countries to strengthen their traditional friendship. The Iranian initiative in converting what was only to be refuelling stop of the President on his way to Ukraine into an occasion for a summit meeting was a welcome gesture. Moreover, India and Iran seem to have taken a concerted step towards a new entente cordiale with the visit of Prime Minister Mr. P.V. Narsimha Rao to Islamic Republic of Iran on 20 September 1993. The two MOUs that India and Iran have signed to enhance the cooperation in such spheres as surface transport and science and technology may appear less impressive on paper. But their spin off potential for wider economic cooperation cannot be missed. The Iranian President was appreciative of the fact that Indian democracy had functioned well and that its political experiment coupled with sagacity of the leadership had shown that they were both proficient and competent in dealing with the situation. He said: cooperation between his country and India could play a significant role in ensuring the economic and political stability of the Central Asia region.

India and Iran had been engaged in discussions on economic cooperation in diverse forms and fields in recent times. In his talks with Indian Prime Minister, Mr. Velayati mentioned various possibilities in Iran-India economic cooperation such as the gas pipeline project. A major joint venture being considered a gas-based Fertiliser plant—envisages the purchase by India of the entire production of Urea and ammonia. Also under consideration are schemes for joint exploration of cooking coal, manufacture of equipment for the power and oil refining sectors and cement plants etc. Recently under President Khatami Indo-Iranian ties have flourished further.

7. The Mecca Incident of 1987

The instability in Gulf politics is increasing before our eyes today. The region's political system seems to be breaking down. Its socio-religious and economic cohesion is diminishing. It's weight in world affairs is declining. This deterioration is manifested in the clashes at Mecca between Shite fundamentalists and Saudi riot police in which 275 Iranians, who were among 402 people dead.

What accounted for this situation and what are its implications? In considering these questions it can be said that in the last week of July (1987) Ayatollah Khomeini, the spiritual leader of Iran addressed 153,000 Iranian pilgrims, the largest ever national contingent to take part in the annual Mecca pilgrimage.

Every year there is trouble with the Saudi hosts insisting that the pilgrims confine themselves to strictly religious rituals, and with the Iranians insisting in line with the basic Khomeini principle, that without politics, (that too militant politics) religion is no religion.

The Iranian leadership laid emphasis on "two splendid demonstrations" in Mecca and Medina, to "disavow the infidels". According to Khomeini, Iran has a divine mission to bring about true Islam by weakening and undermining the evils of western influence wherever they appear. In the above message to pilgrims Khomeini exhorted to "export our experiences to the whole world".

The riot started with the contrived pathos of a rally of the disabled, who in Medina shouted anti-American and anti-Israeli slogans from their wheel chairs. Asked about the Saudi prohibition, pilgrim leader Hojatoleslam Mahdi Karroubi opined: "We obey Imam Khomeini's views in relation to the pilgrimage". Besides the Iranians were accused of planning to seize the grand mosque and proclaim Khomeini the leader of the Islamic world. Whether Saudi police opened fire on the pilgrims, as the Iranians claim, or whether most of them were crushed in a general stampede, as the Saudis claim, the outcome—an official Saudi death toll of 402, mainly Iranian women shows how deep is the schism between two Islams, Sunni and Shite. It also witnessed just what dishonour their rivalry can bring on both sides in the shadow of Islam's most important holy place.

Here it is necessary to understand the historical roots of the Saudi-Iranian differences. The struggle between these two countries is rooted in prejudices that have long been part and parcel of the West Asian culture. The Shites' prejudice against the Saudi rulers of Mecca stems from the alleged intolerance of Saudi Islam. The doctrinal forbears of the Saudi state, the Wahabis committed atrocities against Shites in the 19th century, earning an enduring reputation for cruelty. But after their conquest of Mecca in 1924 the Saudis tempered their fervour with pragmatic tolerance. The Shites have not forgiven the Saudis for their excesses. The old libel survives today in the belief that Iranian pilgrims come to Mecca not to worship but to offend the Sunni (Wahabi) sense of propriety by glorifying Ayatollah Ruhollah Khomeini. Thus, the respective sectarian tradition the deaths in Mecca will be interpreted within.

Iran had gone into three days of national mourning, the Saudi and Kuwaiti embassies were ransacked, and the speaker of the Iranian parliament, Ali Akbar Hashemi Rafsanjani called for the overthrow of the Saudi monarchy from the region. Iran warned all international shipping to stay out of Iranian territorial waters for seventy-two hours (immediately after the incident took place in Mecca) while it conducted naval manoeuvres code-named *Operation Martyrdom*. Yet it remains to be seen whether the Iranian leaders are really starting to implement in practice what they have always called for in principle: the destruction of all those tyrants, and despots who, by their definition, are Islamic in name only.

The incident in Mecca emphasised the vulnerability of Arab States to terrorism and subversion. They fear Iran and don't trust the Reagan administration, which turned tail in Beirut. Moderate Arab governments dreaded Khomeini's long arm. The Tunisian authorities had stepped up security measures around the resort towns of Sowse and Monastir, after a series of bomb explosions in hotels there. Leaders of the Arab Sheikhdoms that line the southern Persian Gulf also expressed alarm over Iran's threat to hit economic targets in the event of an escalation in the Gulf war.

The intervention of US naval forces in the Gulf to protect Kuwaiti shipping apparently had prompted Iran to escalate its threats. Rafsanjani declared a "new policy of retaliation", which meant that, "if Iranian economic centres and installations" are attacked, Iran will strike of economic centres of Iraq's allies". These threats had been taken as a grave warning in the Emirates. Largely untouched by the Gulf conflict these Emirates have in fact prospered during the war by offering crude oil at Premium prices to customers who do not want to send their oil tankers through waters made dangerous by Iran. They have supported Iraq out of Arab solidarity and as members of the GCC, but have maintained their strong trade and cultural links with Iran.

Iran's relations with non-Islamic governments are wary at best and subject to sudden breakdowns. Recently Teheran concluded a general agreement with the Soviet Union to cooperate on large economic projects including new rail and pipeline connections between the two countries. But Moscow had been cautious, in its new dealings with Teheran.

The Western countries particularly Germany and Japan, have managed to maintain workable ties with Iran but France didn't succeed in improving its relations with Iran. The US and France alerted their embassies worldwide against expected terrorist attacks following Iranian charges that Saudi guards opened fire at the instance of the US. (The US role in the Mecca clashes seems to be a matter of speculation.) However, the US condemned as 'baseless' the charges that Washington was behind the violence.

In the Arab sphere, President Hosni Mubarak of Egypt and Mr. Yasser Arafat the chairman of the Palestine Liberation Organisation have described the Mecca incident as "painful" and renewed their call for the convening of an Islamic Summit meeting to discuss the death of over 400 pilgrims there and to find out ways and means for ending the Gulf war.

Addressing a Press Conference at Dhaka, Mr. Arafat made an "urgent appeal" to all Islamic countries to hold a Summit conference to find out ways and means for ending the Gulf war (1980-88). He also appealed to Iran and Iraq to stop the fratricidal war for the sake of Islamic unity. "The continuation of the war is against peace, the Islamic world and also against the Palestinian people", he said.

The Arabs seem to be no more interested in a confrontation

with Iran. They want the war to finish because it is now getting too dangerous for them and they don't want the whole Gulf to explode.

Whatever the truth today, Iran stood to profit from the tragedy at Mecca. Threatened by the United States in the Gulf, it felt isolated and vulnerable. Iran sought to portray Muslim anguish over these deaths as support for its struggle against the United States, and an evidence that a move against Iran is tantamount to a move against all Islam. There is no doubt that the Khomeini regime has now entered the climatic phase of its appointed mission, however, one defines that—and that the Meccan mayhem grew out of that. Iran's effort will be rewarded if the United States mistakes Iran for Islam, and loses its resolve for fear of provoking an apocalyptic war with Islam. Although a mere awareness of these developments encourages actions to prevent their repetition, the shattering of the regional order will not be easily repaired. It's the high time the US, the Russia, the NAM, the UN, and the Arab League should contribute towards the speedy solution or easing of the tension in the Gulf. Even though they cannot wave a magic wand and usher in total peace and stability to the area, they can do a great deal more diplomatically to solve the festering problem in the Gulf.

Gulf

8. The Protracted Gulf War (1980-88)

The Gulf war is the bloodiest and the most brutal of all armed conflicts between minor powers since the Second World War. This is said to be the crux of the inter-Arab relations today. It is an event that Arabs and Iranians must come to terms with on the basis of the politics that they have created in the post-colonial era, and on the basis of their own histories and political traditions.

Fighting between the two countries began after Iran ignored Iraqi demands for the withdrawal of Iranian forces from Zain-ul-Qos in Diali province on the border between the two countries. Iraq maintained that this territory should have been returned to Iraq under the 1975 agreement with Iran. Iraq abrogated the 1975 Shatt-al-Arab agreement and invaded Iran on September 22, 1980. Most observers now believe that this was no more than a pretext on Iraq's part, that is, the real objective of its President, Saddam Hussain, being to topple the new threatening but vulnerable Iranian regime.

Iranian resistance was spirited and a position of statements was soon reached along a 300-mile front. Various regional and international peace missions proved of no avail, and in the spring of 1982 the Iranian forces broke the stalemate by launching two offensives, the first in the Shush-Dezful area in March and the second on a 60-mile front south of Susangard to Khorramshahr at the end of April.

In February 1983 Iran began a major offensive in the area of Iraq's Misan Province, but the impetus was soon lost. A further Iranian offensive in July saw its forces entrenched 15 km within northern Iraq. The attack seemed to be consistent with Iran's policy of waging a war of attrition, keeping Iraq busy with war and thereby exerting pressure on the weakening Iraqi economy which might lead to the ouster of the regime of Saddam Hussain.

During the second half of 1983, Iraq stepped up missile and air raids against Iranian towns and petroleum installations. Iran countered by promising to make the Gulf impassable to all shipping (one-sixth of the Western world's petroleum requirement passes through the Gulf) if Iraqi military action rendered it unable to export oil from the Gulf via the Strait of Hormuz. Besides, Iran boycotted the Islamic Conference Organisation (ICO) meeting in Morocco in January 1984, and in Kuwait in January 1987, in protest at its apparent lack of concern over Iraqi bombing of Iranian civilian targets. At the end of the Morocco session of the peace committee of the Islamic Conference Organisation, the President of Gambia was asked to visit both sides. Rafsanjani, the Speaker of the Iranian Parliament, had made it clear that the trip would be pointless, saying: "They meet to discuss a peace plan. What we say is clear. The day you accept that Saddam (Hussain) is the one who started this blaze, that he is the aggressor and war criminal who should be tried in a credible international court, we will be ready to take our finger off the trigger".

In March 1984 a further Iranian offensive succeeded in taking part of the marsh land around the southern Iraqi Island of Majnoun, the site of rich oilfields, though only at a great cost in lives. The Iraqis subsequently retook some of the territory which they had lost. A team of UN observers, sent in at the request of the Iranian government, found that Iraq had used mustard gas to counter the offensive.

The long-discussed Iranian offensive against Iraq and for which it is estimated that Iran had massed between 500,000 and one million men has not materialised. Asked why Iran had changed its strategy, Col. Ishmad Sohrabi, the Chief of Staff, said: 'Out blitzes are planned so as to make it hard for the enemy to redeploy its forces to the area(s) attacked. In our various operations, while we aim to avoid sustaining heavy casualties, we seek to surprise the enemy and to wear him out psychologically.... We wish to render almost impossible for the enemy commanders to plan properly; our operations enable our man to fight an enemy with superior hardware".

Despite its military and economic limitations, Iran's strategy, on the whole, has been to maintain the offensive while Iraq has for the most part remained on the defensive. Iran's successful offensive occurred in February 1986, when its forces surprised the defenders of the port city of Fao by forcing their way in small boats across the snatt-al-Arab waterway. Iran's first major territorial capture, Fao, was a psychological defeat for Iraq. This was followed by the visit of President Hosni Mubarak of Egypt and King Husain of Jordan to Iraq. There the leaders issues a joint statement calling upon the Arabs to stand by Iraq against Iran.

Besides, the moderate Arab solidarity with Iraq over the Gulf war has been strengthened after disclosures of Washington's attempted contacts with Teheran and supply of American arms and spare parts to Iran. The Arab media as a whole condemned the US's secret deals with Iran as an outrageous sell-out of their Arab friends. The response of the Gulf countries was different. The Amir of Kuwait issued a brief tame statement merely saying that the American secret deals with Iran do not conform with the American declared policy in the Gulf area. The long awaited harsh Saudi response never came up.

However, the Gulf war, the longest major conflagration of the century, has been alternatively dismissed or has become the subject of fears. Iran's apparent plan to prolong the war until the Iraqi economy collapses, bringing Saddam Hussain down with it, depends for its success on the extent to which it is able to sustain its own economy. This war may now be entering a phase of 'no war no peace'. Whatever, the immediate results, the war will not end in practice. What we are seeing there is another hundred year's war. The blood treasure and political capital invested by both sides make any pacific resolution almost inconceivable.

What, then, are some of the lessons of the war? The war was provoked and welcomed as a blessing. It has been used to consolidate the regimes, unite and divert the people, repress the opposition and provide a platform for the regime on which to perform. Personalism has reached a hitherto inexperienced pinnacle in these countries, so that the war is not really a war between Iran and Iraq, it is a Saddam-Khomeini war. It is a person-to-person war in which entire nations, entire peoples, are being made to pay the price of the criminal ambitions of one minority government and a crazy individual and the stubbornness of another.

Another noteworthy fact is that the West Asian states have evinced deep, if unworthy interest in the outcome of this war. From Morocco to Oman, or to that extent Pakistan, West Asian governments have shown greater interest in preserving the status quo than in defending national sovereignty or serving the common good. So Saudi Arabia has expended much greater sums of money in saving Saddam Hussein than it has been willing to do to save the lot of Palestinians in the West Bank and Gaza, or to protect the sovereignty and integrity of Lebanon or even to protect the sovereignty of Jerusalem and assure excess for both Muslims and Christians to that sacred city. It betrays the question of humanity and the costs to common people.

We have also seen through this war the harmful effects of the emergence of *rentier states* (i.e. states that have become rich on the basis of one product; or rather, one source of profit, since in West Asia only the peasants and some artisans produce anything. The elite profit a great deal without producing. They have oil, gas and many minerals. Some foreign company comes and extracts these for them) in West Asia and North Africa.

Moreover, there is a frightening absence on the world scale of any mechanism to pursue or ensure peace in the world. This senseless war has been going on for a long period and the world has watched callously and with indifference. The United Nations, along with other Third World forums, which pretends to be concerned and probably is concerned, has been reduced to an expensive cipher.

What interests has the war served? First, the regime in Iran has profited. The Iraqi invasion helped Ayatollah Khomeini and his mullahs to mobilise popular support around nationalism. Khomeini needs the war badly. His regime can now claim that it has succeeded, at least temporarily, in consolidating power.

Second, the war has helped the elite in Iraq to profit from it. Businessmen on both sides of the war are getting rich.

Finally, the war has profited the super powers and their multinational corporations. The losers are the two countries and their inhabitants. Their resources depleted, their cities destroyed and their economies in ruins, Iran and Iraq are countries of orphans and widows, of sacrificed youths whom those in power have entitled martyrs.

In conclusion, this much can be said that the world will not be safe to live in as long as through the power of public opinion and the power of movements, we do not produce new institutions, and new ways of ensuring peace between madmen who drag in large numbers of decent people because they are powerless.

9. Cease-Fire in the Gulf (1988)

What can be described as the most profound and touching message from the Islamic leaders of Iran was the recent broadcast to the nation and the people of the world, namely. Teheran accepted a call by the United Nations Security Council (Peace Resolution 598) for a Gulf war ceasefire. Indeed, Ayatollah Khomeini's unprecedented approval of the ceasefire ushers in a new era in the Iranian history and marks a significant phase in the politico-military developments of West Asia and world at large. This is one of the most delicate peace decisions of this century.

The UN Resolution 598 (adopted on July 20 last year) demanded that both the parties cease all conflict and withdraw to their borders. Iran's decision to accept the UN ceasefire has rightly provided a chance to end the eight-year-old Gulf war (which has left at least 360,00 soldiers dead and about 1 million civilian casualties). But hard work will be needed to make the long desired peace take hold. And there is still a space for thought here which should not be wasted.

Against the background of intense diplomatic activity at the United Nations, it is perhaps useful to rehearse some of the main factors responsible for the Iranian decision to agree to the ceasefire and put them into the proper perspective of events.

To start with, all attempts to end the war by the UN, the Gulf States, the Islamic Conference Organisation, the Non-Aligned Movement, the Organisation of African Unity (OAU) and by other Islamic and European bodies had failed. It was thought that the stumbling block to peace was Iran's insistence that a condition of peace would be the fall of Saddam Hussain in Iraq. However, the terrible Iranian losses in the US cruiser *Vincennes's* deliberate shooting down of Iran's civilian Airbus with 290 people on board (July 3, 1988), preceded by Iraqi victories in recapturing Fao Peninsula (April 17, 1988), Shalamcheh Marshes east of Basra (May 25, 1988), Majnoun Islands (June 25, 1988), followed by Iraq's recapturing of Zubeidat areas south-west of Baghdad and the recent damaging Iraqi raids (with the use of chemical weapons) on Iranian cities along with the new pragmatic Iranian leadership under Hojatoleslam Rafsanjani forced the regime in Teheran to seek the new moderate approach of peace to the war.

It is rightly believed that Rafsanjani, who was appointed Chief of Staff of the Iranian armed forces in June this year, viewed the continuation of the war and its effect on the economy as a greater threat to the regime's long-term chances of survival.

Another factor may have been a growing dissatisfaction on the part of some Iranian officials with their countries isolation from the rest of the world. Moreover, there was speculation that Iran's change of heart might be related to the 88-year-old Islamic leader Khomeini's deteriorating health. Whether or not Khomeini's health is falling, Iran's sudden ceasefire move confounded, the widespread prediction that the hostilities would not cease until he died.

The UN Resolution 598 on a ceasefire adopted on July 20 last year and which Iran accepted on July 18 this year and Iraq agreed to abide by the terms set out in the resolution from the outset, contains the following main points:

(i) UN Secretary-General Javier Perez de Cuellar invited the Foreign Ministers of Iran and Iraq to New York last week (July 1988) to discuss a *truce agreement*. The UN also dispatched a military team to Teheran and Baghdad to begin arranging the details;

(ii) Neither side now holds any significant parts of the other's *territory*;

(iii) Prisoners to be exchanged. Iran has about 50,000 Iraqi prisoners of war, and Iraq holds about 20,000 Iranians.

(iv) With August 20 set for a truce, UN Secretary General would open *negotiations* (he has already started *for a comprehensive Peace treaty*;

(v) A UN *commission* will be established *to determine who started the war*. Iran drops its early refusal to stop fighting until Iraq is labelled the aggressor and President Saddam Hussain of Iraq is ousted;

(vi) Another UN commission will be set up to study international aid for post-war reconstruction of both countries;

(vii) Calls upon Iran and Iraq to cooperate with the Secretary General in implementing this resolution and all other states to exercise the utmost restraint and to refrain from any act which may lead to further escalation;

(viii) Besides, requests the Secretary General to examine in consultation with Iran and Iraq and with other states of the Gulf region, measures to enhance the security and stability of the region;

(ix) Requests the Secretary-General to keep the Security Council informed on the implementation of this resolution;

(x) Decides to meet again as necessary to consider further steps to ensure compliance.

Iran's announcement of the acceptance of UN Resolution 598 and agreeing to have direct talks with Iraq was welcomed in West Asia, starting from moderate Arab states like Egypt, Saudi Arabia, Jordan, Oman to radical Arab states like Syria, Libya, Algeria and others.

In Israel, which has long taken great comfort from the thought that two of its avowed enemies were busy fighting each other, there was a sense of foreboding. The prospect of the battle tested Iraqi army turning its attention to the Jewish state is unsettling to Israelis. Shimon Peres, the Israeli Foreign Minister, said that a ceasefire could pose a new threat to Israel if Iran or Iraq decided to turn its fire power against the Jewish state.

Washington called it "a major breakthrough", opening the way for the end of the war. However, for Washington, one of the big questions is whether an end to the Gulf war will allow Washington to reduce its formidable naval buildup in the area. The US has no intention of completely ending its naval presence in the area which goes back to nearly 40 years.

Besides, in both Teheran and Baghdad, the people received the news with astonishment and joy. In Teheran people handed over sweets to celebrate the announcement. An end to clashes would lessen hostility between Iran and Iraq's main Gulf Arab backers—Kuwait and Saudi Arabia which have suffered missile hits, attacks on ships, and attacks apparently linked to their support to Baghdad. It would remove a major threat to countries that provide much of the world's oil supplies.

Moreover, most of the Asian and European powers welcomed the Iranian decision for a UN ceasefire in the Gulf war, saying an end to the war could create new business opportunities.

The sign of goodwill and peace intentions shown by the Islamic Iran deserves encouragement. The world powers should feel happy to deal with a pleasant, prosperous, moderate regime in Teheran. Iraq and Iran must be freed to use their massive oil wealth to rebuild their war-ravaged economy and return to normalcy.

10. US Policy in the Third World

The Third World region, particularly the Arab nations, is today faced with the most serious challenge to its integrity and independence. With the Arab moderate regimes stubbornly aligning with the US Imperialists and the West, the United States and Zionist Israel are now poised to exert massive military, physical and economic influence and control in the region. From the outset of the Israeli invasion of Lebanon (1982) and the freedom struggle of the oppressed Arab-Palestinian children, i.e. *Intifadeh*, the Iraqi revolutionary leader President Saddam Hussein had rightly urged the Arab rulers to mobilise their defence against the US Imperialist and Zionist designs.

Under the cover of Kuwaiti liberation, the United States has quietly moved to step up its military presence in the Arab homeland. The brutal bombardment of the thousands of Iraqi and Kuwaiti women and children in the recent times has again highlighted the dangers facing the Third World.

Viewed against the background of the events in Eastern and Central Europe, the tide of recent radical Arab nationalism espoused by President Saddam Hussein or President Yasser Arafat of Palestine Liberation Organisation (PLO) or Colonel Muammar Gaddhafi of Libya has been rolled back by the muscular and economic diplomacy of United States and its direct intervention in the Gulf.

Besides, nowhere outside Europe is the revolution in Soviet foreign policy under President Mikhail Gorbachev more tangible than in the way Gorbachev has reached to US armed intervention in the Gulf and destruction of the Arab state of Iraq. Once the champion of the anti-Western and anti-colonial forces in the Gulf, the Soviet Union now projects itself as a partner with the US in destroying the Arab socialist state of Iraq.

The US President George Bush along with the Western and Zionist leaders had spoiled the plans of anybody who brought into the idea that a new "Era of Universal Peace" was dawning.

Taking into account the recent armed might of the US Imperialist army in the Gulf, the US has re-established its political, economic and military hegemony over the region more fully than at any time since the post-World War II period.

Since 1945 the US has initiated and taken part in most armed conflicts and staged interventions in different parts of the Third World, i.e. not only in Latin America (Cuba and Panama recently) but also in the Mediterranean (Libya), Africa, Asia and the Arab region.

Not long ago in October 1983, the US Imperialists invaded Grenada, a tiny island of the Caribbeans, violating the UN Charter and defying the international law and norms of conduct. Following it the US took vigorous steps for a large-scale invasion of Lebanon and butchered the state in concert with its ally the Zionist Israel. All this found reflection in the brazen statement by a highly placed US dignitary who claimed that the world looked to America for leadership while America, for its part, looked to its marines.

The rash US action in the Gulf shook the lakhs of Arab people there. Though the outcome of the US ambitions in the Gulf is very much predictable, it has already elicited a series of threats to the Third World. It has lasting ramifications for the reconstruction of the Third World, particularly Gulf region, US-Soviet relations, credibility of United Nations and other international and regional organisations.

It has its impact on other conflicts such as Lebanon, Cyprus, Western Sahara and last but not the least the Arab-Israeli crisis i.e. the Palestine question. 'The present crisis', rightly says Prof. K.R. Singh of Jawaharlal Nehru University, 'has once again exposed the ever volatile Gulf region to the multiple regional and international imperialist pressures that threaten to unleash yet another violent conflict'.

Decades after formal independence, Third World countries including the West Asian region still find themselves under severe restrictions to fully exercise their sovereignty as nation states. In the post-1945 period, the colonial territories have by and large attained independence. As a bloc, the Third World countries are supposed to be free and equal participants in the shaping of world development. Yet in reality the big Imperialist powers particularly the US maintain a dominant grip over international relations—including the international organisation i.e. the United Nations.

Despite pious declarations of non-interference and non-intervention, Imperialist powers like the US can choose to invade or attack other countries under various pretexts such as "self defence". Besides, the Third World countries' right to take back control over their own natural resources, and to nationalise industries in order to do so, has also been blocked in many cases including the Gulf region by the US and Zionist Israel who want to maintain their stranglehold over the world resources and wealth (as the case of Zionists' forcible occupation and exploitation of Arab-Palestinian resources and wealth).

Moreover, behind the facade of the United Nations, sheer US military might is still the force around which the system of international relations revolves.

The eyes of the world are now focused on what sort of Peace will emerge from the debris of the recently concluded Gulf War. Will it be one whose modalities have been worked out carefully and impartially by the UN Security Council—already suspected of being influenced by the UN's biggest paymaster, the US—or will it be one imposed on a toothless Iraq by the US and its Western partners. To consider this point here one needs to delve into the past and to find out the real reasons for the US entry into the Gulf conflict which has claimed more than 150,000 lives, military and civilian.

It would be foolish to believe that the US attacked Iraq out of brotherly love for the Kuwaitis, or on sympathetic grounds. If this was so, why did it not raise a finger to save the people of Hungary, Czechoslovakia or Afghanistan when the USSR forcibly intervened in their territories? And did it protest when Zionist Israel grabbed the whole of Arab-Palestinian territory?

Oil, the most valuable resource, was the motivating factor, especially since US's domestic resources of this liquid gold are fast drying up what more effective way could have been found of ensuring an unlimited supply of oil than by becoming the dominant dictating power in the largest oil-producing store in the world?

The US under President George Bush has lost a great deal of prestige in the Comity of Nations by the indiscriminate bombing of the civilians, women and child population in Iraq. One lesson of the war is very clear: unless and until the United Nations can be provided with more effective means of enforcing its decisions, it might as well be wound up, as was the League of Nations during the inter-war (1919-1945) period.

The UN should be freed from domination by the two Super Powers. It should play a major and positive part in the improvement of the situation in the West Asian region. It would be logical for the UN to lay the main emphasis on care for the interests of all sides concerned and, from this viewpoint, on a fair settlement of the situation and practical steps towards peace in that region.

A de-escalation of the conflict and some positive settlement are better than the encouragement of a conflict pending its comprehensive settlement. Immediate priority should be given to the long lingering Palestinian problem. It is time for the UN, US and the West to accept the reality and seriousness of the Palestine question.

It is also the time to realise that a peaceful settlement of the Palestine question in the shape of the establishment of a Palestinian state at West Bank and Gaza with its capital at Jerusalem. The establishment of a Arab-Palestinian state would be in the best interest of the UN, US and the West as well as regional and world peace.

11. US-Iraq Confrontation

It was with a collective sigh of relief that the Arab World, Russia, France, China and India greeted the Iraqi decision on the unconditional return of United Nations weapons inspectors in an apparent bid to avert an imminent US military strike on Baghdad.

The confrontation between Iraq and the US has come to an end with Baghdad responding positively to the letter of UN Secretary General Kofi Annan appealing to them to allow United Nations arms inspectors to resume work of eliminating Iraq's weapons of mass destruction.

The crisis in Iraq over the UN inspection of suspected weapons sites again escalated with the United States reported to be weighing the option of an air strike early in November, 1998. A similar crisis in the early part of 1998 which appeared more serious was resolved by the active intervention of Annan.

By preventing the outbreak of a dangerous war in the Gulf region, the UN Secretary General has again achieved a rare victory for peace.

Annan's latest deal with the Iraqi leadership certainly elicited an enormous sigh of relief from an anxious world. Three out of five UN Security Council permanent members—Russia, China and France—expressed support while the US and UK did not reject it.

However, it is unfortunate that the US leadership still thinks in terms of deposing Iraqi President Saddam Hussain by force. The presence of US soldiers, ships and war planes poses a serious threat to peace, stability and security of the Gulf region.

Besides, the US is still contemplating a more imaginative set of new options than simply threatening to bomb Iraq in a way that might not do so much good. No country except Kuwait sees real necessity for prolonged presence of massive US troops in the region.

The developments in the Gulf are a direct consequence of

the old US hardline stance demanding an unrestricted access for UNSCOM weapon inspectors to inspect all possible chemical and biological weapons storage sites in Iraq.

United States' desperate attempts to rally support among its European and Arab allies for a possible military strike against Iraq over arms inspections had caused concern all over the world, with Russian President Boris Yeltsin even warning that the use of force could trigger another 'world war' and do untold damage to the stability and security of Gulf region.

It was also a matter of anxiety as tension was created by the flexing of muscles by United States to launch what is termed a "substantial" attack on Iraq.

"We face a new cold war in the Gulf", said Middle East expert Anthony Cordesman. The US is in for a long stay in the Gulf. Neither the use of force against Iraq nor its search for a peaceful solution would make the US come out of the region. It could not ignore its economic and military strategic interests in the region.

In retrospect, Iraqi President Saddam Hussain's refusal to allow United Nations access to inspection sites within Iraq led to this situation which international experts said was unfortunate.

The United States and Britain have more fire power trained on Iraq than at any time since the 1991 Gulf war, and had been rallying support for military action.

Across the Arab world, from Egypt to the Arabian Peninsula, popular unease at the prospect of an attack was mounting along with anger at United States which is seen as arrogant and blindly loyal to Israel and possible US military strikes at Baghdad without the Security Council mandate as an act of naked aggression.

To many Arabs, Iraq is more an object of pity. While the west formulates the conflict as one with Saddam himself, Arabs tend to see it as bullying of a people made to suffer needlessly.

"The Arab leaders feel the opposition in their bones" said Michael Hudson, an expert on the Arab world at Georgetown University. "If that opposition were actually articulated in the political process, I think many of these governments would be even more opposed".

The Arab states accuse Washington of double standards in its West Asia policy and felt that west should exert the same pressure on Israel to respect international law as it does on Baghdad.

President Bill Clinton's entanglement in Monicagate affair prompted an opinion in Europe and Arab world that he is seeking to divert attention from his domestic troubles through a confrontation with President Saddam Hussain. Arab diplomats point that Iraq is not the only country in the world with weapons of mass destruction.

According to military sources, some 10 countries including Israel in West Asia have more efficient biological and chemical weapons technology.

The Arab League has warned the US against a military attack on Iraq saying that the use of force on Arab state was unacceptable. The League cautioned the US against embarking on a new military attack on Baghdad and asked Washington to evolve diplomatic solutions to end the crisis.

Egyptian foreign minister, Amre Moussa, also came out against the military solution in Iraq and said the use of force will only add to the problems. He agreed with the Arab League that diplomacy and dialogue should be engaged to solve the Iraqi crisis.

Jordan along with Turkey, Algeria, Morocco and Tunisia also renewed its opposition to any military action against Iraq.

In an interesting reaction to possible punitive US military strike against Iraq, Iranian foreign minister, Kamal Kharrazi, said his country opposed any escalation of the present crisis and use of military forces as such a move would not only further increase the agony of the Iraqi people but also worsen regional situation.

The Times, London, citing western intelligence and security sources, said the security officials from Iran and Iraq had met secretly to forge an alliance in the face of growing US military buildup in Gulf.

The meeting, if confirmed, would provide evidence that the once bitter foes are developing new contacts and putting aside, for the time being at least, obstacles that have blocked normalisation of their ties after the 1980-88 war.

Russia and China, strongly backed by France, issued a stark ultimatum to the US, warning that they would do their utmost to block the threatened Anglo-American attack on Iraq, including use of their vetoes in the UN Security Council.

However, Kuwait has said, it will not oppose military option against Iraq if all peaceful efforts to solve the current imbroglio in the Middle East fail.

Kuwaiti ambassador in India Abdulal SO Al Ganaei said, "We want a peaceful and diplomatic initiative to help ensure peace in the region but if the military action becomes the last resort, Kuwait and other GCC countries would not come in the way".

India, well-known for its initiatives on peace, also raised a strong protest against America's muscle flexing over Iraq.

Kofi Annan has shared India's concern about the situation in Iraq and backed New Delhi's readiness "to contribute to the process of finding a peaceful and diplomatic solution to the present crisis".

Former Indian Prime Minister I.K. Gujral said India would not tolerate a military attack on Iraq as it would jeopardise peace in the entire west Asian region, where more than three million Indians live. Gujral further stated that disruption of peace and stability in the Gulf would have serious effect on India's economy and national welfare.

The Congress party said it was committed to the territorial integrity of Iraq and would like to see Iraq play its rightful role in regional and world affairs.

The central secretariat of the Communist Party of India also expressed deep concern over the continued threat of the US imperialists to attack Iraq in the name of forcing the UN Security Council resolutions about destroying weapons of mass destruction allegedly still in the possession of Iraq.

Since March 1991, Iraq has been living under UN resolutions and sanctions which stipulated conditions for ceasefire in the Gulf war and elimination of weapons of mass destruction in Iraq.

The economic and other sanctions imposed on Iraq have caused immense hardships to the 20 million Iraqi people, particularly the aged, women and children.

Children are malnourished, hygiene conditions are appalling and the threat of diseases looms large. Over 5,000 children die every month.

India's anxiety, shared by others, is to ensure against destabilisation of the sensitive but fragile Gulf region.

It is clear that India has no other stance to take except to oppose and eliminate the possibilities of war in the Gulf. In the first place America's threat to Iraq and the prolonged presence of

US troops goes against India's long-standing stance of peace and co-existence.

India perceives that any military initiative in Iraq is bound to have its repercussions in Kuwait. To India, the repercussions in Kuwait means turmoil, destability and chaos in a neighbourhood with which it has political, economic, social and cultural relationship.

Therefore, India's compulsions are very obvious. It wants to uphold on the one hand its moral prestige as an apostle of peace while on the other it wants to ensure that no harm comes to its friendly neighbours. An end to UN sanctions in Iraq will go a long way to bring stability to the whole region.

12. Operation Desert Fox

It is matter of much relief that the American and British missile and air attacks on Iraq have been halted. It was with a collective sigh of relief that the Arab world, Russia, India, France and China greeted this development. The US President, Mr. Bill Clinton had said that "significant damage" had been inflicted on Iraq's weapons of mass destruction programmes, on command structures that protect the capacity and on that country's military and security infrastructure.

But has the American mission in launching the attacks been really achieved, as Mr. Clinton claimed? And at what cost? The American propaganda aimed at serving the single-minded purpose of dethroning the Iraqi President, Mr. Saddam Hussein, has always been suspect. All the talk about so-called Iraqi "weapons of mass destruction" have become even more suspect than before. The Clinton administration obviously hopes that the four-day military barrage would bring palpable change to Iraq's political landscape. That probably will be a long-range goal. But there can be no doubt that the four-day long military aggression code-named Operation Desert Fox will alter the political and diplomatic landscape elsewhere.

The UN Security Council and the office of the Secretary-General (Mr. Kofi Annan) are still in shock at how callously and casually they were sidelined by the US. The unilateral action has truly made the world body irrelevant in the global decision-making process. Besides it seems certain that the UN Special Commission (UNSCOM) would become irrelevant. The latest American strikes have virtually ended the possibility of the UN Special Commission resuming its work of weapons inspection. Iraq cannot be expected to take kindly to the commission's return after all that it has gone through.

It is ironic that the US attack is sought to be justified on the ground that it is in keeping with UN security Council resolution. When this sudden US-British attack was carried out, three permanent members of the Security Council—France, Russia and China—expressed their opposition to it. The demand of Russia and China that the attack should be immediately halted was fully supported by India. It was only to be expected that the sense of outrage of India's general public and members of Parliament, belonging to all political sections, found immediate expression in the Houses which were in session.

The Prime Minister, Mr. Atal Behari Vajpayee, deplored the Anglo-American aggression by pointing out that the use of force would be counter-productive. India's call for resolving the issue diplomatically, through peaceful means and dialogue, is likely to have little impact on the United States at this time, but should be sincerely pursued in concert with like-minded nations in various international fora including the United Nations.

The American-dominated Security Council, dealing with Iraq, have to undergo a change if the tensions have to come down. The call for a review of the eight-year-old UN embargo on Iraq, made by the President of France, Mr. Jacques Chirac, is very timely. Mr. Chirac, whose country is a permanent-member of the Security Council, had urged that the living conditions of the Iraqi people "who have suffered for so many years" had to be improved very quickly. Pope John Paul expressed his bitterness at the US-led raids on Iraq, saying hopes that international law could be upheld had been dashed.

"Not only do I feel profound sorrow for the Iraqi people, I am also bitter to see how often the hopes invested in the power and validity of international law and in the organisations meant to guarantee its application are disappointed", he said in his Angelus speech to pilgrims in St. Peter's square. Coming from a non-political personality like the Pope, the remarks are significant.

Russian President Boris Yeltsin also expressed strong condemnation of the military strikes on Iraq, describing the decision to strike without the backing of the Security Council—where Russia has a veto—as a violation of the United Nations Charter. Russia, along with China, demanded the resignation of Richard Butler, UNSCOM chief, for distorting the key UN report and playing "a dishonourable role in this crisis".

Butler is being increasingly seen by several countries as complicating the problem by assuming a political role for the UN Security Council itself, instead of abiding by the task assigned to him of certifying Iraq's compliance with UN resolution. In the wake of the attacks on Iraq, Russian Prime Minister Yevgeny Primakov, in his recent visit to New Delhi, called for a "strategic triangle" between Russia, India and China to ensure regional geo-political stability and to "set new parameters" to bilateral relations.

Arab governments and newspapers fiercely criticised the US air strikes on Baghdad. A common theme of the Arab protests was that all Arabs, and not just Iraqi leader Saddam Hussein, are being targeted by the US and British attacks. "The aggression on Iraq is an aggression on the whole Arab nation", said Aziza Fadhel, a university student in Damascus.

Sheikh Sabah Al-Ahmed Al-Sabah, the Kuwaiti Foreign Minister and deputy Prime Minister, expressed his point by saying that the current crisis was between Iraq and the United Nations. "We are not part of it, and we have nothing to do with it whatsoever", he was quoted as saying. The Kuwaiti comment has special relevance since it was the Iraqi attack on Kuwait that set off the present crisis.

Malaysia, Indonesia, North Korea along with other states deplored and condemned the US air attacks on Baghdad saying that such military action would destroy stability and peace in the region. It was a brazen act of international terrorism conducted by a beleaguered American President a day before the impeachment debate was due against him. With scant regard for civilian lives or property, the Anglo-Americans have unleashed a new imperialist war against Iraq barely hiding their contempt for the sovereignty of Afro-Arab-Asian and Latin American nations and the basic rights of citizens who are not Americans. This is a sad moment for the United Nations and the world.

It is imperative that developing world, including India, takes a timely stand against this unilateral American action and exerts unified pressure through the Non-Aligned Movement, the United Nations and other organisations.

If the US air strikes against Iraq have achieved anything outside the battered country and people it is to devalue the developing world and its dignity as perhaps never before. It is high time that the international opinion asserts itself.

13. Sanctions Against Iraq: How Long will People Suffer?

From the issue of economic, military and social sanctions on the people of Iraq, Libya, Sudan and Iran to the Arab-Israeli peace process not one of the major problems of the Arab-African region has been resolved in the new millennium. The prospects are that the coming months too would be every bit more turbulent than the early part of the millennium.

The George Bush (Jr.)-Tony Blair new policy on Iraq involves nothing more than the use of brute military force and economic sanctions to contain President Saddam Hussein. This in turn, causes immense suffering to the people of Iraq, particularly women and innocent children. The Anglo-American resolution to maintain a massive military presence in the Arab-African region exposed their political, economic, military and strategic aims against the people of the region.

The economic agenda of maintaining strategic and military control over the giant oil resources of the Gulf region is obvious to anyone. While it is true that the sanctions policy has been imposed on Iraq through the United Nations Security Council, it is very clear that the US and Britain have remained its strongest and consistent proponents.

Since March 1991, Iraq has been living under UN embargoes and sanctions which stipulated conditions for ceasefire in the 1991 Gulf War. The economic and other sanctions imposed on Iraq have caused immense hardships to the 23.5 million Iraqi people, particularly the aged, women and children. Children are malnourished, hygiene conditions are appalling and the threat of diseases looms large. Over 5,000 children die every month.

A striking example of the reality in Iraq came to light in an interview with Dennis Halliday, the former UN assistant secretary-general responsible for implementing the UN's "oil for food programme". Discrediting the myth of consensus among UN officials, Halliday confessed that in his view sanctions were "undermining the moral credibility of the UN" and "in contradiction of the human rights provisions in the UN's own charter".

UN Secretary-General Kofi Annan has, from time to time, reported to the Security Council on the devastating and tragic effects of sanctions on the civilian population of Iraq, and also as recently as December 2000. He gave a detailed account of dramatic increase in infant mortality due to the sanctions and then admitted in his report that the implementation of the oil for food deal did not redress the severe health and nutrition conditions of Iraqis because of the UN embargo imposed on them for more than a decade now.

At the time of the Kuwaiti crisis the UN Security Council was led by the US and the West into imposing sanctions on Iraq. After the end of the conflict, many have seen and realised the futility of the sanctions imposed on Iraq. The US attempt to keep up the pressure on Iraq for toppling President Saddam Hussein does not have international support. The continuing UN sanctions against Iraq have only prolonged the misery and sufferings of the people of Iraq. They are being used as a political, military and economic tool for US policies and interests in the Arab-African region.

There is a total disintegration of the Iraqi society, a complete failure of the infrastructure and all necessities of life-water, sanitation, medicine, hospitals, communication, transportation and others. It is not only the environmental and sanitary conditions which are deteriorating, the agricultural viability of farmlands have also decreased. To quote Bert Sacks, representing one of the humanitarian organisations, although the UN sanctions are "intended to eliminate weapons of mass destructions in Iraq, they themselves have become a weapon of mass destruction.... Legally what sanctions are doing is an act of terrorism".

The US should realise that any unilateral use of force against Iraq will not only be illegal under international laws but will also have serious socio-political, economic and geo-strategic consequences. The double standards of US policy in the Arab-African region are now fully out in the open. The way it is siding with Israel against the Arab Palestinians and the way it has been dealing with Iraq, has made it clear that it has now fully assumed the job of the global policeman.

The former Iraqi foreign minister Mohammed Saeed al-Sahhaf

suggested that Iraq could allow less intrusive UN monitoring of its weapons facilities if the decade-old sanctions are immediately lifted and if Israel and other countries in the Arab-Africa are similarly monitored for proscribed weapons.

Russia's President Vladimir Putin met Mr Taha Yassin Ramadan, the Vice-President of Iraq, to step up efforts to lift UN sanctions on Iraq. The last few years have seen the UN spending huge resources on committees to monitor "weapons of mass destruction", issues relating to the Iraqi-Kuwaiti border and the plight of Kuwaitis missing since the Gulf War, but no UN Body has been formed to assess the impact of the sanctions on the civilian population of Iraq, Libya, Sudan or Iran. In order to comply with the spirit of the UN Charter, the Security Council must take upon itself the task of monitoring the humanitarian effects of its own policies.

The continuous US-sponsored UN sanctions do not have the sanction of international community. It's a unilateral US decision. The US is so powerful today that it is able to get its way through. That does not mean there is international support for the policy. Even the US had to agree to the 1996 UN "Food for Oil deal" for Iraq. But the food for oil deal is serving a limited purpose. Even the US allies, except Britain, do not support the UN sanctions on Iraq.

The so-called smart sanctions idea of the US is an attempt to satisfy the allies of the US who are opposed to the sanctions. There is no logic behind this. The plain motive is to topple President Saddam Hussein of Iraq. The international community will have to convey to the US its disagreement with such policies. One hopes over a period of time good sense will prevail.

It's not Saddam's Iraq alone against which the US policy is directed. The Americans have targeted Libya, Iran, Sudan, Cuba and other states in a highhanded fashion. But they have not been successful in toppling their leadership. It would be the same with Iraq. Because in all these cases the leadership enjoys the support of the people. That is their strength. It is high time that the international opinion asserts itself. It is time to end the economic sanctions on Iraq and the politically motivated UN arms inspections.

14. Uneasy Moves to Market Economy

At present the world economy is on a slowly accelerating growth path. It has not yet attained the more rapid and sustainable rate of growth that it is capable of. The twin processes of liberalisation and globalisation are shaping a new system of international economic relations. Privatisation or Liberalisation has become the acid test for the commitment of the governments of Developing and Under-Developed States, (DUDS) to the creation of a market-based economic system.

Liberalisation or globalisation of national economy has been continuing in the last two decades through flows of trade, finance, information and technological change. More than just a change of ownership of individual companies, privatisation involves the restructuring of entire sectors and a total overhaul of the domestic economy in order to create an environment conducive to the development and growth of private enterprise. Privatisation policies imply a complete reform of the fiscal system, involve numerous institutional and legal reforms, address the creation of financial markets and shake up the system of relative prices by slashing subsidies and removing price controls.

The primary motives for privatisation or liberalisation can be divided into the following categories, viz. introducing a market economy; increasing economic efficiency; establishing a political system based upon private property rights and individual freedoms; and boosting state revenues. Naturally, the abandonment of traditional central planning and simultaneous introduction of a set of market-oriented economic reforms is far from a smooth process.

Globalisation on the other hand could be defined as increasing inter-relationships through movement of factors of production among nations and economies. Although the process of globalisation began during the late 18th and early 19th centuries, the present day system has certain distinct features. A salient feature of this is the fragmentation of the production process, with facilities scattered around the globe in pursuit of access to cheap sources of labour and other inputs, growing markets and financial concessions etc. It envisages closer all-round integration of a developing economy with the international market. Such integration is sought not only through expanding trade and foreign direct investment, but also by way of free mobility of finance capital.

The globalisation as we are witnessing it today, has created a paradox: increasing wealth creation and profitability of business is accompanied by job losses and often lower wages at the non-executive levels. Scepticism about globalisation is growing not only in the developing and under-developing countries but also in the developed world, where widespread unemployment and other human and social costs are causing public opinion to turn against the globalised economy. It is becoming harder for the industrialised countries to ask their public to go through the pains and uncertainties of structural economic adjustments for the sake of benefits in a distant future.

Some in the developed world are also pointing out the lack of an ethical dimension to the system of globalisation. In many developing and transition economies, however, economic adjustment programmes are beginning to bear fruit. Developments in Arab Gulf States are quite significant. Professor Girijesh Pant's book *The Arab Gulf Economies: From Crisis to Reform* explains this process lucidly.

Professor Pant's timely publication constitutes a distinct contribution to the literature on international economic relations, reforms and global economic changes with special reference to Arab Gulf States. This book reflects the changing economic policy scenario. It tries to establish the nature of the longer-term economic trends that have shaped the Arab Gulf States in the recent times.

The book comes at a time when it is needed the most. It looks into the nature and dimension of the economic changes and the initiatives taken by the states for crisis management. It also probes, in the words of the author, into the political and social ramifications of the reform process. Though the focus of the study is on Arab Gulf countries, its findings are equally relevant for the developing world.

The book has five chapters with a span of 193 pages, inclusive of a selected bibliography of about three pages. The first chapter opens with a discussion of the globalisation process and the evolutionary path of the national economies particularly of the Arab Gulf States. Here, Dr. Pant argues that global pressure on the Arab Gulf economies is going to be determined by the changing power dynamics of the 'new world order' the structural and behavioural changes in the oil industry and the peace-security matrix of the Arab Gulf region. With the globalisation process gaining momentum the Arab Gulf countries have little choice but to restructure their economies.

The second chapter talks about the unprecedented economic boom triggered by the rising oil prices which led to basic transformations in these Arab societies. However, the upward swing of the Gulf economy did not last long. By 1986, with oil prices touching the lowest, prospects of stagnation started looming large. Though the regional economies started growing in 1990s, they remained much smaller in size in 1995 as compared to the earlier period. The core of Dr. Pant's text is his projection of the demographic changes and labour market on the one side and the oil market, oil reserves and production ratio on the other.

The performance of the Gulf economies during the period under review, was also influenced by two devastating and tragic wars—the eight-year war between Iran and Iraq and the Iraqi-Kuwaiti war in 1991—and their impact on the economy of the region. The military expenditure of the region has gone up from $15.6 billion in 1979 to $46.5 billion in 1995.

In the third chapter the author lays emphasis on the fiscal policy of Arab Gulf states which influences their national agenda. In negotiating the fiscal crisis, the Arab rentier states find it difficult to revise their fiscal contract with the society. Oil exporting economies of the Arab Gulf region are the most obvious and appropriate test case of a rentier economy, says Dr. Pant. The vast volume of oil reserves with lowest production cost has provided these economies enormous amount of finance exceeding their capacity to absorb them.

Pant has devoted the whole of chapter four to the social implications of privatisation has been on the national agenda of the developing countries since the early eighties. However, not many governments have been able to implement it effectively. Reservations and resistance have come from different segments of the society including industry, merchants, labour, politicians and bureaucrats. Besides, the initiatives regarding privatisation policy taken by the six Arab Gulf countries (Saudi Arabia, Kuwait, Oman, Bahrain, Qatar and UAE) suggest that the pace and level of privatisation process has not been identical in all these States.

Dr. Pant's special highlight in chapter five is the process of transition from a regime of 'over developed' centralised State to competitive market. It is a complex process and a number of factors contribute in determining the transition process. In the case of oil exporting Arab Gulf countries, the external factors have been of decisive importance.

The State in these countries, argues Dr. Pant, has enjoyed much higher degree of autonomy due to power disparity between the State and the market. The civil society has been either non-existent or at best very feeble. Political liberalisation and democratisation has become one of the leading issue on national debate both at official and non-official levels in the Arab Gulf region in the 1990s. The State has taken initiatives in most of these countries creating space for political debate and a semblance of sharing of power.

Kuwait is the most advanced form of democracy, concludes Dr. Pant. Besides, what is important for the Arab Gulf state is to extend the parameters of debate as it moves towards market culture by engaging the political and social segments into dialogue and if need be by coopting them into the mainstreams of the debate.

Professor Pant's book is a valuable contribution in the study of developing economies particularly of Arab Gulf countries in their various dimensions. It is quite useful and interesting for the students of West Asia and Gulf. It adds a new and demanding perspective to scholarship on new economic policies of nations.

West Asia Peace

15. Quest for Peace

While East-West relations appeared to dominate international relations in the early part of the 1970s, world politics had many other crucial subjects on its agenda. The latter part of the 1970s and early 1980s witnessed a series of regional happenings in the Middle East and South West Asian regions, viz., the Camp David Agreement between Egypt and Israel, the Islamic Revolution in Iran, the Gulf War, Soviet intervention in Afghanistan, Israeli invasion of Lebanon and the subsequent departure of the Palestine Liberation Organisation from Lebanon, the Islamic resurgence in the Middle East and other regions, the crisis in Western Sahara, and the Great Palestinian uprising (Intifideh) in the Israeli-occupied Arab-Palestinian territories of the West Bank and Gaza.

Attributes of Regional Conflicts

Clearly there is a great variety of political conflicts and inter-state tensions in the region. It is hard to generalise about them, especially those—primarily domestic in nature. But the major overt conflicts, do appear to have some common characteristics.

First of all, they are generally of long-standing. The major inter-state and civil wars raging today have been going on for years. The above mentioned Palestinian-Israeli conflict, the Sahara and Lebanon wars began in the late and mid-seventies. The Iraq-Iran war and internal strife in the Sudan and Afghanistan conflicts go back to the early 1980s.

Second, conflicts in this region are basically reflections of internal weaknesses, which had been exploited by the big powers for their own interests (e.g., the United States role in Palestine and the Soviet role in Afghanistan). Internal weaknesses are the result of a troublesome process of gradual or sudden decolonisation. They arise because of political struggles among various groups, whether based on ideological, religious or ethnic grounds (Lebanon and Afghanistan provide examples).[1] They may also be brought about by socio-economic revolution, focusing on the problems of change, in the country's leadership (Egypt and Algeria), coupled with an ideological movement such as Islam (in Iran) or democratic socialism (in Algeria, Libya and Tunisia) in the recent times.

Besides, the conflicts in the region today are far more destructive than those of earlier years (e.g., the Gulf War between Iraq and Iran and its disastrous implications).[2] Domestic conflicts are also more dangerous than they used to be. Syria and Egypt gained a certain reputation for instability in the years before Abdel Nasser or Hafez Assad seized power, but the Egyptian regime (1970 onwards) and the Muslim radicals, between the Assad regime and the Muslim Brothers killed many thousands including President Anwar Sadat of Egypt. More recently, the turbulence in Lebanon, Palestine and the upheaval in South Yemen (in January 1986) vastly exceeded earlier struggles in destructiveness.

Another significant and disturbing attribute of current major conflicts in West Asia is what one might call their populistic base. These populistic ideologies (in Iran) and a certain public rhetoric that often drives leaders into conflicts, notwithstanding the authoritarian nature of most regimes (Iraq and Iran). Regional wars and certainly most of the domestic conflicts now elicit the engagement of large numbers of people who are mobilised by highly emotive ideologies and slogans (Iran and Iraq). Nationalism, territorial *irredentism*, religion, sectarianism and ethnicity have their own way of extending and intensifying West Asian conflicts. Accordingly conflicts become more difficult than before to contain, much less to solve the same.

Besides, conflicts between countries in the West Asian and South-West Asian world also arise because of territorial disputes, often dating back to the arbitrarily drawn boundaries of the colonial period (for e.g., the British colonial division of Palestine).[3] Many ethnic groups which for historic socio-political reasons have become separated and are living as minorities (like the Kurds in Iraq, Iran, Turkey, etc.) in different border countries have found a new urge to seek unification (*irredenta*), largely because of their dissatisfaction with the governments of the countries in which they are now living. These problems are often allied to internal instability and political struggle and are complicated by the involvement of the neighbouring countries. Such situations prevail in South-West Asia, between Afghanistan, Pakistan and Iran, in connection with the demands of the Kurds to have a substantial degree of their independence.

Another characteristic of today's conflicts in the West Asian and South-West Asian region is the blurring of the differences between internal and "external" types. Political boundaries in this region are highly permeable. Domestic disputes are usually affected by interested outsiders, as Syria and Iran in Lebanon, Iran and Pakistan in Afghanistan and Israel, Syria and Jordan in Palestine. Inter-state conflicts are often driven by factors arising out of the domestic political process, ideological notions, dynastic, historical or state-to-state differences as in the case of Iran's war with Iraq or Libya's border war with Chad. These are the fertile sources of instability today.[4]

Conflicts in the West Asian and South-West Asian region also have their roots in nationalism and problems associated with the survival of nation states. These conflicts are not only politically motivated but include economic interests and the struggle for resources like the Moroccan role in the Western Sahara region.[5]

Another common and important characteristic pertains to the involvement of the great powers from outside the region, especially the two Super Powers in the Middle East conflict.[6] The big powers are playing a negative role in such conflicts. Their intervention basically pertains to three things, viz., (a) Their military and economic capabilities are suited to the condition of these countries and their conflicts (the role of US in Israel and since the 70s in Egypt); (b) World opinion is hardly taken into account by these Great Powers (the case of US bombing of Libya); (c) The use of force by these big powers in this region has escalated their conflict into global confrontation (US in Libya and USSR in Afghanistan). In the Arab-Israeli dispute, the United States not only actively backs one side (i.e. Israel), but also plays the so-called role of a mediator. The Soviet Union for its part has a major political investment in Syria, Iraq, the PLO (to some extent) and Afghanistan. Both the Big Powers circled warily around the punch-drunk protagonists in the Gulf War.

To explain this point further, the Super Powers are working out rules of their engagement in this region that protect their interests but do not unduly disturb their existing relationships with regional states. The unstable regional political environment provided tempting opportunities for super power intervention, invasion and enhancement of their interests. The Russian intervention in Afghanistan in December 1979[7] thrust into the headlines a country which the world had overlooked for almost forty years. Besides, the United States' raids on Libya[8] since 1981 (more prominently in mid-April 1986 and early January 1989) till today provoked immediate outrage in Europe, Afro-Asia, Latin America and in the Arab world. Of America's European allies only Britain supported the raid. The American attacks are not only a violation of the spirit of the United Nations but also indicated an erosion of the rule of law in the world. Forty years ago, the United States was one of the founders of the United Nations. Today, the continuous US violation of the UN Charter exposes the limitations of this world organisation when faced with a rich and military determined Super Power and the danger to world peace from such acts as the brutal raids on Libya. A new dimension of complexity thus is added to this region's tensions.

More important to the above mentioned attributes are the range of forces unleashed by the rapid embrace of new technology and new ideas, made possible by the oil wealth in the 1970s. The rise in oil wealth also coincided with the (i) rapid rates of population growth with a large proportion of restive young; (ii) the movement of the society from rural areas into towns and cities which entailed urbanisation, and the decline of traditional society; (iii) the adoption of new political institutions; (iv) the diversification of economies away from reforms to destruction; (v) the manpower shortages, immigrants and their political implications and finally (vi) the reconciliation and synthesis of traditional moral values with new norms and socio-politico organisation.[9]

Another essential point to be taken into account is the rise of pervasive and deeply felt religious fundamentalism in this region. These fundamentalist movements seek radical transformation in the existing society.[10] The general conditions which are propitious to the rise of these fundamentalist movements are, viz.:[11]

(a) the behaviour of a regime;
(b) the discrepancies between the distinctive socio-religious-economic order;
(c) the self-worth, and the incapacity of the society to provide for the basic human needs and the growing population outstripping the food supplies and resulting in imbalanced diets.

The gap in living standards between the industrialised capitalist states and the Imperialist-dominated Third World countries is also widening. For the latter, the situation has become more intolerable (e.g., the population crisis in Egypt, the recent socio-politico-economic crisis in Algeria, Jordan, Sudan, etc.) and explosive. More than a billion people in the Third World suffer from hunger, malnutrition or inferior nourishment and hunger-related diseases.

The situation has become critical in North Africa and Sudan. Hunger and poverty in this Afro-Asian region, whether stark and overt resulting from natural disasters (e.g., the rise of locusts in mid-east and North Africa), wars and harvest failures, or chronic social and economic problems, has its roots in external and internal crisis. The aggravated situation in this region is largely due to its dependent status (the Egyptian and Israeli dependency on the United States[12]) with the capitalist states. The so-called "development strategies" of the Imperialist system has strengthened the factor of foreign control and capital. Industrialisation expansion in this region instead of being a liberating force has subjugated and integrated their economies into the Imperialist system. The traditional colonial form of dependency gave way to a neo-dependency with a deformed type of industrialisation. The domination of the trans-national and multinational monopolies and bands has led to vast financial tributes from the Third World to the developed capitalist countries.[13]

Factors Intensifying Existing Tensions

Taking the above general attributes into consideration, here it is possible to identify a set of crucial factors present throughout this area which had tended to exacerbate and intensify the existing tensions:

(a) The end of the great oil boom in the early 70s created an atmosphere of frustration and alienation. It also led to the decline of the "political morale" in the West Asian region. Confidence in the established order is eroding. On the one hand, opportunities are fewer and development is slowing. On the other, there is increasing scarcity in the states' resources and capabilities for dealing with growing domestic problems.

(b) The rise of radical and violent religious organisations and movements (since the early 70s) challenges the very established *status quo*. Although these currents were evident in several West Asian and South-West Asian countries in the early 1970s, it was the Egyptian food crisis in 1978, Egyptian-Israeli Treaty in 1979 and September Radical Islamic Revolution in Iran in 1979 that gave the momentum to the Islamic resurgence movement. It is also important to track the rise of violent Islamic and Jewish extremism in the West Bank, Gaza region and Israel respectively.

Related to both the above mentioned factors is the:

(c) Problem of political participation in many of the countries of the Arab and South-West Asian world. While there are few exceptions, the general picture is one of authoritarian regimes that feel so insecure that they must limit or suppress basic political and civil rights. Few of the states (recently—Tunisia, Algeria and Libya) have opened up the political process in recent years but most have resisted such a development. Many regimes seem to cut off from genuine linkages with their people.

(d) For the West Asian and North African states particularly, the stagnation is the so-called peace process for finding a solution to the long-standing Palestinian problem. The ineffectiveness and the inability of the so-called pro-American moderate regimes and elites to generate progress cannot but diminish their authority and political legitimacy in the eyes of their people. At the same time, the radical Arab states' betrayal (particularly Syria) of the Palestinians facilitated the growth of violent religious movements.

Besides,

(e) the extraordinarily destructive Iraq-Iran War has perpetuated the constant threat of spillovers and the general uncertainty generated by it carried political risks of their own. The recent end of the war had also set in motion a number of diplomatic challenges to the involved states.

Last but not the least, the emergence of terrorism, particularly state terrorism, under the United States and Israel, as an instrument of normal political action feeds upon itself in this region. The new technologies of violence, viz., the car bomb, the use of plastic bullets, poison gas, mustard gas, plastic explosives by the Israeli state against the Palestinians pose tough challenges to the peace and security of the region. Massive and indiscriminate violent reprisals by the Israeli authorities against Palestinian aspirations for independent statehood and freedom generally play into the hands of the radical Arab factions and encourage their destructive response.

Finally, the competition between the Super Powers, as mentioned above, for strategic position in this region further aggravated the regional insecurity and tensions. Whatever may be the latest moderate American response to the Palestinian cause, the picture therefore, is not entirely gloomy. But if one could weigh the relative causal importance of the conflict-generating factors against the limited conflict-mitigating factors, the general guess could be that the tendencies favouring continued or increasing turbulence are still stronger.

Crisis-Ridden Issues

The crux of the Inter-Arab confrontation today lies in the above mentioned variety of socio-economic, politico-military factors. It would be appropriate to deal with two main crisis issues, that is the Palestine Question and the Gulf War coming up in the last four decades (1950-1980s) which indicate that the Arab system is more oriented toward state power. These issues revolved around pointers like state security v/s regional security, inter-Arab tensions, parochial Super Power interests, and the diffusion of regional unity.

Palestine Question

Starting with the Palestine Question, one could fix the origin point at the end of World War I, or even earlier in 1882, when the First Zionist Settlement was established on Arab soil. This was followed by the Balfour Declaration (2 November 1917),[14] which promised to work towards "the establishment in Palestine of a national home for the Jewish people". It is said to be one of the most calamitous document's of colonialism in modern history. The allotment of a major part of Palestine to the Jews who constituted only eight per cent of the total population amounted to denial of basic rights to the 92 per cent Arabs (both Muslims and Christians).

But in the mid-thirties when the European Jewish immigration increased dramatically after Hitler's rise to power in 1933, Palestinian resistance to British control and Zionist settlement culminated in the Arab revolt of 1936-39,[15] which was suppressed by the British Army with the help of Zionist militias and the complicity of the Arab regimes. The Palestinians started their active national struggle and launched this Arab revolt which was basically aimed at overthrowing the British mandate. For the Palestinian Arabs, the task of national liberation was much more difficult than the other Afro-Asian peoples who were fighting only one enemy, British colonialism. The Palestinians were facing two enemies at the same time: the British Mandatory Authority and the Zionist colonisers. National liberation, therefore, has a deeper meaning for Palestinians than others.[16] But they could not succeed because leadership was under Haj Amin Husseini, who represented the feudal class.[17] Their defeat in 1936-39 prompted the sympathetic neighbouring Arab countries to take over their cause, which only suited the Jewish perceptions of the Palestinians as an externally generated force. In the 1940s the United States joined Britain against the Palestinians in their struggle for protecting their homeland. By the end of World War II, the new American-Zionist-British alliance had forced the Palestinians to move to partition. The 1948 (First) Arab-Israeli War[18] led to the total collapse of the Palestinian society.[19]

During the Pan-Arab or Nasserite era (1952-70) the Palestinian national upsurge took a new but broader shape of an anti-imperialist struggle. Here the struggle was of an indigenous population against the occupation of its territory by invading foreigners who came to the area to colonise the land and displace its inhabitants. In the 1960s, a coherent Palestinian movement began to emerge when the Second Arab Summit in Alexandria under President Nasser's leadership (1964)[20] decided to establish the PLO (Palestine Liberation Organisation) and the PLA (The Palestine Liberation Army).

The defeat of the Arab states in the June Arab-Israeli War (1967) increased the prestige of the Palestinian freedom fighters in the Arab world. It reinforced their claim that they alone were capable of realising their peoples' aspirations. However the June 1967 War—which led to the occupation of the West Bank and Gaza by the Israelis[21]—did not bring any change in the existing perceptions of mutual hatred. Since the 1967 War, Israel has, in violation of the Geneva Conventions, seized more than 53 per cent of West Bank land from 800,000 Palestinian inhabitants for the benefit of 50,000 Jewish settlers forcing the 650,000 Palestinians into a fetid slum with a population density approaching that of our own city of Calcutta. The inability and rigidity of the Israelis to the Palestinian's just cause, is said to be central to the understanding of this Palestinian impasse.

Apart from the above historic reasons, the latest uprising (started since October 1987) among the Palestinians is believed to have been triggered by a series of socio-economic *factors*,[22] including increasing unemployment, lack of adequate financial resources and the continued oppression by the Israeli forces. To go into some details, it can be said that economic relations between the occupied territories and Arab and other countries were cut and their markets flooded with products from Israel's light industry and agriculture. Home agriculture and industry suffered great losses. In addition, Israel's expansionist policy resulted in a militarisation of the economy and consequently in growing rates of inflation. This aggravated the situation of Arab populations and unemployment escalated. Besides this, working conditions in Israel's enterprises are very bad. Wage increases and social security do not exist for Arab women, although taxes are regularly deducted from the wages. Arab workers get a total of two-third the wages of Israeli workers for equal work in equal working hours. Again Arab holidays are not paid as they are not recognised by Israel.[23]

The revolt in Gaza and the West Bank[24] after 20 years of Israeli occupation is truly perceived as a protest against neglect, understood by the world at large as a demand from the Palestinian Arabs remarkably similar to that what the Jews fought for 40 years ago—a national state. The Israeli occupation and its repressive policies have led to the emergence of a helpless yet vibrant revolutionary community. Young Palestinians who were born into the Occupation manifest stronger resistance to the Occupation. Three out of every four Gazans are under the age of 25 and have never tested self rule; increasingly they despair of doing so. The total ban on political activity and harassment and deportation of Palestinians seriously hinder the life process. Along with this, threats of reprisals, intimidation and assassination of Palestinians who challenge the Zionists, discourage the whole peace process. The sole purpose of this calculated Zionist terror policy, unleashed on a defenceless and peaceful population, was to drive the majority of Palestinian Arabs out of their country to oblivion.

The Palestinian uprising in the West Bank and Gaza marked an escalation in the violent acts conducted by the Israeli soldiers against the Palestinians. In the last week of November 1987, a glider-borne attack by a Palestinian on an army camp in northern Israel had been perceived as a severe blow to the Israeli military and political establishment.[25] This took a toll of six Israelis dead and seven injured. For the first time the uncommon resolve displayed by the lone Palestinian attacker created shock waves in the Israeli military circle and exploded the myth of Israeli soldiers as supermen. However, all these events have been marked by demonstrations, with the Israelis responding firmly.

The above actions were followed by trials of Palestinians accused of taking part in the riots in the occupied Arab areas, observance of a sad and quiet Christmas, Israeli raided Lebanon, the Israeli decision to deport Palestinians, resignation of 400 Arabs from Israel 1,000 Arab Police Force, indefinite closure of some 800 schools, sending of 250,000 students home until further notice, an underwater explosion of the PLO peace voyage ship to Israel attack on the PLO headquarters in Tunisia resulting in the assassination of PLO's Commandoes in Chief, Abu Jihad by the Israelis,[26] and the flurry of diplomatic activity all over West Asia and beyond including the recent PLO recognition of the state of Israel and the moderate UN response to the PLO leader Yasser Arafat. Around 604 or more Palestinians are said to have been "martyred" and 20,000 wounded by the Israelis in the last sixteen months of disturbances. About 20,000 Palestinians are said to have been detained.[27] Besides, there have been indulgence in killings, beating, breaking of limbs, burying alive and demolition of houses and other acts of terrorism (wider use of live ammunitions such as new kind of plastic bullets and steel balls fired from guns) against innocent unarmed civilians. The Israeli authorities placed refugee camps, towns and villages under a virtual seige, so as to deny the people access to food, water, medicine and other essential items.

Israel had come under sustained national, regional and international attacks for its handling of the latest unrest in the occupied West Bank and Gaza Strip. The Israeli Press castigated the government for continued inactivity on the political front while the military campaign against Palestinian unrest in the occupied territories built up. Shimon Peres, the Labour Party leader and Finance Minister of Israel, has proposed that the Gaza Strip be demilitarised, and the Jewish settlements there removed. Peres opined that, "Israel has only two choices in resolving its conflict with the Arabs—either to accept an international conference on the Middle East or hold direct negotiations with the PLO to resolve the continuing unrests".[28] According to him, the first move is for the United States to seek Soviet support for an international conference in which to set the local arrangements needed under the US Peace Plan.

Itshak Shamir, Prime Minister since October 1986 and leader of the Likud Party in Israel however opposed the idea of an international peace conference.[29] Recently, Shamir has introduced fresh collective measures to try to end the Palestinian uprising in the occupied West Bank and the Gaza Strip. The new measures include a ban on fuel supplies to the occupied territories, a night-time curfew, severance of international telephone and telex links, a ban on international media, a ban on travel between Gaza and the West Bank and restrictions on currency flows into the territories.[30]

At the regional level, Yasser Arafat, Chairman of the PLO described the events in the Gaza Strip and the West Bank as "a popular uprising" which would yet teach the Israelis the strength of people's power. People's power had achieved results in Mahatma Gandhi's India and Aquino's Philippines, so why not in Palestine? He asked. He further said, "no matter what the sacrifice, no matter how ruthless (the Israeli actions), we will continue the uprising until occupation is eliminated".[31] He had earlier proposed to the United Nations Force and to the Security Council to protect the political and human rights of the Palestinians and ensure them safety from the organised official Israeli terrorism. Libyan leader, Colonel Gaddafi has also asked the UN Secretary General to take immediate and energetic action to put an end to the "terror against the Palestinian people in occupied territories". Moreover, Israel's violent repression of the Palestinian uprising in the occupied territories has put strains on Egypt's unstable peace with the Jewish state and exposed it to the dangers of entrenched domestic opposition to the treaty.

The Arab would, when it was awash with oil money, could have afforded to improve life in the Palestinian camps had it really wanted to do so. But, unfortunately it didn't choose to do the same. They care very little about them as was clearly demonstrated during the Israeli invasion of Lebanon in 1982 and thereafter. In fact, after the 1978 Camp David Agreement,[32] Egypt promised to develop Sinai to provide work for the refugees of Gaza—but has done nothing.

However, the Algeria Arab Summit (7 June to 9 June 1988) and the address of Yasser Arafat delivered before the 43 Session of the UN General Assembly meeting in plenary at the United Nations office in Geneva on 13 December 1988 and the recent American response to the PLO's peace overtures, were a remarkable reversal for the PLO which had been snubbed at the Arab Summit in Amman just thirteen months earlier. The PLO Chairman Yasser Arafat's reception in Algeria contrasted with the PLO setbacks of the past six years. The five page statement said, the Algeria Summit condemned Washington's policy in the Middle East as "biased in favour of Israel and antagonistic to Palestinian national rights". It hailed the *Intifida*, or the Palestinian uprising, saying the assembled Kings, Presidents and Emirs expressed "honour and pride" in the Palestinian people's resistance to the Israeli occupation of Arab-Palestinian land.[33]

In the European sphere, Pope John Paul II criticised the Israeli Police for clashing with Muslim demonstrators on Jerusalem's

Temple Mount and said it was unacceptable to attack people while they were at prayer. He called for internationalisation of the occupied city of Jerusalem, stressing the Palestinian right to statehood and identity.[34]

The British Minister for Middle Eastern Affairs, David Mellor, in his four day visit to Israel (January 1988), expressed mounting concern about the new situation in the occupied territories. Mellor was shaken by his visits to the refugee camps in Gaza and the West Bank, which he described as an "affront to civilised values" and accused the Zionist regime of flouting international law and putting a "blot on the face of civilisation".[35]

Besides, the 12 nations of the European Economic Community, and recently the United States, also deplored Israeli tactics in its occupied territories as illegal and repressive. The European nations, "deeply deplore the repressive measures taken by Israel, which are in violation of international law and human rights", EEC Foreign Ministers said in response to tactics used by the Israeli Authorities to quell unrest in the occupied territories during the past month "These measures must stop", the Ministers said in a joint statement.[36] Besides, the European Parliament refused to ratify new trade accords with Israel that would have given Israel early access to European markets and loans.

At the international level, Soviet leader Mikhail Gorbachev has denounced that Israel Authorities' continued reprisals against the Palestinians in the occupied Arab lands. On January 1988, he said, these are "illegal occupations" and part of Tel Aviv's "campaign on terror and reprisals against the Palestinians".

The United States Administration has a major responsibility for this distorted state of violence on the West Bank and Gaza. By failing to act incisively it undercuts those farsighted moderate Palestinians and Arabs who see their region's current course leading towards disaster. It dismisses the right of Palestinians to exercise self-determination guaranteed by the United Nations Charter.

It has become increasingly clear that efforts to end this unrest will be futile unless a direct and immediate negotiating process leading to some form of Palestinian self rule is started. The last US initiatives for peace in Middle East failed to break the deadlock on Palestine. If the American initiative on West Asia succeeds, it is likely to be the opening hand in a lengthy diplomatic game. However, the US political initiatives[37] that were introduced after the uprising began are viewed critically by the Palestinians. These are seen as an attempt to abort the uprising and stop the political momentum that has been generated in favour of Palestinian national rights. They are seen to have been diverting attention from the occupied territories and the aspirations of the Palestinians. It would have been worthwhile if the latest American initiative on West Asia had done two things: edged the Israeli Administration in some way towards dealing with the Palestinians through their true representative (that is PLO) and making it plain to Washington that an international conference of the kind that is now advocated by the entire world is both right and necessary.[38]

India has commanded the framework of the Palestinian peace initiative, as presented by the PLO chairman Yasser Arafat to the 43rd Session of the UN General Assembly in Geneva. Indian Minister of State for External Affairs, Natwar Singh rightly stressed the need for the world to grasp this present opportunity for peace in the Middle East with flexibility and openness.

President R. Venkataraman said: "Arafat's recent bold and courageous initiatives for peace had entirely transformed the West Asian equation and deserved universal acclaim". The President also emphasised that India was convinced that the most appropriate forum for durable peace in the Middle East was the United Nations-sponsored peace conference with full participation of all concerned states including Palestine (PLO) and the permanent members of the Security Council.[39]

A just and *lasting settlement* of the Palestinian Issue needs priority. The Super Powers (particularly the United States which is also an ally of Israel) must recognise the urgency of developing a broader and deeper understanding of this underlying problem. The Bush Administration should also demonstrate its will and leadership, while recognising that America can only act effectively if it adopts a posture of objectivity essential to a just mediator. If America does not seriously seek to bring the parties together, there is a danger that the Arab-Israeli fighting will spread and intensify.

The Gulf Crisis (1979-1988)

The latter part of the 1970s also witnessed one of the fastest socio-politico-economic and military transformation in West Asia particularly in the Gulf region's history. As it happened the tension generated by these changes exploded in a series of upheavals (mentioned above), viz., the overthrow of the Shah of Iran culminating in Khomeini's Islamic revolution (1979),[40] the seizure of the Grand Mosque at Mecca and the grisly eight-year-old Iraq-Iran War which ended recently (20 July 1988) with the acceptance of the United Nations Security Council Peace Resolution 598 for a Gulf-War ceasefire by the Islamic Republic of Iran.[41]

The Gulf War, which officially began with Iraq's 22 September 1980 invasion of Iran, was the bloodiest and most brutal of all armed conflicts between minor powers since the Second World War. It was the crux of the inter-Arab and Arab-Iranian relations till the recent times. In its duration, scale, casualty rates and physical damage, it already ranks as one of the most serious and dangerous wars between states in the world since World War II. It was the most tragic because the warfare, reminiscent of the First World War in Europe, caused heavy casualties for no obvious advantage to either side. The war entered its ninth year last year, but despite a certain war-weariness on both sides, the fundamental sticking point remained: Iranian leaders refused to agree to any resolution that did not provide for the condemnation of Iraq's President Saddam Hussein, while the Iraqi leader showed no signs of being willing to accede to his own demise.

Fighting between the two countries began after Iran ignored Iraqi demands for the withdrawal of Iranian forces from Zain-ul-qos in Djali province on the border between the two countries.[42] Iraq maintained that this territory should have been returned to it under the 1975 Algiers Agreement it had concluded with Iran.[43] Iraq abrogated the 1975 Shatt-al-Arab Agreement and invaded the newly born Islamic Iran on 22 September 1980. Most observers now believe that this was no more than a pretext on Iraq's part, that is, the real objective of its President Saddam Hussein being to topple the newly threatening but vulnerable Iranian regime.[44] But what was expected to be a week-long Iraqi-Iranian walk-over turned into a nine-year nightmare in which both states fought for their destruction. Iraq took it as a fight for its national existence and its supporters in the Gulf and Arab region, Saudi Arabia, Egypt, Jordan and the PLO for the preservation of their political systems threatened by Iranian-backed Islamic radicals. Both the states responded by bombing each other's cities and disrupting oil flows by attacking tankers and oil terminals. This mutual battering continued for a long time and was decided by the parties' moral attitudes, interest and capacity contain each other at home as on the battlefield.

One important outcome of this prolonged war was to strengthen the standing of the regimes in Iran and Iraq. In both the countries the war helped to consolidate the domestic political scene and enabled the governments to gain massive support for a vigorous confrontation of the invader. The determined, uncompromising attitudes of Iran and Iraq has paid ample dividends as demonstrated by the failure of the UN Secretary General's earlier peace initiatives and the direct US military intervention in this area. Iran and Iraq have emerged the two most destructive powers in the Arab (Persian) Gulf by holding the key to the solution of the war.

In the Arab sphere, this war has shifted attention from the Arab-Israeli conflict and diluted the efforts of the Palestinians to sustain their struggle for an independent state of Palestine. Besides, the war has relieved much of the pressure from Egypt which had been isolated from the general Arab scene. As the tide of war turned against the Baghdad regime the Iraq found it necessary to seek Egyptian support. This led to a complete reversal of the Iraqi position from being one of the major sponsors of Egypt's isolation to becoming the main advocate of Egypt's readmittance to the Arab family. The impact of the war on Egyptian foreign policy has been an increase in importance of the Gulf Arab States. Of equal significance are the economic benefits that Egypt derives from cash sales of arms to Iraq and from the remittance of so many Egyptians working there. Besides, the war prevented Iraq from achieving hegemony in the Arab Gulf by slowly exhausting its strength. It also forced the Baghdad Government to look to the West, for material assistance. Agreements were reached with France, US and other West European countries providing for deliveries of war materials and related technology.

Again, the war increased the threat of direct US involvement in the region. It soon became obvious that the United States would increase its existing military involvement in the region at least as the so-called protector of the Gulf Arab friendly states, and to protect vital interests in the region. The United States assistance and direct military action would accepted by the Gulf States as long as they felt threatened.

Another important consequence of this unending war has been creation of plans the oil-producing countries to protect their oil exports from war operations. The plans engaged a gradual shift of oil shipments from the Arab (Persian) Gulf.

For the Soviet Union the outbreak of the war was an unwelcome development. Given mood of intense hostility in Iran towards the US military intervention and American Administration's idea of imposing sanctions on Iran, there appeared good prospects for greater Soviet influence. The Soviet Union had warned the United States of the deployment of an American atomic cruiser in the Gulf "as a step along the dangerous path". In the words of the Soviet Foreign Minister, Eduard Shevardnadze, "The safety of navigation in the Gulf can and may be ensured by the entire world community, in whose behalf the United Nations will be active. If necessary, appropriate and sufficient forces should be made effectively available for it. The Soviet Union would agree to such a decision". It is here that for the first time Moscow supported the idea of a United Nations Force in the Gulf. Besides, the Soviet Foreign Minister suggested that an "impartial body" should be formed to "investigate responsibility" for the outbreak of the war "within a clearly established time frame". Unfortunately this proposal was rejected by Iraq.

Unlike its rival, the United States continued to face fundamental questions about its political, military and strategic postures in this area. In spite of the revelations of secret US-Iranian arms deals in November 1986, US strategy towards the Gulf War had consisted primarily of three interrelated strands, viz.: repeated public commitments to freedom of navigation in the Gulf; the reassurance of local allies like Saudi Arabia and Kuwait; and the maintenance of the regional balance of power. Underlying these strands was an awareness of the need to limit potential Soviet gains without at the same time provoking a Soviet response that could lead to confrontation.

Referring to the case of the middle powers, the interests of Western industrialised nations in the Gulf were largely commercial in the early years of the war. These nations have distanced themselves politically from both sides and have neither affected nor been affected by the war (except in placing themselves along with the United States, to a certain extent, in a dangerous position where the options seemed limited to humiliation).

In the domestic sphere, the war has come to involve the two nations to a greater and greater extent calling upon them to sacrifice not only their sons but also to mortgage their countries' future. The combined cost to the belligerents' economies, in terms of lost oil revenues, may have been as high as $50 billion in the first year alone. Thus its economic losses can be measured in hundred of billions dollars. More important, the cumulative effects of fighting would dominate the planning and the patterns of government expenditures for many years to come. Indeed the war has left permanent scars on both countries' development prospects. It had in fact become a political and economic liability to both the countries. Even with the recent end to the war, it may take as much as a decade for these two countries to rebuild and restore what has already been destroyed.

In the social sphere, the war has been used (as mentioned) to consolidate the regime, unite and divert people's attention and repress the opposition in both the countries. Besides, it has affected the institutions of society, extending to each government in the countries. A large element of coercion, accompanied by the propagation of myths has been used to mobilise the people. Moreover, the dictates of the war have accelerated the concentration of absolute powers in the hands of the rulers in both these countries.[45]

At the international level, both the countries, militarily weakened, have left the field of confrontation to the Super Powers, particularly the United States. Besides, the Palestine issue has receded to a secondary position. And finally, the Arabs seemed to have lost Iran as an ally in their struggle against the Zionist enemy and US imperialism.

One reason that the Gulf War lasted so many years is that the combatants were in a sense evenly matched. Another reason is that no one, either the immediate Arab or Gulf neighbours and great powers alike, wanted either side to win. The war had enabled the West, principally the United States, Great Britain, France, Israel and also the Soviet Union to sell enormous quantities of deadly weapons to the warring Gulf states, Saudi Arabia, Kuwait, etc., thereby consolidating the political and military ties while making lucrative transactions.

However, this unending Gulf War came to an end when the Iranian Government under the leadership of Ayatollah Khomeini was finally persuaded to agree to a ceasefire; it announced on 18 July 1988 its acceptance of the one-year old Security Council Resolution 598 (1987). Iraq agreed on 6 August 1988 to a truce before direct negotiations got under way. Both sides adhered to the call by the Secretary General, Javier Perez de Cuellar for an armistice which took effect from 20 August. Both parties drew back to their pre-war frontiers. The Americans may claim they won up to since Iran failed to defeat its opponent. But the question is at what cost? The cost of millions of dead and wounded.

Yet in the stillness that followed the ceasefire as the dead are unearthed by the plough shares over the coming months and years, there will be time to speculate on the shifting balance of power in the Gulf region. On the domestic scene of the wary states there was a darker and more frightening picture.

However, it can be said that the world will not be safe to live in as long as we do not produce new institutions and new ways of ensuring peace through the power of public opinion and the power of movements. Peace and security of the Gulf region depends very much on the responses of the states concerned, particularly Islamic Iran and Iraq and the responses of the United Nations, the Super Powers, the Arab governments and the Non-Aligned Movement. The sign of goodwill and peace intentions must be encouraged among all the states of this region.

Conclusion

The above analysis makes it clear that the degree of disintegration is now outrunning that of reform, reconstruction and regrowth in the West and South-West Asian region. The search for peace is still a complex task more than in other regions because of the inter-state confrontation, big power intervention and of the socio-political and economic stages of development of this region.

The events of the recent years mark a significant turning point and change in the crisis-ridden history of West and South-West Asia. Peace has become a factor to be reckoned with all over the world. The tiny territory of Namibia has moved step closer to freedom, a ceasefire has been reached in the Gulf, the Soviets have already withdrawn from Afghanistan, negotiations have been started between the Sharawi independence fighters and the Moroccans and signs of movement towards peace are also seen in Cyprus, Kampuchea and Palestine. "The overall climate of international relations is positive and for the first time the confrontational atmospheres of the first few decades has given way to dialogue and consultations", Cante Caputo, President of the United Nations General Assembly said rightly. However, a just and lasting settlement of the existing problems particularly the Palestinian impasse must be considered immediately. The Super Powers must recognise the urgency of developing a broader and deeper understanding of this underlying problem.

REFERENCES

1. For details see Naomi Joy Weinberger, *Syrian Intervention in Lebanon: The 1975-76 Civil War* (New York, 1986). Here the author presents a fresh look at the motives, strategies, levels of state commitment and unpredictable results which fuel the dynamics of intervention in the West Asian scene. Also see Edward E. Azar, *et al.* (eds.), *The Emergence of a New Lebanon: Fantasy or Reality* (New York, 1984), pp. 3-55. On Afghanistan, see Prof. Baldev, *Global Impact of Afghan Crisis* (New Delhi, 1980), pp. 39-100.
2. Shahram Chubin and Charles Tripp, *Iran and Iraq: War, Society and Politics 1980-86*, PSIS Occasional Papers, No. 1/86 (Geneva). Also see J.P. Sharma, "Eighth Year of Gulf War", *Indian Nation* (Patna), 7 October 1987.
3. *The Origins and Evolution of the Palestine Problem, Part II: 1947-1977* (United Nations, New York, 1978). Also see Ralph H. Magnus (ed.), *Documents on the Middle East* (Washington D.C., American Enterprise Institute For Public Policy Research, 1969) and J.P. Sharma, "The Palestinian Imbroglio", *Indian Nation*. 18 April 1987.
4. Shahram Chubin (ed.), *Security in the Persian Gulf: Domestic Political Factors*, (England, 1981), p. 1.
5. See K.R. Singh, "The Sand Wall is Crumbling", *Strategic Analysis* (New Delhi), Vol. XII, No. 5, August 1988, pp. 579-95. Also see Robert Rezetti, *The Western Sahara and the Frontiers of Morocco* (Paris, 1975), pp. 9-15.
6. Harold H. Saunders, *The Super Powers in the Middle East* (Washington D.C. and *AEI Foreign Policy and Defence Review*, Vol. 6, No. 1, 1986), pp. 14-43.

7. For more details see, John C. Griffiths, *Afghanistan: Key to a Continent* (London, 1981).
8. E.P. Thomson, Marry Kaldor, *et al., Mad Dogs: US Raids on Libya* (London, 1986).
9. Shahram Chubin, *Security in the Persian Gulf* (ed.), n. 4, p. xi.
10. J.P. Sharma, "Islamic Resurgence in Egypt and Tunisia", *Indo-Africana: Collected Research Papers on Africa* (Department of African Studies, University of Delhi, Delhi), Vol. 1, No. 2, October 1958, pp. 67-83.
11. Ian S. Lustick, *Jewish Fundamentalism in Israel: For the Land and the Lord* (New York, 1988), pp. 1-40.
12. For details see Gabriel Sheaffer (ed.), *Dynamics of Dependence: US-Israel Relations* (Boulder, London, 1987). Also see Marvin G. Weinbaum, *Egypt and the Politics of US Economic Aid* (Boulder and London, 1986).
13. Cheddi Jagan, "Poverty: Cause and Cure", *World Marxist Review* (London), Vol. 31, No. 8, August 1988, pp. 28-34.
14. Balfour was British Secretary. The Balfour Declaration was issued from the British Foreign Office in November 1917. See George Antonius, *The Arab Awakening: Study of the Arab National Movement* (London, 1938), pp. 262-70.
15. See Ahmed M. Gomaa, *The Foundation of the League of Arab States: Wartime Diplomacy and Inter-Arab Policies 1941 to 1945* (London and New York, 1977), pp. 36-37.
16. For details, see Mehmood Hussain, *The Palestine Liberation Organisation* (New Delhi, 1975). In this context, he discusses the role of three Zionist gangster groups—*Irgun, Hajanah and Stern* which ultimately merged to become the Israeli Army.
17. *Ibid*.
18. The First Arab-Israeli War (15 May-1 June 1948) laid the foundations for the confrontation that has continued until the present day. The foundation of the state of Israel (which occupied 77 per cent of the Palestinian/Arab territory) on 15 May 1948 sealed the defeat of the Palestinian nationalist movement. See Abdallah Frangi, *The PLO and Palestine* (Translated by Paul Knight) London, 1983), pp. 81-85.
19. As a result of the war, historic Palestine was divided into three parts: the new Jewish state occupied 77 per cent of the Arab-Palestinian territory; Jordan occupied the "West Bank" of the Jordan River and East Jerusalem and Egypt were given the temporary control of the area surrounding the Gaza city. The Palestinian Arab State provided for in the UN Partition Plan was never established.
20. On Nasser's initiative, the First Conference of Arab Heads of State, on 16 January 1964 in Cairo had passed a resolution calling for the

founding of an organisation, i.e. Palestine Liberation Organisation (PLO) to 'embody Palestinian existence'. Here it was proclaimed that the Arab people of Palestine had the right and the duty to assume responsibility for their national cause and the liberation of Palestine. See (Edited): *The Palestinian Problem: Aggression, Resistance, Ways of Settlement* (Moscow: USSR Academy of Social Sciences, 1984), pp. 169-73.

21. In the June 1967 Arab-Israeli War, Israel decisively and quickly defeated the Egyptian, Syrian and Jordanian armies. In this war, Israel had captured the remainder of the historic Arab-Palestinian territory, as well as the Sinai Peninsula from the Egyptians and the Golan Heights from the Syrians. The newly captured parts of Arab-Palestine had come to referred as the West Bank and the Gaza Strip after 1948, and since 1967 have generally been referred as the occupied territories.
22. The current unrest is the most powerful explosion of Palestinian dissatisfaction with what their lot has been reduced to by brute power, both in the West Bank and the Gaza Strip. See "Palestinians on a Way Round" *Pakistan and Gulf Economist* (Karachi), 12-18 March 1988, pp. 28-30. Also see, "In the Compromising Land", *The Guardian* (Manchester), 6 March 1988.
23. Arabs in the occupied territories were considered as cheap labour for Israeli industry. See "Palestinian Women under Occupation", *Jerusalem* (Tunis), No. 32, November 1987, p. 22.
24. In 1967 Israel occupied the West Bank and the Gaza Strip. The West Bank occupies an area of 2,165 square miles to the West of the Jordan River. Its population is swelled by an estimated 400,000 refugees. The Gaza Strip with the twenty-five by six-mile strip is said to be the most densely populated areas in the world. It has a population of approximately 210,000 refugees. See "Under Occupation—The West Bank and Gaza", in (ed.), *Third World Affairs 1987* (London, 1987), pp. 171-206.
25. The attack perceived as a severe blow to the Israeli establishment also displayed the uncommon resolve of the lone attacker and introduced an entirely new element into Israeli military calculations. See "Palestinians Pose a New Kind of Threat", *Middle East International* (London). No. 314, 5 December 1987, pp. 5-6.
26. See *Jerusalem* (Tunis), No. 38, May 1988, p. 4.
27. The war in the occupied territories is in its sixteenth month. The official toll of Palestinians killed by shootings is now more than 600 if the deaths from beatings and tear gas are added. See, "How Stones Can Beat Guns", *Middle East International* (London), No. 321, 19 March 1988, p. 16.

28. Israel's former Foreign Minister and present Finance Minister, Shimon Peres stated on 30 December 1987 that the PLO was ready to embark on direct negotiations with Israel. Replying to two *Knesset* (Israeli Parliament) floor motions, Peres attacked the Likud Party of the present Prime Minister Yitzhak Shamir for its stubborn rejection of peace and its fear of any progress towards a peace accord. See *Israel Press Briefs* (Tel Aviv), No. 57, February 1988, p. 2.
29. I. Belyaev, "Middle East: One Hundred Year War?", *Soviet Review* (New Delhi), Vol. XXV, No. 1, January 1988, pp. 35-39. Also see *Keesing's Contemporary Archives*, Vol. XXXIII, No. 8, 1987, p. 35351.
30. *Middle East Economic Digest (MEED)* (London), Vol. 32, No. 12, 19-25 March 1988, p. 10.
31. F.J. Khergamvala, "Arafat Emerges Sole Leader of Palestinians", *The Hindu* (Madras), 4 February 1988.
32. Late Mohammed Anwar el-Sadat, President of the Arab Republic of Egypt and Menahem Begin, the then Prime Minister of Israel, met with Jimmy Carter, then President of the United States of America at Camp David from 5 September to 17 September 1978. They signed the Camp David Accords at White House on 26 March 1979. As soon as the Camp David Accords were publicised, the PLO strongly condemned the documents. The PLO leadership said that they were not basically acceptable to the Palestinians because of several factors, the most important being that they ignored the legitimate national rights of the Palestinian people as confirmed by the 29th Session of the UN General Assembly in Resolution No. 3236 of 22 November 1974. For details see, A.G. Mezerik (ed.), *Arab Refugees in the Middle East* (New York), p. 60. Also see Mohammed Ibrahim Kamel, *The Camp David Accords—A Testimony* (London, Boston, Sydney, Henley, 1986).
33. See author's article, "PLO Victory at Algiers Summit", *Democratic World* (New Delhi), Vol. XVII, No. 28, 10 July 1988, p. 11.
34. See "Vatican Plays Role in Search for Settlement", *The Times* (London), 5 February 1988.
35. There has been a reaction in Israel over the vocal criticism voiced by the British Foreign Office Minister, David Mellor, while touring the occupied territories. The Israeli media carried a prominent report on Mellor's visit to the Jabaliya Refugee Camp near Gaza on 4 January 1988 and his characterisation of conditions there as "an affront to all civilised values". See *Middle East International*, No. 316, 9 January 1988, p. 4. Also see "Jabaliya Camp is the Worst in the Region", *The Times*, 6 January 1988.
36. See *The Times of India*, 10 February 1988. Also see *Times*, 21 March 1988, p. 22.

37. The American Plan calls for a token international conference this year as a prelude to direct Arab-Israeli talks on interim Palestinian "self rule" in the Occupied West Bank and Gaza and a final settlement before the end of the year. It provides for bilateral negotiating sessions, independent of each other, between Israel and a joint Jordanian-Palestinian delegation, Israel and Syria and Israel and Lebanon and stipulates that the five permanent members of the UN Security Council will provide an "international umbrella" but none will have any arbitration or veto authority over any agreements reached in the negotiations. The Plan makes it reference to the PLO but provides for no direct role for the organisation which is the sole legitimate representative of the Palestinians. See *Times* (Chicago), 21 March 1988, p. 22. Also see *Newsweek* (New York), 14 March 1988, p. 36.
38. *Middle East International*, No. 320, 5 March 1988, p. 2.
39. *The Hindustan Times* (New Delhi), 15 December 1988. Also see *Patriot* (New Delhi), 10 March 1989.
40. The revolution in Iran, which led to the overthrow of the Shah in February 1979 and the emergence of a new religious regime, had profound consequences both in the Gulf region and beyond.
41. J.P. Sharma, "Ceasefire in the Gulf", *Democratic World*, Vol. XVII, No. 333, 14 August 1988, pp. 12-13.
42. Iraq and Iran have long contested their common river borders.
43. J.P. Sharma, "Iraq-Iran War to Peace", *Democratic World*, Vol. XVIII, No. 4, 22 January 1989, p. 14.
44. J.P. Sharma, "The Never-Ending Gulf War", *Democratic World*, Vol. XVI, No. 18, 3 May 1987, p. 13.
45. For more details see *Adelphi Papers*, No. 219, Spring 1987. Also see *Middle East Review 1988* (Essex, England), pp. 25-28; Tareq Aziz, *Iraq-Iran Conflict: Questions and Discussions* (London and Baghdad, 1981) and Shirin Tahir Kheli and Shaheen Ayuki (ed.), *The Iran-Iraq War: New Weapons, Old Conflicts* (New York, 1983), pp. 195-200.

16. The Palestinian Imbroglio

The question of Palestine became a symbol of Arab unity. Egypt's commitment to the Palestine cause has become a historical part of her strategy in seeking the resolution of the Arab-Israeli conflict. Nasser's policy has been characterised as adhering to the strategic goal i.e. the establishment of an independent Palestinian entity.

No one can fail to recognise Egypt's contribution which is greater than that of any other Arab state in sustaining Palestinian entity. It pursued that policy through the establishment of the Provisional Government of Palestine under Multi al-Husseini which existed in Gaza till 1956 and which shifted its headquarters to Cairo after the 1956 war. In 1964 Egypt too a major part in the establishment of the PLO it was also a major step towards its recognition as the sole and legitimate representative of the Palestinian people. The achievements of the PLO would be inconceivable without Egypt's initiative support and ongoing activity especially during the Nasser era.

To start with the Egyptian-Palestinian relations have a background of their own. The Arab struggle against Zionist designs and British policies in Palestine can be said to be the most important of all factors which had contributed to the sense of Arab unity. The Palestine Arab Revolt of 1936 was the most serious expression of Arab discontent made so far, and had its repercussions all over the Arab world.

Palestine was held by Britain as a League mandate. Her task was to prepare the people of Palestine for self-government. Since 1936, the question of Palestine began to intrude into the Egyptian domestic politics. Being Arabs, the Egyptians had a natural sympathy for the Arabs in Palestine. The Islamic organisations were attracting an increasing number of disenchanted youths and were using the Palestine issue to embarrass the contemporary WAFD government. Nahas Pasha the Wafd Party leader saw the benefit to himself and to Wafd in championing the Arab cause in

Palestine. The maiden speech of the Egyptian Minister of Foreign Affairs after Egypt's admission to the League of Nations in 1937 dealt entirely with the Palestine question.

Egypt played an important part in the Arab League on the Palestine question. It was under Egypt's insistence that the Arab League had taken over the conduct of Arab cause on Palestine. Egypt being a founder member of the Arab League, and being its leader, was honour bound to defend the cause of Palestine.

On 29 November 1947, the General Assembly of the United Nations passed the resolution recommending the partition of Palestine. The Arabs including Egypt totally rejected the recommendation, but the Zionists accepted it. Britain announced its decision to relinquish its mandate for Palestine on 15 May 1948.

Partition

The partition of Palestine was a staggering blow to Egypt's prestige. So, on 15 May 1948 Egypt sent her armies into Palestine to forestall the establishment of a Jewish state. When the war broke out in Palestine, Egypt contributed the largest single contingent of Arab troops. It played a significant role in the 1948 war. But the Arabs were defeated.

The humiliating defeat of Egypt in Palestine had a profound and immediate effect on Egypt's public life. Prime Minister Nokarashi Pasha tried to conceal from public the disastrous course of the war but failed. The government's inefficiency, corruption and cowardice was exposed. Frustration humiliation and anger caused the outbreak of violence and destruction.

The post-1948 period gave rise to the new factors: the creation of a provisional government of Palestine in Gaza and the Refugee problem. Egypt was interested in keeping in fact the legal point of a Palestinian government especially after the absorption of the West Bank by Transjordan. Hence a government of Palestine was set up in Gaza with Egyptian assistance under the leadership of Mufti Haj Amin al-Husseini. It was formed in October 1948.

The Palestinians were frustrated by the half-hearted attitude of the Arab countries towards their problem. The Husseini group decided to launch Fedayeen raids, and by 1951 they started active operations. The increase in the encounters between the groups of the Palestinian Fedayeen and the Israelis forced the latter to adopt a policy of massive armed retaliation. In 1955, large scale Israeli raids on Fedayeen bases in Gaza were engineered. This involved Egypt directly in military confrontation with Israel, for Gaza was under Egypt's patronage. The Fedayeen raids and Israeli retaliations became a pretext for the war of October 1956.

After the war of 1956 the Palestine government in Gaza moved to Cairo and continued to operate from there till Mufti Husseini moved to Beirut in 1959. In the sixties the Government in exile ceased to be of any relevance and its place was taken by the PLO in 1964.

The military elite, that came to power after the 1952 COUP D'ETAT in Egypt was influenced by the events in Palestine and their repercussions in Egypt. Gamal Abdel Nasser who emerged as the leader of Egypt was an Arab nationalist who was committed to the Palestinian cause. Nasser had fought in Palestine in 1948 and it was a significant factor in galvanising his Arab policy. He felt that a great injustice was committed against the millions of Palestinian Arabs who were now refugees.

After the Arab defeat in Palestine in 1948, the only Palestinian organisation tolerated in the Arab world was the Palestinian Student's Federation in Cairo. It was founded and led by Yasser Arafat, Abulyyad Farouk Kaddoumf and also by the members of the Baath Party. Parallel to this, Palestinians in Gaza Strip now began to form underground groups. They were led by Khalid Wazir (Abu Jihad) and Abu Youssef Najjar, who was killed in an Israeli Commando operation in 1973. The aim of these groups in the Gaza Strip was to form a common front of all Palestinians. They were no longer content to pin their hopes of Arab armies or UN resolutions. Accordingly, they formed the National Unity Front (AL-FATAH) in 1955.

Nasser's rise to Arab leadership and popularity among Arab masses had in large part rested on his promise to act in restoring Arab rights in Palestine. The Palestinian problem occupied a key element in Nasser's policy of Arab Unity Radio Cairo was developed into a powerful instrument through which 'Nasserism could be communicated throughout the Arab world, and by 1954 the Palestine Service of Radio was on the air daily. That represented something of a commitment to the Palestinian cause. Radio Cairo expanded its Palestine Service greatly in the early 1960s and by January 1962 was broadcasting two hours in the morning and thirty minutes in the afternoon.

At the Arab League Council session of March 1959 Egypt initiated a discussion on Palestinian entity. From the outset laid the stress on the erection of institutions, or representative bodies, which would speak in the name of Palestinians.

Arab League Council

The Arab League Council deliberated Egypt's proposals for the adoption of operative resolutions on the establishment of such institutions. Egypt's plan for reviving the Palestinian entity was thus a turning point in its process of solving the Palestine problem.

Under Egyptian influence the Arab League Council Session of September 1933 decided to appoint Ahmad Shequeiri as representative of the Palestinians in the League until the Palestinian people were able to choose their own representatives. Thus seeds were sown for the creation of Palestine Liberation Organisation (the PLO). The first Arab Summit held in Cairo on 16 January 1964 at Nasser's initiative resolved that Ahmad Shequeiri as Palestinian representative, would continue his contacts with Palestinians. It led the way for Shequeiri to establish the Palestine Liberation Organisation (PLO) in May 1964, following the first meeting of the Palestinian National Council (PNC) held in East Jerusalem.

The Second Arab Summit Conference, held in Cairo in September 1964, formally welcomed the creation of the PLO as the basis for the Palestinian entity. The setting of the PLO marked the fulfilment of the Egyptian initiative for the establishment of and the Arab recognition of the formal Palestinian entity. The Summit also affirmed the decision of the PLO to establish the Palestine Liberation Army (PLA).

For Nasser, the establishment of the PLO was the turning point in the Arab effort to liberate Palestine. Cairo allowed Shequeiri to use Gaza and its inhabitants to conduct the PLO's political and organisational activities. Moreover, in March 1965, Radio Cairo began broadcasting the Voice of Palestine Programme.

Egyptian Decline

Defeat of Egypt in 1967 June war resulted in the decline of Egypt's role in the Arab world, though from the Khartoum Summit of September 1967 to the Casablanca Arab Summit of 1969, Nasser had sought to win Arab support for a policy of confrontation with Israel. Besides the Arab defeat in the 1967 war completely discredited the traditional leadership of the PLO on 24 December 1967 Shequeiri resigned as chairman of the PLO and as representative of Palestine in the Arab League. He was succeeded by Yanya Hammouda as PLO chairman for the time being. In February 1959, Yasser Arafat, the leader of al-Fatah was elected chairman of the PLO.

Nasser's support for the Fedayeen organisation was reflected in his declaration that the standing of every Arab country determined in terms of the struggle (with Israel) and by its relations with the Palestinian resistance movement. He described the Palestinian organisation as a national liberation movement and both, he and his spokesman Mohammad Hussein Heikal, referred to the West Bank and Gaza as occupied Palestinian territories. He lobbied with the countries of the Eastern Bloc and the Third World for the recognition of the PLO and to project it as the legitimate representative of the rights of the Palestinians. It was he who introduced Arafat, the PLO leader, to the Soviet leadership in July 1968 which paved the way for Soviet military aid to that organisation.

Nasser played an important role as a mediator between the Palestinian guerrillas and the Arab governments. Lebanon was in the grip of civil war in 1969 on the question of the Palestinian presence there. The Cairo agreement was signed between the Lebanese government and the Palestinians on 3 November 1969 following Nasser's mediation which recognised the presence of Palestinian guerrillas in Lebanon.

Besides, when the civil war broke out in Jordan between the Palestinians and Jordanian army, resulting in the massacre of 3,000 Palestinians in September 1970 Nasser played his last role as a peace keeper. An agreement was signed in Cairo on 26 September 1970 between Yasser Arafat and King Hussein of Jordan in the presence of President Nasser.

However, the death of President Nasser in 1970 led to a gradual shift in Egypt's Palestine policy. Nasser might have failed to do much for the Palestinians yet he was a father figure who always provided protection for them. Palestinians mourned his death.

17. The Palestinian Problem Since the 70s

With the death of President Nasser on September 28, 1970 an entire page of Egypt's Arab history came to an abrupt end. It ended an era on contemporary Egyptian history. Within less than a year after his death, his political lieutenants were ousted from all positions of power by his successor Anwar al-Sadat. The policy of Egypt under President Sadat underwent significant change.

In the Arab sphere, the policy of President Sadat, while seemingly similar to that of Nasser during 1967-70, has exhibited subtle differences in emphasis which indicate basic shifts in the underlying elements of the policy. He tended to keep a low profile in Arab politics. His Arab Policy as also his policy towards the great powers underwent a total reversal. Egypt's ties with the PLO and the Fedayeen organisation reached the lowest point during the Sadat period.

New Foreign Policy

By July 1972, Sadat had expelled thousands of Soviet military advisers, signalling an about-face in Egyptian foreign policy. At the same time has moved closer to the United States and the oil rich and conservative Arab States of Saudi Arabia. The paralysis in Egyptian-Soviet relations has deprived Egypt of the capability to manipulate the competitive nature of the bi-polarised global system. Besides, while gaining the support of the conservative Arab elements, Sadat's anti-Soviet orientations have equally alienated the radical and 'leftist' forces inside Egypt and in the Arab world generally. These trends truly projected Sadat's policies as a flagrant reversal of the Nasserite socialist, pro-Arab, anti-imperialist crusade.

As his domestic power and authority increased, Sadat began to gradually modify the Nasserite principles. Indeed, Nasser's vehement anti-western orientations has been reversed. This is exemplified in the case of the United States, which had constituted the major focus of Nasser's anti-imperialist campaign; but which now replaced the Soviet Union as Egypt's trusted ally. Similarly, as Egyptian attitudes towards the Eastern block grew more ambivalent, Egypt's relations with the Western community as a whole became warm and cordial.

Egypt's Arab or Palestinian involvement has also reflected a change. Sadat began to gradually shift Egypt's position regarding the Arab world towards an increasing emphasis on Egyptian affairs. Sadat's earlier adherence to 'Arab Unity' in the period following Nasser's death had by 1972, became subordinate to the value of Egyptian patriotism. In his speech, made in July 1972, Sadat declared that in the forthcoming 'battle' with Israel, 'Egyptian Patriotism and Arab nationalism will, if necessary be alone in the field. This imposes on us an organised programme of action regarding Egyptian patriotism, and to safeguard it with domestic unity. Such a statement was indeed, a far cry from Nasser's often repeated assertion that his, and Egypt's responsibility was to the Arab nation and Palestinians as a whole.

Sadat's relative success in the 1973 war did not permit him to regain the Arab position which Nasser had held in the past. In any case, under Sadat Egypt rapidly moved towards a settlement with Israel in spite of the objections of the other Arabs. It began with the two agreements on troops disengagement signed in 1974 and 1975, under the US mediation. Replying to the Syrian accusation that he had abandoned the Arab cause by signing the Interim Agreement with Israel Sadat asserted that his first responsibility was to Egypt. Thus Sadat's indignation at Syrian and Palestinian hostility to Egypt's interim agreement with Israel indicated that the Egyptian leadership had expected their policies to be met with wholehearted and unequivocal support.

Turning Point

The US mediation between Egypt and Israel was later followed by the visit of President Sadat to Jerusalem between 19-21 November 1977 and his address to the Israeli Knesses, it was followed by the summit meeting in America in September 1973, and the Camp David accords leading to the signing of the Egypt-Israel peace treaty in March 1979. This visit of Egyptian President Anwar Sadat to Jerusalem between November 19-21, 1977 marked a turning point in the history of the Arab-Israeli conflict. It reversed the Egypt's earlier policy of commitment to Pan-Arabism and a total support for the Palestinians. For half a century since the meeting between the Emir Faisal, son of Sherif Hussein of Mecca and the Zionist leader Claim Weizmann in June 1918 no Arab leader had publicly met with any Zionist or Israeli official.

Sadat's visit to Israeli stirred many angry reactions in the Arab world as a whole. It undermined Egypt's role as a leader of the Arab world. It found expression in noisy demonstrations in various Arab countries and cities, especially Beirut, Damascus, Baghdad, Aden, Tripoli and Algiers. Popular disgust reached its apex in Damascus, Baghdad and Tripoli. The day Sadat arrived in Israel was declared a "Day of National Mourning" in Syria, where flags were flown at half-mast, citizens stopped working at noon for five minutes, church bells rung and muezzins sounded the call to prayer throughout the mosque's of Syria.

In Iraq, celebrations of the Al-Adha feast, which coincided with the day of Sadat's visit to Israel were cancelled in protest. Libya withdrew its recognition of the Sadat Government and also severed its diplomatic relations with Egypt, and imposed upon it the terms of Arab-boycott against Israel, calling on countries to follow suit. Besides this, several Arab newspapers and broadcasting stations both official and semi-official, described Sadat as a 'traitor' a 'capitulator', a 'conniver' with the 'enemy' and an 'agent of imperialism'. The visit was seen as an indication of a desire to abandon the Palestinian cause in particular and the Arab cause in general.

Arab opposition to Sadat's visit first realised in Egypt itself. In protest to this, Egypt's foreign minister Ismail Fahmy submitted his resignation, declaring that "Arab sovereignty over their lands is not subject to compromise". Sadat then appointed Mohammed Riad, Minister of State for Foreign Affairs, as Foreign Minister, but he too resigned. These events marked a turning point not only in the history of the Arab-Israeli conflict but also the end of Nasser's policy of Pan-Arabian and total support for the Palestinians.

Outside Egypt, the Palestine National Liberation movement Fateh also condemned Sadat for his visit. On November 17, 1977, Fateh issued a statement calling upon Sadat to forego that step as it would be a dangerous turn-point and a gain for world Zionism and its imperialist allies, headed by the US. In its statement, Fateh maintained that the visit would place the Palestinian people and the PLO in a dangerous position in the face of an aggressive Israel which is more intransigent and is declaring on every occasion that the people of Palestine have no rights, that there can be no independent Palestinian state and no total withdrawal from occupied Arab lands.

Besides this, a meeting of the Syrian and Palestinian leaderships resulted in a Syrian-Palestinian communique, stating that the visit "along with the Sadat-Begin plan, has no other aim but to impose a fait accompli on the Arab nation and thereby invalidate all genuine efforts to achieve a just peace based upon total withdrawal from all the occupied Arab territories and the safeguarding of the rights of the Palestinian Arab people to return, to self determination and to establish an independent state". For the Palestinians in general and the PLO in particular, Sadat's visit to Jerusalem represented a grave threat to their independence struggle. In reaction to Sadat's visit a conference was held in Libya. It was attended by Syria, the PLO, South Yemen, Libya and Algeria. The five leaders accused Sadat of attempting to create "an alliance between the Zionist enemy and the present Egyptian regime with the object of liquidating the Arab and Palestinian causes fragmenting the Arab nation and endangering its national interests. The Tripoli conference announced their refusal to take part in any Arab league meeting held in Cairo and also discussed about the relocation of League headquarters presently located in Cairo.

Camp David Talks

Moreover what Sadat did in going to Jerusalem was to recognise Israel de facto without anything in return. He also violated the basic Arab position regarding Jerusalem itself. By going to Jerusalem he recognised Israel's claim to that city as its capital.

The Camp David talks which began on 5 September 1978 under the auspices of US ended with the signing of documents, on 17 September 1978 between Egypt and Israel. These documents (1) A framework for peace in the Middle East; (2) A framework for the conclusion of a peace treaty between Egypt and Israel. The first of these documents contains the Egyptian-Israeli declaration of their intent to reach an agreement covering all aspects of the Middle East problem on the basis of the UN resolution 242 and 333. It called for an Israeli withdrawal from the Sinai, including the dismantling of the air bases. The second document envisioned a five year period of autonomy for the Palestinian of the West Bank and Gaza. An administrative body, or authority would be elected. And at the end of the first three years, negotiations would begin over the question of eventual sovereignty. But there was no mention of Palestinian self-determination nor did Israel commit itself to eventual withdrawal.

The peace treaty between Israel and Egypt was formally signed in Washington on 26th March 1979 under the auspices of the United States. The treaty guaranteed normal relations with full diplomatic recognition, economic and cultural relations and end to the state of war between two countries. Far from achieving the much promised honourable and comprehensive peace based on total Israeli withdrawal from Arab lands occupied in 1967 and Palestinian self-determination the Camp David agreements provided the grounds for a separate Egyptian-Israel peace treaty. In the light of the Camp David framework these following observations can be made:

To start with all the basic decisions relating to the procedures to be followed in seeking solution have been made at Camp David in the absence of Palestinian representatives and without regard for the known wishes of the Palestinian people. Besides, the Camp David Framework divides the Palestinian people into separate categories and offers different formulas for dealing with their respective situations. The dismemberment of the Palestinian people which is itself a feature of this tragedy has been transformed at Camp David into final solution to the Palestine problem. Moreover the Camp a permanent feature of the pro-David formula exclude the three posed Egyptian-American-Israeli basic rights of the Palestinian people which have been recognised and affirmed by the United Nations as the foundations of a just and lasting solution of the Palestine problem viz.—the right of the Palestinian people to self-determination and independence in Palestine; its right to designate its own national representative and to participate through the PLO—its sole representative in all efforts aimed at achieving a settlement of the problem.

Criticism

The serious Arab criticism of the Camp David agreements came from the inhabitants of the occupied territories themselves. The announcement of the signing of the agreements was met with an uprising. On 1 October 1978 a national Congress, attended by 150 West Bank figures and political representatives, met 'officially to give Begin, Carter and Sadat a definite response: an absolute rejection and a formal condemnation of the Camp David agreements. The PLO too rejected the agreements categorically. In April 1979, a distinct hardening of the whole of the Arab world was perceptible, the Arab countries broke their relations with Egypt, and decided on an economic boycott of Egypt and the transfer of the Arab league headquarters to Tunis.

Sadat also faced a drumbeat of criticism at home. Opposition newspapers sharpened their attacks: Friday sermons in the mosques raged against the "separate peace". Police were called out to control public protests. By September 1981, Sadat had lost his nerve and cracked down on the dissidents in Egypt, jailing hundreds of people from all walks of life and this alienating virtually every element of Egyptian society. All these factors culminated in Sadat's assassination at the hands of his own soldiers on 6 October 1981. It was ironic that he was mourned mainly in the West. Begin managed to isolate Sadat even in death. By insisting on attending his funeral. Begin kept the other Arab leaders except Sudan's former President Numeiri away.

There are many lessons to be drawn from Sadat's odyssey. As far as Camp David is concerned, it has been a complete disaster for the Arab world. Sadat's peace initiative could only have succeeded if he had been able to get the minimum that the other Arabs would accept. What the Americans and Sadat seemed to forget was that while the Arabia could not make war without Egypt, neither could Sadat make the peace he desired without the other Arabs. During the years since Sadat's assassination, tension in the Middle East have multiplied. Most are ahead results of Camp David.

Iran-Iraq War

The Egyptian-Israeli talks on Palestinian autonomy were destined to go nowhere. The war between Iraq and Iran created new divisions within the Arab world and has drained billions of dollars from the economies of the region. Arab disunity, exacerbated by

Egypt's isolation has made the Arab states individually vulnerable to foreign enemies. The Israeli invasion of Lebanon in June 1982 was another direct outcome of the Camp David. The tragedy in Lebanon gave Arab states and others new cause for anger at the United States and a new sense of their own helplessness.

Several peace initiatives have been put forward since the Israeli invasion of Lebanon. There is the Arab Fez plan, the Reagan plan, and the PLO-Jordanian peace initiative. All have been rejected outright by Israel. However, these efforts have not acquired any point of solution. Besides, Palestine might have contributed at times, to a general form of Arab solidarity, but on its own it has not provided any basis for Arab political unity.

The key lesson of Camp David for the Americans to ponder lies in what happened to Sadat. None of the promises made to him were kept. Besides, the Palestinian issue has been deliberately made into an obstacle by the Americans and the Israeli's. The Israelis use it to buy time, further absorbing the territories, while the Americans use it to justify their own inaction.

Arafat on several occasions has said that he accepts all UN resolutions pertaining to Palestine. The importance of this has been both overlooked and down played. By accepting all UN resolutions pertaining to Palestine Arafat has, for the first time, also accepted the 1947 UN partition resolution, which called for the creation of a Jewish and a Palestinian state in Palestine.

Now it is time the Americans and the Israelis fulfilled the promise made to the Palestinians in that same resolution. The Palestinian problem is not one of terrorism as the Americans and Israelis perceive it, but of a people deprived of their homeland, responding out of desperation.

The United States must draw lessons from the warnings of Arab leaders that time is running out. The American administration should not take moderation for granted in the Arab world or the friendship of its Arab allies. Moreover, Russia, the United Nations and the West European and Non-aligned powers should put pressure on the Americans and Israelis and see that the Palestinian problem is resolved at the earliest time possible.

18. Arab Disunity

The events of the past marked a significant turning-point in the turbulent history of West Asia. Manoeuvrings around UN Resolution 598 (to end the Gulf war (1980-88)), the American-Russian dialogue or the Arab-Palestinian talks on the West Bank and Gaza uprising displayed the depth of each component of the crisis.

The Palestinians, in the aftermath of Abu Jihad's brutal assassination by the callous Israelis, had demonstrated that the decades of hopelessness and neglect have not produced cowed and quiescent Palestinian population. And, they remain a struggling nation later through the four-part crisis—the combined challenge of the years of bloody Israeli repression in the occupied West Bank and Gaza, the continuing Israeli military intervention there and the developments in Gulf and Afghanistan.

Along with this, the Kurdish question, the declining role of the Arab League and the Islamic Conference Organisation (ICO), the urge for nuclear power, the Islamic-militant threat to the stability of regimes in Syria, Egypt, Saudi Arabia, Tunisia, Sudan, Kuwait, Jordan, Lebanon, Morocco and other existing regimes, the increasing defence spending of Egypt, Syria, Jordan, Iraq, Iran, Libya and Saudi Arabia have also contributed to the turmoil in the region.

The disunity among the Arab states and the Palestinians is both a cause and a consequence of these factors.

The split within the Fatah, the largest of the bodies grouped within the Palestine Liberation Organisation, has ensured that moves towards a resolution of the Arab-Israeli conflict and the Palestine problem would be put on the backburner. In the Arab sphere, Syria intervened in Lebanon after 1975, Libya and Egypt entered into a small border war since July 1977, Algeria and Morocco have great differences concerning the Polisario issue.

Jordan and Syria have experienced periods of tense relations with their armies being put on the alert at least twice. Syria and

Iraq, Syria and Egypt, Syria and the PLO could not develop co-operative relations during this time. Their discussions continue to be the most damaging aspect of the Arab system's overall political cohesiveness.

The Palestinian uprising in the West Bank and Gaza, that started since November 1987, now appears to be entering a crucial period. Two developments in the occupied territories have thrown up indications that the revolt has entered an important, new phase. First, the Israel's brutal killing of Abu Jihad leading to Syrian-PLO (limited) reconciliation and, second, a wave of increasingly repressive measures by the Israeli authorities designed to beat down the Palestinians.

Amidst all this, it is hard to find a realistic reason to hope for success in the US and West's belated foray into West Asia. The American political initiatives, that were introduced after the Palestinian upsurge in the Israeli occupied territories began, are being viewed with legitimate cynicism by the Palestinians and even the Israelis, besides the Arab states.

These are widely seen as an attempt to abort and stop the political momentum that has been generated in favour of Palestinian national rights. They are seen as a ploy to divert attention from the occupied territories and the aspirations of the Palestinians.

It would have been worthwhile if the latest peace proposals had sought also to edge the US and Israeli administrations toward dealing with the Palestinians through their true representatives, the PLO, and their leader Yasser Arafat.

The modern map of West Asia is in many respects an arbitrary creation of imperialist history. It is hard to envisage restoration of peace in the region unless the map is redrawn by its people in the process of rewriting history.

Arab Nationalism and Palestine Question

19. Arab Nationalism

I

Arabism is said to be a concept based primarily on emotional and sentimental attachment to a nationalist entity called 'the Arab nation'. Nationalism is a social concept that expressed the bond existing between individuals of one nation. It is the bond which relates the individuals of one nation in a common Partrie. Arabism in this context presupposes a high level of homogeneity among the inhabitants of the Arab states based on mutual perceptions of a common cultural, linguistic and religious heritage. It is also identified with the Arab existence, its past, present and future.

Arab nationalism is an attitude of mind which almost all Arabs share. It is unique in two important respects. First, it is linked to memories of past glories. It recalls a golden age of Arab greatness which is said to be the true image of the Arab genius. The second, is its Pan-Arab aspiration.

The Arab nationalists argue that all Arabic-speaking people from the Persian Gulf to the Atlantic constitute one nation. They conceive of the Arab world as single homogeneous whole and of the Arab people as a single nation bound by common ties of language, territory, economic life, religion and history. Pan-Arabism constitutes the intellectual mainstream of Arab nationalisation.

To the radical Arab nationalists, Arab nationalism is the outcome of excessive fragmentation, under-development, exploitation and subjection. It represents the motor-force of the Arab nation in its struggle. Besides, it gives rise to awareness of the link welding together the Nation's past, present and future and the personality common to all Arabs.

Today, the term "Arab" generally designates the Arabs as a cultural entity. The cultural evolution which the Arabs set in motion was the resultant of two processes viz: the religious and social. The first was the process of Islamisation whereby the new faith preached by the Prophet Muhammad, transformed their spiritual life. It is essential to consider Islam which had outgrown its Arab peoples. That God chose, to reveal His most perfect word to Arabs, in Arabic, and that by God's will or historical circumstances it was the Arabs who spread Islam throughout the world is of great significance to Arabs. Moreover, it permeates the daily life of the individual with its ritualistic obligations. It is an important part of socialisation and serves to integrate the Arab society by inculcating a sense of the Arab special relationship with God.

The other result was the process of Arabisation which had two aspects: Linguistic Arabisation that is the process by which the conquered people gradually acquired Arabic as their mother tongue; and racial Arabisation, caused by entry into those countries of masses of immigrants of pure Arab stock, whose absorption gave the conquered races a predominant admixture of Arab blood.

In formulating the postulates of Arab nationalism, Arab writers have drawn upon two principal sources, the first one (mentioned above) is the legacy of the past. The community of language, of tradition, and of historical experiences have all been stressed as common denominators of an Arab nation. The second source of inspiration is the cultural impact of the West (the term west stands for modern European civilisation in its totality).

The principal factor constituting Arab nationalism is said to be the language. A language is the medium through which people express their minds and emotions. It is linked to the national idea and acts as a symbol of Arab unity.

The second most important factor among the constituents of Arab nationalism is historical tradition. It is said to be the living memory of the nation. The unity of Arab history generates uniform sympathies, leads to a sharing of pride in the glories of past and creates identity of aspirations for the future.

The third factor constituting Arab nationalism, is said to be the community of interest.

The major ideological currents during the early phase of Arab nationalism (1800-1945) were Westernisation, Islamic revivalism, combining nationalism, reformism, and revolutionary activism, constitutionalism inspired by the winds blowing from Europe and finally, nationalism in its modern sense, that is on the basis of language, race, and culture in contradiction to Pan-Islamism or ottomanism.

From the nineteenth century onward, Western concepts have been incorporated into Arab nationalist thought and seems to have formed an integral part of the Arab tradition. The conquest of Egypt by Napoleon Bonaparte of France in 1789 initiated a chain of events and ideas. The above, in its totality constitute Arab nationalism. The first and foremost result of this was the general Arab awakening. A second result was the introduction of the printing press, which gave impetus to Arab classics and to national consciousness. A final result was the introduction of the European idea of nationality, which among other, led to the reaction against ottoman tyranny.

Next in line it was Mehmet Ali (1805-1849) who was instrumental in sowing the seeds of intellectual awareness, and the belief in the freedom of all peoples, and their right to national self-determination. Mehmet Ali's conquest of Egypt (1805), strove to serve his own ends by building up a strong modern army on the lines of Napoleon's renowned forces. Having learned from his French advisers that he would ultimately have to rely on Egyptian recruits, Mehmet Ali turned his energies to an educational movement designed to provide the military institutions with the educated elements amongst Egypt's indigenous population. As part of such a campaign, he sent a number of Egyptians to further their education in France, to assimilate western ideas, and to master the French language.

However, Mehmet Ali and his successors projection of carving out an Arab empire for themselves was never realised. It crashed on the rock of British hostility, economic crisis, moral decline and above all the absence of Arab national consciousness.

II

The story of the rise of a specifically Arab national movement, writes George Antonins "opens in Syria in 1847, with the foundation in Beirut of a modest literary society under the American patronage". The first organised effort in the Arab national movement can be traced back to the year 1875, when five found men who had been educated at the Syrian Protestant College in Beirut formed a secret society. They established branches in Damascus, Tripoli and Sudan. The main points of their programme were: (i) grant of independence to Syria in union with the Lebanon; (ii) recognition of Arabic as an official language; (iii) removal of censorship; (iv) employment of local recruited units on local military service only. Whatever may be, the society's appeals were the first trumpet-call by the infant Arab movement. It was the earliest organisation to be founded with a primarily political object. One of the earliest representatives of Islamic revivalism was Jamal al-Din al-Afghani to whom goes great credit for disseminating a new and vigorous nationalist spirit. He was the founder of the modern Pan-Islamic movement combining a nationalist interpretation of Islam with modernism and reformism. Another leading representative of Islamic revivalism was Muhammad Rashid Rida, a Syrian living in Egypt, whose book *The Caliphate* is the most systematic exposition of the Islamic theory of Government. To him, the authority of the people is meant the authority of those who represent the people. The third leading representative of modern Islamic revivalism was Abdul Rahman al-Kawakabi. He combined the four principal ideological currents which prevailed in his era; Islamic revivalism, Arab nationalism, westernisation and constitutionalism.

The distinguished representatives of the school of constitutional reform were Francis Fatuallah Marrash al-Halabi and Shibli al-Shumayyil who believed in the eventual triumph of popular sovereignty.

Modern Arab nationalism owes it birth to a movement, which had, as its principal aim the overthrow of autocratic rule. It started as protest against centralisation and as a plea for the introduction of democratic processes. One of the most important exponents of Arab nationalism was Adib Ishaq (1856-1885), a Christian (born in Damascus). He was also one of the staunchest advocates of Liberalism and constitutionalism. Ishaq was conscious of the obstacles which stood in the way of a free democratic society. Besides, he gave emphasis on equality which he considered indispensable to the success of a democratic system of government.

The other prominent exponents of nationalism were Mustafa

Kamel, and Sheikh Mohammed Abdou of Egypt representing the radical and moderate school of thought. The British occupation of Egypt (1882) led to the growth of a separate and intense feeling of nationalism. Abdou believed in reform as the ideal method to achieve national aspiration whereas Kamel (the leader of the Nationalist Party) believed that reform would be of no avail until the complete evacuation of the occupying forces. Kamel was an ardent supporter of popular sovereignty. He believed that participation of the people in their own government was a prerequisite to progress.

In Egypt, the Ottoman empire was viewed by both nationalists and ulema as Egypt's naturally against British domination. Ever since the British occupation of Egypt the wave of nationalism, demanding the evacuation of the country continued. Every Egyptian nationalist leader was working towards the aim of putting an end to the foreign domination with which the country was afflicted. The Arab nationalists in Syria and Iraq moved further away from the concept of Islamic solidarity, which the Ottoman Caliphate represented, and toward independent Arab nationalism. The Arabs in these countries, with their sincere love of independence, had been showing symptoms of a budding national consciousness. However, the striving for total independence did not take place until after the young Turk revolution of 1908 had frustrated all hopes for an autonomous Arab existence.

The First World War (1914-18) indeed offered opportunities to the Arab nationalists and led to the collapse of the Ottoman empire. Five new states were created from the ruins of the Ottoman empire—Iraq, Syria, Lebanon, Trans Jordan and Palestine. However the net result of the war, was the transformation of the Arab peoples from the status of citizens to that of subjects. No sooner did the war terminated than most of the Arab countries found themselves occupied by their wartime allies. A system of colonial rule in the guise of mandatory trusts, was imposed on them against their wishes.

III

Besides, the Balfour Declaration of November 2, 1917, which called for the establishment of a national home for the Jewish people in Palestine, created frustration and dismay among the

Arabs. It was during this time that a new basis for mutual sympathy and the aspiration for Arab unity in the struggle against foreign domination was established. It was accompanied by national uprisings in Egypt, Iraq and Syria.

In the 1920s, and still more in the 1930's, there began to grow up a new sort of nationalism, more thorough-going and revolutionary than that of the pre-First World War generation. As late as the Second World War, Arab nationalism really had two important centres, Damascus and Baghdad. However, Egypt played a major role in the movements of literary and intellectual revival. During this period the aim of all political action was to gain independence from Britain and France. Unity was the goal to be achieved after foreign domination had been brought to an end. To secure independence and make proper use of it, help was looked from Europe. Mustafa Kamel of Turkey hoped that in its own interest the French government would check the growth of British power. Said Zaqulul Pasha (a moderate leader of Egypt) appealed to the liberal conscience of England.

In Egypt, this was the period when 'Pharonic' nationalism was at its height, and Egyptians were concerned primarily with their own problem of independence from the British. The influence of monarchy was declined. The 1936 Anglo-Egyptian Treaty gave her comparative freedom in foreign policy. Besides, some Arab leaders were looking to her as a possible source of help in the complicated problem of Palestine. At the Bludan Conference, the then Egyptian Vice-President stated that a Jewish state in Palestine would be a danger to Egypt as much as to its neighbours.

In the 1930s Arab nationalism had taken the shape of a secular movement. The Arab leaders wished to deprive the Europeans of their most powerful weapon, that is the existence of Christian and dissident Muslim minorities who looked to them for protection. They wished to state their opposition to Zionism in national terms i.e. in terms of Christian and Muslim Palestinians alike.

In the 1940s, political changes in the Arab world took place (which were more radical than those occurring after the end of the first World War. Efforts were initiated to establish some concrete manifestation of Arab unity and cooperation. The result was the Arab League, which came into being on March 2, 1945.

The Arab League aimed at encouraging progress towards regional cooperation and unity and to formulate a joint Arab response to the Zionist colonisation of Palestine (1948). It represented the Arab movement of synthesis aiming at the liberation of Arab territories states from foreign domination. There were seven founder members: Egypt, Lebanon, Iraq, Syria, Jordan, Yemen, and Saudi Arabia. Membership has since expanded to include 21 independent Arab states plus Palestine, which is represented by the PLO at League meetings.

The end of second World War shattered the European dominance in the Arab world and led to the emergence of the United States and the Soviet Union as the world's two Super Powers. In 1945, France was forced to evacuate the republics of Syria and Lebanon, and by the end of the following decade, to grant independence first to Tunisia and then to Morocco. The Algerian revolution, which broke out in 1954, brought about Algeria's independence in 1962. Libya, which had been put under United Nations trusteeship after the war, achieved independence in 1951.

Britain's withdrawal from the Arab world was carried out gradually and without bloodshed except in Palestine where the mandate was formally terminated in 1948. Trans Jordan was recognised as an independence monarchy in 1946; Sudan was granted the right to self-determination in 1953 and became independent in 1956, became fully sovereign after the Baghdad Pact in 1955 stipulated Britain's evacuation. In 1961 the oil-rich Sheikhdom of Kuwait was declared independent and became the state of Kuwait.

In the post-war period another radical change took place: the domination of the old-guard nationalist leaders came to an end and was replaced in most Arab countries by a new type of nationalist leadership. The post-1952 period gave rise to a more militant form of Arab nationalism and Arab unity under the dynamic leadership of President Nasser in Egypt. He was said to be the Paladin of Pan-Arab nationalism and was identified by many in the West as well as in the east as the personification of the quest for Arab unity.

It was from this time that Nasser began to assume the stature of the hero of the Arab nationalism. Most Arabs felt that here, at last, was the leader they had been waiting for, who could stand up to the imperialist powers. Some looked further ahead to see him recovering Palestine for the Arabs. It was Nasser's

Egypt that breathed life into the Palestine Liberation Organisation (PLO), and it was Ismail Fahmy, the Egyptian Foreign Minister, at the 1974 Rabat summit, who proposed the PLO as the sole legitimate representative of the Palestinian people. It was since Nasser's time, that the struggle for unity and nationalism symbolised the quest for Arab unity and Arab nationalism.

20. New Facets of Arab Nationalism

The Iraqi thrust into Kuwait can not be viewed in isolation as a case of Iraq's nascent sub-imperialist desire in the Gulf region. The Iraqi move has its wider ramifications—which ultimately led to the resurgence of Arab Nationalism and Palestine question. The Iraqi effort to arouse Arab Nationalism through its action in Kuwait is a new attempt to challenge the Western or US imperialism. Before one comes to the present-day crisis one has to take into account, what Arab nationalism actually means. Arab Nationalism or Arabism is said to be a concept based primarily on emotional and sentimental attachment to a nationalist entity called 'the Arab Nation'. Nationalism is a social concept that expressed the bond existing between individuals of one nation.

It is the bond which relates the individuals of one nation in a common *Patrie*. Arabism in this context presupposes a high level of homogeneity among the inhabitants of the Arab States based on mutual perceptions of a common historical, cultural, linguistic and religious heritage. It is also identified with the Arab existence, its past, present and future.

The death of Nasser in 1970 led to a gradual shift in the rapid movement of Arab unification. After the death of Nasser, this nationalism manifested through Palestinian revolution in the seventies-eighties and nineties. Palestinian *intifedah* is also a new dimension which, since November 1987, has been added to the Arab Nationalism. *Intifedah* in fact is Arab nationalism of the oppressed Arab-Palestinian people. When this four-year old Resistance Movement went unheeded by the US, Iraq had to take a step to put an end to the West Asian impasse. Nationalism is now manifested in a different way.

The questions and the issues raised by President Saddam Hussein of Iraq have not been answered by the US and other western countries. The US finds itself in the most uncomfortable position when Saddam Hussein linked up the Kuwait issue with the central question of Palestine. If Israeli occupation on the

Arab-Palestinian territories is supported by the US then why is this occupation of Kuwait being actively opposed by it? Saddam Hussein's declaration that Iraq would withdraw from Kuwait if Israel withdraws from the Arab territories and Syria from Lebanon is the central point raising once again the Arab Nationalism which has more or less dominated the major part of this century revolving around the question of Palestine.

Viewed against the background of the recent events in Soviet Union, Eastern and Central Europe, the tide of recent radical Arab nationalism espoused by President Saddam Hussein or President Yasser Arafat of Palestine Liberation Organisation (PLO) has been rolled back by the muscular and economic diplomacy of United States and its direct intervention in the Gulf. Besides, nowhere outside Europe is the revolution in Soviet foreign policy under President Mikhail Gorbachev more tangible than in the way Gorbachev has reacted to US armed intervention in the Gulf and destruction of the Arab state of Iraq. Once the champion of the anti-western and anti-colonial forces in the Gulf, the Soviet Union now projects itself as a partner with the US in destroying the Arab socialist state of Iraq.

The US President George Bush along with the Western and Zionist leaders had spoiled the plans of anybody who brought into the idea that a new "Era of Universal Peace" was dawning. Taking into account the armed might of the US Imperialist army in the Gulf, the US has re-established its political, economic and military hegemony over the region more fully than at any time since the post-World War II period. Since 1945 the US has initiated and taken part in most armed conflicts and staged interventions in different parts of the Third World, i.e. not only in Latin America (Cuba and Panama recently) but also in the Mediterranean (Libya), Africa, Asia and the Arab region. Not long ago in October 1983 the US Imperialists invaded Grenada, a tiny island of the Caribbeans, violating the UN Charter and defying the international law and norms of conduct. Following it the US took vigorous steps for a large scale invasion of Lebanon and butchered the state in concert with its ally the Zionist Israel. All this found reflection in the brazen statement by a highly placed US signatory who claimed that the world looked to America for leadership while America, for its part, looked to its marines.

The rash US action in the Gulf shook the lakhs of Arab people there. Though the outcome of the US ambitions in the Gulf is very much predictable, it has elicited a series of threats to the Third World. It has lasting ramifications for the reconstruction of the Third World, particularly Gulf region, US-Soviet relations, credibility of United Nations and other international and regional organisations. It has its impact on other conflicts such as Lebanon, Cyprus, Western Sahara and last but not the least the Arab-Israeli crisis i.e. the Palestine question. 'The present crisis', rightly says Prof. K.R. Singh of Jawaharlal Nehru University (JNU), 'has once again exposed the ever volatile Gulf region to the multiple regional and international imperialist pressures that threaten to unleash yet another violent conflicts'.

Decade after formal independence, Third World countries including the West Asian region still find themselves under severe restrictions to fully exercise their sovereignty as nation states. In the post-1945 period, as mentioned above, the colonial territories have, by and large, attained independence. As a bloc, the Third World countries are supposed to be free and equal participants in the shaping of world development. Yet in reality the big Imperialist powers particularly the US maintain a dominant grip over international relations—including the international organisation, i.e. the United Nations.

Despite pious declarations of non-interference and non-intervention, Imperialist powers like the US can choose to invade or attack other countries under various pretexts such as "self defence". Besides, the Third World countries' right to take back control over their own natural resources, and to nationalise industries in order to do so, has also been blocked in many cases including the Gulf region by the US and Zionist Israel who want to maintain their stranglehold over the world resources and wealth (as the case of Zionists' forcible occupation and exploitation of Arab-Palestinian resources and wealth). Moreover, behind the facade of the United Nations, sheer US military might is still the force around which the system of international relations revolves.

The eyes of the world are now focused on what sort of peace will emerge from the debris of the recently concluded Gulf War. Will it be one whose modalities have been worked out carefully and impartially by the UN Security Council—already suspected of being influenced by the UN's biggest paymaster, the US—or will it be one imposed on a toothless Iraq by the US and its western partners? To consider this point here one needs to delve into the past and to find out the real reasons for the US entry into the Gulf conflict which has claimed more than 150,000 lives, military and civilian.

It would be foolish to believe that the US attacked Iraq out of brotherly love for the Kuwaitis, or on sympathetic grounds. If this were so, why did it not raise a finger to save the people of Hungary or Czechoslovakia when the USSR forcibly intervened in their territories? And did it protest when Zionist Israel grabbed the whole of Arab-Palestinian territory?

Oil, the most valuable resource, was the motivating factor, especially since US's domestic resources of this Liquid gold are fast drying up. What more effective way could have been found of ensuring an unlimited supply of oil than by becoming the dominant dictating power in the largest oil-producing store in the world?

The contradiction in American policy was highlighted by its firm and repeated denunciation of Soviet forces in Afghanistan. Although the Israeli army occupied Arab Palestine (1948), Golan Heights, the West Bank, Gaza, Jerusalem (1967) and had repeatedly violated both human rights and international law in their occupation policies in Lebanon and Palestine, there was never a US criticism of the occupation itself, much less any suggestion of a boycott. Israel was cited for systematic violation of human rights in the occupied Arab-Palestinian territories by a myriad of organisations, including the *UN Commission on Human Rights*, the London *Sunday Times*, *Amnesty International*. Yet the US refused even to acknowledge that Israel had systematically violated the human rights of the Arab-Palestinians, much less criticise or withhold aid.

Though the Iraqi action has cost much consternation and insurmountable difficulties for the Arabs and foreigners in the Gulf the time has come to solve the major West Asian problems once for all. Iraqi action has generated the tremors of Arab Nationalism among the Arab masses which is crystal clear from the demonstrations in various Arab capitals in support of Saddam Hussein. This is ostensible because relatively a small country like Iraq, without the support of any big power, has defied the world's biggest Super Power the US. This has definitely raised the prestige of the Arabs and has given a new direction to the Arab Nationalism. Unless the Palestine problem, which is the crux of the West Asian crisis, is solved and the Palestinians get back a state of their own on their native soil West Asia will continue to endanger the world peace.

21. Palestine: Peace Without Justice

The recent two stages of the Arab-Israeli negotiations at Madrid accomplished little substantial for the Palestinians. These negotiations wound up after a lot of handshake ceremony, gratuitous public rudeness, pronouncements and well-established ritual political stands. Nothing much was accomplished concerning the Palestine question. The unfinished business of the recently concluded Gulf War, i.e., the Palestine question still looms large. The great powers by their support of the Balfour Declaration (1917), and the United Nations, through its resolution of 1947 in favour of the partition of Palestine, created the Palestine problem.

Israel was recreated in the map of West Asia after an absence of about 2,000 years in 1948. Those Israelis who live today in Israel are all emigrants whereas the Palestinians are there in Palestine for generations. Even the Israeli Prime Minister Mr. Yitzak Shamir who, it might be pointed out, was born in Poland and emigrated to Palestine only in 1935. The Palestinians are the natives of the Palestinian soil. There are more Jews in New York city than in the state of Israel. At the end of the First World War, Palestine was among the several former Ottoman Arab territories which were made mandated territories by the League of Nations. The mandate for Palestine was formally allotted in 1922 to Great Britain by the League of Nations without having ascertained the wishes of the Palestinian people, as required by the League covenant.

During the twenty-five years of Palestine mandate, from 1922 to 1947, large-scale Jewish immigration from abroad, mainly from Eastern Europe, took place. The number swelled in the 1930s with the Nazi persecution of Jews. Over this period the Jewish population of Palestine, composed principally of immigrants increased from less than 10 per cent in 1917 to over 30 per cent in 1947. Palestinian demands for independence and resistance to Jewish immigration led to an Arab rebellion in 1937. This was followed by continued Jewish terrorism and violence during and immediately after the Second World War. Great Britain, as the mandatory power, tried to implement various formulas to bring independence to Palestine. A partition scheme, a formula for provincial autonomy, a unified independent Palestine, were all considered and abandoned. In 1947, Great Britain in frustration turned the problem over to the United Nations. Meanwhile, violence continued to spread in Palestine as Zionist terrorist groups stepped up their attacks and sabotage of Arab-Palestinian people and their property. It was at this stage in the tragic history of Palestine the Arab-Palestinians debilitated by thirty years of British suppression proved incapable of withstanding the assault of the violent Zionist community (trained, armed and supported by the European-American international onslaught of the day).

The first special session of the UN General Assembly was convened on April 2, 1947, to consider the question of Palestine. On 1st May 1947 the United Nations set up a UN Special Committee on Palestine (UNSCOP). At the same time, the UN rejected an Arab resolution to end the mandate and declare independence for Palestine. In November 1947, by which date the situation had seriously deteriorated, the majority recommendation of UNSCOP was embodied in a resolution of the General Assembly 181 (ii) dated November 20, 1947. This resolution recommended partition of Palestine into Jewish and Palestinian states. It is quite significant that, during this period of Arab-Palestinian struggle our leaders, particularly Mahatma Gandhi and Jawaharlal Nehru, could realise the injustice being done to Palestinian Arabs by creating a Jewish state in their territory and forcefully raised their protest against it. Even the All-India Congress Committee meeting in 1937 protested against the reign of terror that was being established in Palestine by Zionist and British colonialists.

The Arab states, the Arab League and the Arab Higher Committee, rejected the decision to partition Palestine. The British had now started to withdraw their troops. The Jewish military and terrorist groups—Haganah, Irgun and stern Gang—now intensified their attacks on Arab Palestinians. Between December 13, 1947, and February 10, 1948, 161 Palestinians were killed and 320 injured. The death toll had risen to 2,307 since the partition resolution. In 1948, these Jewish terrorist groups blew up several trains killing 93 Palestinians and wounding many. They also attacked Arab-Palestinian villages hotels, houses and offices.

At the end of the first Arab-Israeli war of 1948, the new state of Israel controlled 77.44 per cent of the country. The UN partition plan had allocated them 56.4 per cent. The Israeli victory in this war brought Israel more land, but it did not bring peace. On the contrary, it laid the foundations for the long confrontation that has been continuing until the present day.

All the peace initiatives undertaken so far have failed because they tried to dodge the real issues and to liquidate the real problem rather than settle it. The Camp David agreements of 1978-79, as far as Palestine was concerned, amounted to little and the subsequent plans initially rejected by Israel sought to weaken the Palestine problem. All the basic decisions relating to the procedures to be followed in seeking solution have been made at Camp David in the absence of Palestinian representatives and without regard for the known wishes of the Palestinians. Besides, the Camp David peace formula excluded the three basic rights of the Palestinian people which have been recognised and affirmed by the United Nations as the foundation of a just and lasting solution of the Palestine problem, viz., the right of the Palestinian people to self-determination and independence in Palestine; its right to designate its own national representative and to participate through the PLO—its sole representative in all efforts aimed at achieving a settlement of the problem. The Israelis are still using it to buy time, abolishing further the Arab territories.

Several other peace initiatives have been put forward since the Israeli invasion of Lebanon in 1982. There was the Arab Fez Plan, the Reagan Plan and the PLO-Jordanian peace initiative, Shultz's peace initiative. All have been rejected outrightly by Israel. Besides, they made the same futile error of ignoring the plight of the real victims, i.e., the Palestinians.

Yasser Arafat, leader of the Palestine Liberation Organisation, categorically recognised the existence of the state of Israel and accepted all UN resolutions pertaining to Palestine. Even, Arafat declared that he was ready to 'smoke the Peace Pipe' with the Israeli Prime Minister, Mr. Yitzhak Shamir, in the run up to the current landmark West Asia Peace Conference. But the importance of this has been both overlooked and down played.

The present adamant Israeli government tries to camouflage its refusal to address the heart of the Arab-Israeli conflict, i.e., the dispossession of the Arab-Palestinians, behind a smokes-screen of moral revulsion at the thought of dealing with what it describes as a "terrorist" organisation, the PLO. And Israeli Prime Minister Yitzhak Shamir, who was himself a leader of the notorious stern Gang, which assassinated UN and government officials before the forcible establishment of the state of Israel and participated in the 1948 massacre of Arab villagers in Deir Yassin, had been a great terrorist as far as terrorism is concerned. Besides, the West has understood the plight of Jews but not of the Palestinians. There is a big Jewish lobby in Western politics and business. Unfortunately, there is no Palestinian lobby in the West either in business, finance or politics.

Now it is time for the Americans, the Israelis, the Europeans and the Non-aligned states, including India, to fulfil the promise made to the Palestinians in the 1947 UN partition resolution, which called for the creation of a Jewish state in Palestine. It is time for the Americans particularly President George Bush to act. At the present juncture of unipolar world scene the US is the only country that can bring peace to West Asia. The Americans must pressurise Israel for accepting independent Palestinian representatives at the international peace table and find a solution to the West Asian crisis. West Asia will continue to be unstable politically, militarily and diplomatically until the Palestine problem is resolved at the earliest time possible.

India's policy should not be dictated by the pro-Israeli lobby. We should depend on our independent foreign policy initiated since the time of Prime Minister Nehru. It is our moral duty to support the Palestinians all the way. Satisfaction in the sphere of Palestinian question should precede India's Israeli policy. For all practical purposes, India has got good political, economic, cultural, diplomatic and historic ties with Arab countries. We must not look at the problem from any other point of view either Arab or West. There is no morality observed here. India must think of its own perspectives. The only solution to the West Asian crisis lies in the establishment of a Palestinian state in West Bank and

Gaza Strip with its capital at Jerusalem. The establishment of the Palestinian state would be also good for Israel from the political, economic and military point of view. This would cut Israel's excessive defence spending, because Israel is spending 89 to 90 per cent of its GNP on defence. Moreover, this would also reduce Israeli insecurity.

22. West Asia Today

The beginning of 1990s has inevitably been dominated by a series of events in West Asia like the Kuwaiti war, unification in Yemen, Intifadeh in Israeli occupied Arab-Palestinian territories, political settlement in Lebanon, imposition of the so-called neo-American order in Arab world and Gulf region, the American shooting down of the Iraqi MIG plane, the Kurdish revolt, Arab security proposals and alliances, Islamic insurgence in Algeria, Egypt, Sudan, Lebanon, Jordan, Kuwait and other Gulf regions. The above events were also followed by the happenings like Saudi-Kuwaiti border crisis, UAE's border clash with Saudi Arabia, elections in Kuwait, Arms build-up in Gulf region and the quake in Egypt. However, the most significant event that made the headlines was the Arab-Israeli peace talks.

The Arab-Israeli peace process that the United States and the erstwhile Soviet Union had set in motion at the Madrid Conference on West Asia in 1991 is not proceeding as well as was hoped, mainly due to the supercilious attitude of the Israelis. The recent illegal and forcible expulsion of 415 Palestinians by Israel and the subsequent killing of Palestinians posed a grave setback for the ongoing Arab-Israeli peace process. Israel had deported a number of Arab-Palestinians from Palestine as a brutal response to their non-violent freedom struggle, i.e. Intifadeh. The deportations both in the past and in recent times by Israel of the Arab-Palestinian people from Israeli occupied Arab-Palestinian territories constituted a severe violation of the basic principles of international law. It also violated, in reality, the provisions of such international instruments and conventions as the Hague Convention of 1899 and 1907, the Charter of the United Nations 1945, the Geneva Convention of 1949 and the universal declaration of Human Rights. Indian minister of state for external affairs condemned the Israeli policy of deportation and expressed the apprehension that such an action would only strengthen forces of extremism in the West Asian region with frightening consequences.

Prior to this, the Israeli policy of expropriation of Palestinian land in the Israeli occupied Arab territories, construction of new Jewish settlements and reconstruction of the existing ones continued unabated during the last decades. The modes of acquiring the Palestinian land included the practice of deliberately confiscating land and declaring it closed for military training purposes, declaring Arab-Palestinian land as 'state land' and expropriating the land for public, i.e. the Jewish use.

When US President George Bush proclaimed a "new world order", the Arab-Palestinians hoped it would include peace, freedom and a permanent land for them. Unfortunately, this was not the case. Spread across the whole of West Asia, North African and Gulf region, the Arab-Palestinians have no country of their own today. Throughout, their homeland under colonial i.e. British and Israeli occupation, Palestinians have faced various degrees of persecution since the beginning of this century.

Achieving peace and stability in West Asia requires Israel to vacate all the Arab-Palestinian territories which it occupied since 1948. The last five decades have demonstrated that any effort at achieving peace and stability in the area that does not offer a practical solution acceptable to the Arab-Palestinian people, shall remain a still-born exercise, if it did not take into account resolutions 242 and 338 of the UN Security Council as the legal basis to a political settlement of the problem and recognise the Palestinians right to independence and sovereignty under the leadership of the PLO—their legitimate representative. If the Palestinians can be satisfied, much of the instability in the Arab-Islamic world will go away. Palestinian self-determination shall rightly be a panacea for resolving all the most complicated socio-politico, religious, military and economic questions.

Besides the Arab-Israeli peace talks, another worst crisis of 1992 in West Asia has been the Islamic resurgence phenomena in Egypt, Algeria, Lebanon, Kuwait, Tunisia, Sudan, Saudi Arabia, Jordan and Turkey. In Egypt, more than 650 suspected radicals were arrested recently during the eight-day sweep of Imbaba district and authorities charged the Islamic extremists of intimidating the area's people to enforce their version of an Islamic society. This is the fourth worst eruption of sectarian strife followed by the killings of 13 Christians in May, four Coptic Christians in October and burning down of 20 shops and a Church subsequently. Prior to this at least 260 militant extremists were taken away from their homes and from the streets in the densely populated suburb of Imbaba this November. Some 12,000-15,000 soldiers and special anti-terrorist troops participated in the above operation, supported by hundreds of armoured combat vehicles. But many residents in the impoverished Imbaba district praised the Islamic radicals and criticised the crackdown by Egypt's secular government. So also, the arrest of two pro-Islamic deputies in Jordan along with almost a dozen other Islamists, on charges of obtaining, maintaining and transporting weapons with the intention to challenge the authority of the state, has sent shock waves throughout the country.

The current trend of Islamic resurgence is large due to the disillusionment in the Arab-Islamic world with other ideologies such as Marxism, Zionism, Capitalism and Socialism, none of which appeared to be ways of meeting their day-to-day difficulties, or finding solution to the ongoing socio-politico, military, psychological conflicts and solving their economic problems. In the contrary, the economic crisis and socio-politico problems that have resulted from these ideologies and conflicts have only deepened and become more complex. This protracted crisis milieu included the disorienting political, economic and social impact of Western, American and Soviet Imperialism, the imperatives of economic development, the disgusting Arab-Israeli conflict, the Arab loss of Palestine and Jerusalem and the ongoing political and territorial conflict within the Arab-Islamic sphere.

In terms of territorial disputes, India recently expressed deep concern at the border clashes between Saudi Arabia and Qatar. While International attention over the past two years has focused on the United Nations' efforts to redraw the border between Iran and the UAE over the island of Abu Musa, border questions in other areas of the Arab-Gulf Peninsula have been largely overshadowed. With the exception of the brief outbreak of hostilities between Saudi Arabia and Qatar in September, mentioned above, considerable progress has been made elsewhere towards defining mutually acceptable frontiers. Two such agreements have already been signed, both concerning Oman. The first was with Saudi Arabia in March 1990, when Riyadh and Muscat agreed on a common border stretching through the southern reaches of the Empty quarter desert and the deadly quicksands of Umm al-Samim.

Shoring up its southwest flank as well, Sultan Qaboos of Oman visited Yemen at the beginning of October and signed another border accord. Oman and UAE have also made slow but some progress towards solving outstanding differences on their border. These border disputes have their roots in a combination of expanding national aspirations, colonialism, imperialism and the competition of control of resources. Until the discovery of oil on the Arab-Gulf Peninsula in 1938 and the promise of much more to come, "borders" were essentially the spheres of influence of dominant tribal leaders.

Another danger that haunts West Asia is that of the arms race. After a brief lull, the weapons sales to the countries of West Asia are accelerating once more with no sign of restraint. Traditional fears and paranoia are paving the way for frenzied purchases of the latest and the most readily available in arms technology, spanning the globe from China, Russia, North Korea, Israel, former East bloc states, Germany, Britain, France, Argentina, Brazil and the record-setting United States. Gulf Arab States and Islamic Iran devote an average $60 billion annually to their military budgets. Following the end of the Gulf war, Israel is said to be the largest importer and exporter of military technology in West Asia. Since the end of the cold war, the great concern today is the fate of thousands of Soviet nuclear weapons possibly up for sale by the various former Eastern republics.

Hence the present problems of socio-economic, politico-military nature stimulate a responsible awareness of the interaction of West Asian events with the international situation in every latitude. The above changes require multilateral responses (non-aligned role), solidarity among West Asian states, and open and indeed concrete solutions. The force of real peace, together with states sincerity, determination and the growing realisation of co-existence on equal terms between the Israelis and Arab-Palestinians shall contribute to the gradual breaking of hated traditional barriers.

The coming decade must see a totally new environment in Israeli-Palestinian, Israeli-Arab, Arab-Arab relations. Foreign policy will need to be extrapolated from the dynamics of internal reforms in Israel, Arab and Gulf region.

23. The New Israel-PLO Accord

The Accord

The signing of the Taba accord (1995) between Israel and Palestine Liberation Organisation (PLO) on transferring much of control of the Israeli occupied West Bank to its Arab-Palestinian residents is hailed as a momentous substantive step toward translating the hope of 1993 Oslo Accords into reality. This second phased interim agreement between Israel and Palestinian National Authority (PNA) which comes about after a year's delay proves the fact that the peace process despite serious setbacks, hurdles and many continuing uncertainties is still on track. It constitutes phase two of the historic agreement signed between Israel and PLO in 1993, which established Palestinian self-rule in Gaza Strip and Jericho in the West Bank.

The main object of the Interim agreement is to broaden Palestinian self-government in the West Bank by means of an elected self-governing authority—the Palestinian Council. This will allow Palestinians to conduct their own internal affairs, reduce points of friction between Israelis and Palestinians, and open a new era of cooperation and coexistence based on common interest, dignity and mutual respect. At the same time it protects Israel's vital interests, and in particular its security interests, both with regard to external security and the personal security of its citizens in the West Bank.

Palestinian Council

In general, the interim agreement between Israel and the PLO, including its various annexes, comprises some 400 pages, setting forth the future relations between Israel and the Palestinians. To the main body are appended six annexes dealing with: security arrangements, elections, civil affairs (transfer of powers), legal matters, economic relations, and Israeli-Palestinian cooperation.

The agreement states that a Palestinian Council will be elected for an interim period not to exceed five years from the signing of the Gaza-Jericho agreement (i.e., no later than May 1999). The negotiations on the permanent status arrangements will begin to later than May 1996. The permanent status negotiations will deal with the remaining issues, including Jerusalem, refugees, settlements, security arrangements, borders, relations and cooperation with neighbouring countries, etc.

The Council is an elected body and, accordingly, the agreement sets out arrangements for democratic elections to the Council by all Palestinians of the West Bank and the Gaza Strip aged 18 year or over who are registered in the population register. The elections will take place 22 days after the conclusion of an IDF (Israeli military) redeployment from populated areas in the West Bank.

The elections to the Council will be personal and by district. A separate election will be held simultaneously for the election of the head of the executive authority of the Council. The candidacy of an individual, a party or a coalition of parties shall be rejected if the said candidate, party or coalition professes racist views or acts in an illegal or undemocratic manner.

Palestinian residents of Jerusalem will be able to participate in the elections according to special arrangements detailed in the agreement.... A Palestinian with a Jerusalem address who wishes to stand for elections to the Palestinian Council will be able to do so only if he or she has an additional valid address in the West Bank or Gaza Strip. All stages of the election process will be open to international observation.

Powers of the Council

The Palestinian Council to be established following the elections will assume various powers and responsibilities in security and civil spheres in the West Bank and Gaza Strip. With the establishment of the Council, the Israeli military government will be withdrawn and the civil administration dissolved. The Palestinian Council will assume responsibility for all rights, liabilities, and obligations in the spheres transferred to it. At the same time Israel will retain those powers and responsibilities not transferred to the Council. The Council, which will have 82 members, will have legislative and executive powers. The agreement provides that the legislative powers will be exercised by a committee of the Council—the executive authority. It should be noted that it will not have powers in the sphere of foreign relations.

The Israeli army or IDF will be redeployed in the West Bank according to the time-table set out in the agreement. In the first stage, designed to facilitate the holding of elections, the IDF will withdraw from the populated areas of the West Bank: the six cities—Jenin, Nablus, Tulkarm, Kalkilya, Ramallah and Bethlchem (in the city of Hebron special security arrangements will apply as provide in the agreement)—and 450 town and villages. At the end of this redeployment, there will be almost no IDF presence in the Palestinian population centres. In general, throughout the West Bank and Gaza Strip, Israel will have overall responsibility for external security and the security of Israelis and settlements.

Three Types of Area

With regard to internal security and public order, the agreement establishes different arrangements for three types of area: *Area A* comprises six cities listed above. In this area, the Palestinian Council will have full responsibility for internal security and public order, as well as full civil responsibilities. *Area B* comprises Palestinian towns and villages of the West Bank. In these areas, which contain some 58 per cent of the Palestinian population, the Council will be granted full civil authority, as in *Area A*. The Council will be charged with maintaining public order, while Israel will have overall security authority to safeguard citizens and combat terrorism. This responsibility shall take precedence over the Palestinian responsibility for public order. Twenty-five Palestinian police stations will be established in specified towns and villages to enable the Palestinian police to exercise its responsibility for public order. The agreement contains provisions requiring that the movement of Palestinian police be coordinated and confirmed with Israel. In *Area C*, which comprises unpopulated areas, areas of strategic importance to Israel, and the Jewish settlements, Israel will retain full responsibility for security and public order.

The agreement contains an undertaking to revoke those articles of the Palestinian Covenant calling for the destruction of Israel, within two months of inauguration of the Council.

The agreement provides for the establishment of a strong police force: 12,000 in number, that will constitute the only Palestinian security force. The Security Annexure specifies the deployment of the police force, the approved equipment, and its modes of action. The Security Annexure specifies the commitment of Israel and the Palestinian Council to cooperate in the fight against terrorism and the prevention of terrorist attacks, according to the following framework. The IDF and Israelis will continue to move freely on the roads of the West Bank and Gaza. Israelis may not, in any, circumstances, be arrested or placed in custody by the Palestinian Police, and may only be required to present identity and vehicle documentation. On roads that are jointly patrolled, any request for identification shall only be made by the Israeli side of a joint patrol.

Responsibility over sites of religious significance in the West Bank and Gaza will be transferred to the Palestinian side. In *Area C*, this will be transferred gradually during the *further redeployments phase*, except for the issues which will be negotiated during the permanent status negotiations. Both sides shall respect and protect religious rights of Jews. Christians, Muslims and Samaritans, etc.

The agreement also contains an undertaking on the part of Israel to increase the amount of water allocated to the Palestinians by 28 million cubic meters. Any further addition to either side will be based on an increase in the available water resources to be developed through international funding and channels.

To foster a positive atmosphere as this agreement is being implemented, and to engender mutual confidence and a basis of cooperation between the two peoples, Israel will release Palestinian prisoners in Israeli custody in three stages according to the following format:

Stage 1: Upon the signing of the agreement.
Stage 2: On the eve of elections of the Council.
Stage 3: According to other principles which will be established separately.

Besides, the agreement defines relations between Israel and the Palestinian Council. Both sides will act to strengthen understanding and tolerance, prevent incitement and hostile propaganda, and will use legal means at their disposal to prevent incitement on the part of groups or individuals. Both sides have pledged that their educational systems will act to advance peace between Israel and the Palestinians.

The above accord signed by Israeli Prime Minister Yitzhak Rabin who was recently assassinated by a young Jewish fanatic and hardliner, Yigal Amir and PLO leader Yasser Arafat on Thursday, September 28, 1995 was praised by US President Bill Clinton as a milestone achievement. Mr. Clinton also urged Syria and Lebanon to join the peace process. Israeli Foreign Minister Shimon Peres said, the agreement *should be judged by its potential, not its content*. The PLO Chairman and head of the Palestinian National Authority said that his self-rule deal with Israel heralded a new era for the Palestinians. *The dawn has started for all Palestinians who dream of and demand a Palestinian State. No doubt it will not be easy but we have to work for it*, he said adding that he hoped *the implementation (of the accord) will be accurate*. However, Mr. Rabin, the Israeli Prime Minister takes a dim view of Arafat's interpretation. The Arab dignitaries, President Hosni Mubarak of Egypt and King Hussein of Jordan, in turn, urged Israel to release Palestinian prisoners from Israeli jails; move along the concurrent peace making *tracks* with Syria and Lebanon, and reach an agreement on the status of Jerusalem, which both Palestinians and Israelis claim as their capital.

Unresolved Issues

So far as the details of the recent accord are concerned, several substantial issues seems to have been unresolved. These are related to the control of electricity grid transformers, control of precious West Bank water resources, a firm time-table for Israeli troop withdrawal from all of the West Bank, and the so-called *Permanent status issues* which include the question of Jerusalem, the fate of the Palestinian refugees (1948, 1967, 1982 and onwards) final borders, status of Jewish settlers and the all-important question on the nature of the Palestinian *entity*. The issues of Hebron (where 53 Palestinians were massacred by a Jewish settler last year) and the release of Palestinian prisoners which held up agreement for so long, have not been resolved properly. The figures on territorial control are malleable. Disappointed Palestinian critics complain that the big towns over which the Palestinian Council will have full control only comprise about 30 per cent of the West Bank—

not to mention the special problems posed by Hebron. Besides, the situation in the bulk of West Bank where Israel will withdraw its troops but retain overall security powers is more complicated. The Palestinian police will have no authority to arrest Israelis even when they are caught red-handed. There also remain differences on the proper security arrangements. Another complication is about Israel's non-implementation of the accord in time. Israel's commitment to 1993 accord had been uncertain at times. A further complication is about the outcome of imminent general elections in Israel.

In such a context, all the quibbling and haggling over the terms of extending self-rule seem bitterly irrelevant. The Palestinian leader, Yasser Arafat does not want the humiliation of ceding control of security to Israel as there can be no constitutional challenge against Israeli military intervention, but he has no real choice. The Jewish militants and the Palestinian radicals like the Islamic Resistance movement or *Hamas* and *Islamic Jihad* are opposed to the Accord and have threatened to boycott any Palestinian elections held under cover of Israeli guns. However, a right-wing Jewish militant. Yigal Amir went to the extent of assassinating the Israeli Premier Mr. Yitzhak Rabin. *I did this to stop the peace process*, he told Israeli magistrate Dan Arbel. Palestinian opponents feel that, for Israelis, the recent Taba accord can also be a prime example of eating one's cake and having it too. In spite of the seeming hopelessness of the Palestinian situation, the Israelis are between a rock and a hard place in relation to their long term occupation of the West Bank, Gaza Strip and East Jerusalem. To avoid unending strife, the logical course for the Israelis would be to return the Jewish settlers to Israel and to completely withdraw from the occupied territories of Arab-Palestinians, Syrians and the Lebanese—A peace based on a permanent occupation under the rubric of limited Palestinian self-government, but devoted to protecting the interests of the Jewish fundamentalism. It is high time to end the Israeli-Palestinian conflict in the best interest of stability, prosperity and social cohesion of the people of the Middle East region. Nations must recognise the primacy of peace in the region. Hence, the solution lies in the realisation of full and practical peace between Arab-Palestinians and Israel and in recognising the right of the Palestinians to self-determination through a state of their own with East Jerusalem as their capital.

24. Israel and Lebanon

"I wholly agree that American partisanship in the Arab-Israeli conflict is dangerous to both the United States and the Free World", rightly wrote John F. Kennedy in a letter to Alfred M. Lilienthal, author of *The Zionist Connection: What Price Peace?* Despite peace talks and shock expressed by the international community at the slaughter of 165 Lebanese civilians by Israeli military shelling, Israeli gunboats continued to fire at the main coastal road south of Beirut and their air craft and artillery pounded areas in the deep South Lebanon. The peace process in West Asia has come under a severe strain due to the continued Israeli military bombing in Lebanon (including the UN Peace-keepers base in south Lebanon) that killed more than 165 people and injured hundreds of civilians. Hizbollah's retaliatory rockets had hurt 50 Israelis, since the fighting began. This Israeli action also forced more than 400,000 refugees in South Lebanon to flee.

The scenes were reminiscent of a similar exodus in July 1993 when Israel launched a week-long air, land and sea blitzkrieg on South Lebanon, killing 130 people and damaging thousands of civilian homes. Some 300,000 people left the South then. The present Israeli military operation is Israeli's fourth large-scale intervention in Lebanon. In a limited invasion in 1978, Israel tried to dislodge PLO guerrillas from near its border. In a broader ground war four years later, it succeeded in expelling the PLO from Lebanon altogether. But the 1982 brutal Israeli invasion degenerated into a costly occupation of the southern half of Lebanon, spawning Lebanese resistance and giving rise to the Iranian-backed Hizbullah, which has rattled Israel ever since.

Unfortunately, the United States turned a blind eye and refused to condemn Israel for its deadly massacre of refugees in South Lebanon saying it would not help restore a ceasefire between Israel and Hizbullah guerrillas. US State department spokesman Glyn Davies rejected suggestions that the United States was maintaining a pro-Israeli stance despite the Israeli shelling on a UN refuge compound. The UN Security Council issued a brief non-binding statement calling for a halt to the fighting in Lebanon, but under US pressure avoided condemning Israel. It was a bitter disappointment for Lebanon and Syria which demanded "swift action" by the UN Security Council to halt Israeli "madness", which they linked to the electoral ambitions of Israeli Prime Minister, Shimon Peres. Throughout, US officials had made it clear in public and private statements that Washington would use its veto to block any concrete action by the Security Council against Israel. While 31 UN members including Egypt, Germany, Indonesia and Russia stressed the "disproportionate" Israeli retaliation to shelling by the Pro-Iranian Hizbullah militia in neighbouring Lebanon, Juam Somavia, Chilean ambassador and this month's (i.e. April) Security Council President, avoided in his statement the slightest criticism of Israel. Each word of his statement was carefully weighed under the close scrutiny of US ambassador to UN Madeleine Albright.

Mr. Rafik at Hariri, the Lebanese Prime Minister, who flew to London for talks with British Premier John Major maintained a tough posture. While Israeli aircraft were dropping bombs on the seventh day and the Hizbullah kept firing rocket shells, a seemingly unperturbed Mr. Hariri claimed that he could, if we wished, subdue the Hizbullah guerrillas in his country, but he would not do it unless the Israeli forces left the South part of his country, of which they were in occupation. He averred that his forces were capable of controlling the Hizbullah guerrillas, but the Israelis, in trying to force him to do so, are in fact asking him to be a traitor to his country, if he helped the Israelis achieve their objective, without their leaving South Lebanon, Mr. Rafik said, he would be, then, making life easier for the Israeli occupiers. Lebanese minister Mr. Hamade furiously denounced Israel as a "war criminal" after the Israeli bloody carnage in Nabatiyah, in which a three-day-old baby was among the dead. "Lebanon, which has been the victim of Israeli aggression for 20 years, is being sacrificed by the US on the altar of so-called American sponsored Middle East Peace", he added. The US has been promising quick action towards a free and stable Lebanon, but has done little to show that its commitment to a belligerent, aggressive and expansionist Israel.

Palestinian President Yasser Arafat called for sanctions to be used against Israel. He called on the US and Russia, as co-sponsors of Peace Process, to use sanctions against Israel. He said Israel should be punished for her crimes in the occupied territories and South Lebanon just as Serbia, Iraq and Libya were being punished by sanctions. He said Israel's human rights violations and her systematic bombing of Lebanon were challenges to the Arab-Israeli Peace Process to which the co-sponsors ought to respond. He complained that the US and Russia remained silent in the face of Israel's crimes. Hanan Ashrawi, the leading Palestinian leader, also accused Israel for deliberately sabotaging the Peace Process. "What is immoral and wrong is deliberately inflicting suffering on a civilian population for political ends. It is not only illegal", she argued, "it is the denial of the idea of civilised behaviour". President Hafez Assad of Syria blamed Israel for the current breakdown in Peace negotiation with Syria and Lebanon, reiterating the accusation that Israel has failed to adhere to UN Security Council resolutions that demand a complete withdrawal from occupied Arab land (Golan Heights, Jerusalem and South Lebanon) in return for secure borders. President Hosni Mubarak of Egypt urged the Arab world, fragmented since the 1990 Iraqi invasion of Kuwait, to close ranks. He warned that if Arab States cannot agree among themselves, it would be difficult for them to "counter dangers and prevent further deterioration in the Arab situation". Palestinian militants threatened to carry out more suicide attacks and drown Tel Aviv "in a sea of blood" unless Israel stopped its bombardment of Lebanon. The threats were made in two leaflets by *Izzedine Al-Qassam*, military wing of the radical group Hamas, which has carried out a series of suicide bombing in Israel in the past two years.

As in 1993, Israel relied on US's unlimited support to stall discussions in the UN Security Council. Israel also rejected France's offer to mediate, use its good offices with Iran to influence Hizbullah, or provide French troops to police the zone. Only US mediation, guaranteed wholly in its favour, would be considered by Israel. The Lebanese Premier said that he had received proposals for ceasefire from both the United States and France but, he preferred the French one. The French plan stipulates assurance by all parties involved, the Israelis, Lebanese and the Hizbullah, that they would not attack civilians. The US proposal does not refer to the UN resolution of 1978, which demanded Israeli withdrawal from the South Lebanon, where it controls a border "Security zone". The Lebanese Premier accused the Israelis of causing immense damage to his country's economy, by bombing power stations, infrastructures and displacing people. If Israeli's state of war with the Arab populace persists, it would lead to more religious fanaticism, suicide bombing, destruction and political and economic instability in West Asia. The Israeli action in Lebanon goes far beyond the limits of counter-terrorist action. It is high intensity war involving indiscriminate causalties among civilian population. It is bound to have its impact on the Arab States. What is accomplished through violence can go in the guise of justice, and for a while the hoax may be successful. But some people will realise that lies, are really lies violence is violence, and both lies and violence will suffer the destiny history has in store for all that is false.

25. West Asia Peace Talks

The problem of West Asia is crucial to world peace today. There are few parallels in history to the injustice done to the Arab-Palestinians. Conflict in West Asia is between the native Arab-Palestinians and the Jewish invaders of the land.

The Palestinian land is regarded as the sacred land of three great religions—Islam, Christianity and Judaism. In 1920, Palestine was made a British mandate by the decision of the League of Nations. But in reality it became a colony of British imperialists. For centuries, the Jews were living outside Palestine.

In the second half of the 19th century, a Jewish movement was started to go back to Palestine. The British imperialists used the Jewish desire for a national home in Palestine, by fanning racial strife between the native Arabs and the Jews.

Before World War I, Palestine was part of the Turkish empire. As many as 6,60,000 Arabs were living in the country in comparison to 55,000 Jews. By the 1917 Balfour Declaration, Britain accepted the Jewish demand for creating a national home for them in Palestine.

In 1922, the Jewish population in Palestine stood at 1,58,000. By 1935, it increased to 3,75,000. Palestinians revolted against the Jewish immigration.

In the 1940s, the United States joined Britain against the Palestinians who were struggling to protect their homeland. By the end of World War II, the American-Jewish-British alliance had forced partition on the Palestinians. The 1948 creation of the state of Israel and Arab-Israel war led to the collapse of Palestinian society.

After the creation of state of Israel in 1948, Israel launched war against the Palestinians and captured 77.4 per cent of Palestine instead of 56.4 per cent allotted to it by the United Nations partition plan.

In 1967 war, it occupied the whole of Palestine. The Israeli occupation of Palestine and its repressive policies have led to the emergence of a helpless yet vibrant revolutionary Palestinian community—the young Palestinians who were born into occupation manifested stronger resistance to the occupation of their land.

Israel had come under sustained national, regional and international attack for its handling and suppression of the latest Palestinian uprising in the occupied West Bank and Gaza Strip in 1980s.

The Palestinian uprising or the Intifadeh set the political agenda for the Arab-Israeli peace process namely the Madrid Peace Conference which started in October, 1991. Israel was compelled to participate in it as the so-called invincible Israeli army failed to suppress the Intifadeh.

The accord that was signed between the Palestine Liberation Organisation (PLO) and Israel was indeed the first serious attempt at coexistence between Israel and Palestine.

The accord stipulated that limited Palestinian self-rule would continue for five years but at the beginning of third year the final status negotiations would start for a permanent settlement of all outstanding issues including Jerusalem.

Many Arab-Palestinians opposed and criticised the accord as it gave too much concessions to Israel and did not deal directly with the central problem.

Since 1993 till today there was a feeling that the Arab-Israeli conflict was progressing towards a settlement.

However, during the past year reversals in the Arab-Israeli peace process have resulted in renewed tensions between Israel and the concerned Arab states in general and between Israel and the Palestinians in particular.

The Israeli-Syrian negotiations on Israeli withdrawal from Golan Heights were suspended in March, 1996. Israel's relations with Jordan and Egypt are rocky. The election of Israel's hardline Prime Minister Benjamin Netanyahu sent shock waves throughout the Arab-Palestinian world.

In his policy guidelines, the former Israeli Prime Minister said, he would expand the Jewish settlements in the West Bank and Gaza Strip and retain Israel's self-proclaimed and aggressive sovereignty over the occupied Golan Heights and all of Jerusalem.

Netanyahu also pledged a get-tough campaign against the Palestinian demand for a state with Jerusalem as its capital. Hopes that the signing of accords between Israel and Arab-Palestinians would lead to a reduction in violent incidents in Israel and Arab-Palestinian territories were frustrated.

The killing of Hamas' senior military leader in Gaza in November, 1996, the Israeli idea of building more Jewish settlements in Arab-East Jerusalem and the violent incidents that followed, have brought the Arab-Palestinian and Israeli region to the brink of explosion.

The suicidal bombings, which killed 16 Israelis and left more than 150 wounded, came on the eve of scheduled visit by US special envoy Dennis Ross in July, 1997 and two days after Israelis and Palestinians agreed for the first time to resume their deadlocked talks.

President Bill Clinton immediately postponed the Ross mission. He deplored the bombs and called on the Palestinians to take "concrete steps" to increase security.

Netanyahu promptly called off the political dialogue with the Palestinians and placed the blame on Yasser Arafat for failing to work seriously against terrorist plans.

Netanyahu sent the army to seal Israel's borders to all Palestinians, putting to all 100,000 day labourers out of work. He ringed the seven self-ruled Palestinian cities with troops to prevent any movement, in or out.

The Israeli government also warned it would stop paying out several million dollars it owes to the Palestinian National Authority in tax refunds.

But, in spite of all these developments, Israeli intellectuals are quite optimistic about the progress of peace in West Asia. They feel the peace process will continue despite problems.

26. Obstacles to Peace in West Asia

"If I was an Arab leader I would never make (peace) with Israel. That is natural: We have taken their country". Words of David Ben Gurion, quoted in Nahum Goldman's *The Jewish Paradox*, Weidenfeld and Nicolson, 1978, p. 99.

The above comment by David Ben Gurion rightly sums up the plight of peace in West Asia today. So far, Arab-Israeli peace talks have proceeded with depressingly little result. The stages of Arab-Israeli negotiations since Madrid peace accords accomplished little substantial for the Arab Palestinians, Syrians and the Lebanese. These negotiations wound up after a lot of handshake ceremony, pronouncements and well-established ritualistic political stands. Nothing much was accomplished concerning the Israeli withdrawal from the West Bank and Jerusalem territory, Syrian Golan Heights and South Lebanon. Every time an administration changed in Washington or Tel Aviv, hopes and concerns arise for a fresh initiative towards the Arab-Israeli conflict. It is rarely fulfilled.

Israel was recreated on the map of West Asia after an absence of about 2,000 years in 1948. Those Israelis who live in Israel today are all emigrants whereas the Palestinians are there in Palestine for generations. Even the former Israeli Prime Minister, Yitzhak Shamir, was born in Poland and emigrated to Palestine only in 1935. The Arab-Palestinian land is regarded as the sacred land of three great religions—Islam, Christianity and Judaism. The Arab-Palestine was among the several former Ottoman Arab territories which were made mandated territories by the League of Nations. The mandate for Palestine was formally allowed in 1922 to Great Britain by the League of Nations, without having ascertained the wishes of the Palestinian people, as required by the League covenant.

During World War I, as many as 6,60,000 Arab-Palestinians were living in the country in comparison to 55,000 Jews. By the 1917 Balfour Declaration, Britain accepted the Jewish demand for creating a national home for Jews in Palestine. In 1922, the Jewish population in Palestine stood at 1,58,000. In the 25 years of Palestine mandate (from 1922 to 1947) large-scale Jewish immigration from abroad, mainly from Eastern Europe took place. The number swelled in the 1930s with the Nazi persecution of Jews. Over this period the Jewish population of Palestine (composed principally of immigrants) increased from less than 10 per cent in 1917 to over 30 per cent in 1947.

Palestinian demands for independence and resistance to Jewish immigration led to an Arab rebellion in 1930s. The Palestinian struggle of 1936-1939 culminated in 15 years of Palestinian resistance to the British mandate. This was followed by continued Jewish terrorism and violence during and immediately after the Second World War. The 1948 creation of the State of Israel and Arab-Israel war led to the collapse of Arab-Palestinian society.

Arnold J. Toynbee, eminent world historian who dealt directly with the Palestine mandate in the British Foreign Office, wrote in 1968:

> All through those 30 years, Britain (admitted) into Palestine, year by year, a quota of Jewish immigrants that varied according to the strength of the respective pressures of the Arabs and Jews at the time. These immigrants could not have come in if they had not been shielded by a British chevaux-de-frise. If Palestine had remained under Ottoman Turkish rule, or if it had become an independent Arab state in 1918, Jewish immigrants would never have been admitted into Palestine in large numbers to enable them to overwhelm the Palestinian Arabs in this Arab people's own country. The reason why the State of Israel exists today and why today 15,00,000 Palestinian Arabs are refugees is that, for 30 years, Jewish immigration was imposed on the Palestinian Arabs by British military power until the immigrants were sufficiently numerous and sufficiently well-armed to be able to fend for themselves with tanks and planes of their own. The tragedy in Palestine is not just a local one. It is a tragedy for the world, because it is an injustice that is a menace to the world's peace.

During the first Arab-Israeli war in 1948, Israel captured 77.4 per cent of Palestine instead of 56.4 per cent allotted to it by the

United Nations Partition Plan. Israel also occupied the larger part of Jerusalem, meant to be internationalised under the UN partition resolution. In the 1967 war, Israel occupied the remaining territory of Palestine. This included the West Bank and the remaining Arab part of Jerusalem, the city being made the Israeli capital. Israel also occupied the Egyptian Sinai Peninsula and the Syrian Golan Heights strip. Israel captured the strategic Golan Heights plateau in 1967 and annexed the same in 1981. Syria has made the return of the Golan area its main condition for peace.

The 1967 war brought a second major exodus of Palestinians, estimated at half a million. The United Nations Resolution 242 of November 22, 1967, called upon Israel to withdraw from the Arab-Palestinian territories it had occupied in 1967 Arab-Israeli war. Syria and Iraq rejected the UN resolution, while Egypt and Jordan demanded Israeli withdrawal from all Arab territories occupied in the 1967 war as a precondition to any negotiations. The Israeli victory in the 1967 war brought Israel more land. But it did not bring peace. On the contrary, it laid the foundations for a long confrontation which has continued without respite till today.

The Israeli repressive policies have led to the emergence of a helpless yet vibrant revolutionary Arab-Palestinian Community—the young Palestinians, who were born into occupation, manifested stronger resistance to the Israeli occupation of their land. The Palestinian uprising or the Intifadeh movement set the political agenda for the Arab-Israeli peace process namely the Madrid Peace talks which started in October 1991. Israel was compelled to participate in it as the so-called 'invincible' Israeli army failed to suppress the Intifadeh. The accord that was signed between the Palestine Liberation Organisation (PLO) and Israel was indeed the first serious attempt at coexistence between Israel and Palestine. The accord stipulated at Limited Palestinian self-rule would continue for five years but at the beginning of third year the final status negotiations would start for a permanent settlement of all outstanding issues, including Jerusalem.

Many Arabs and Palestinians, including the Syrians, Iraqis, Libyans opposed the accord as it gave too much concessions to Israel and did not deal directly with the central problem. From 1993 onwards there were some indications that the Arab-Israeli conflict was progressing towards a settlement. However, during the past few years reversals in the Arab-Israeli peace process have resulted in renewed tensions between Israel and concerned Arab states like Syria, Lebanon, Egypt and Jordan in general and between Israel and the Palestinians in particular.

The Israeli-Syrian negotiations on Israeli withdrawal from Golan Heights were suspended in February 1996. Damascus stressed that the stalled Syria-Israel peace negotiations could not resume unless the Jewish state was committed to the land-for-peace formula. The Syrians consider the 35 Jewish settlements in Golan as Israeli military outposts intended to create a spatial asymmetry in territorial balance in favour of Israel. To the Syrians, if progress were to occur, this would require an Israeli commitment to a total withdrawal from the Golan only then could a formula for resolving the territorial dimension of the Syrian-Israeli conflict be reached.

The official Syrian newspaper *Tishrin* called on Arabs and the international community to exert more pressure against Israel and urged the Palestinians to stop negotiating with the Jewish state. "Arabs must set an example against Israel's intransigence by taking specific measures such as cancelling the normalisation (of relations) with Israel by some (countries) and stopping negotiations between the Palestinians and the government of Israeli Prime Minister Benjamin Netanyahu", *Tishrin* wrote. Since coming to office, Mr. Netanyahu has suspended implementation of the 1995 Oslo agreements on Palestinian autonomy signed by his Labour predecessors and has lifted restrictions on Jewish settlement in the occupied Arab-Palestinian territories.

In one of the latest incidents of expanding their foothold on East (Arab) Jerusalem, Jewish settlers moved into four homes in an Arab neighbourhood early this June and the Israeli cabinet approved a plan for the expansion of Jerusalem setting-off a violent confrontation and heightening tension in the area claimed by the Palestinians as their future capital.

"Our aim is to Judaize East Jerusalem", declared Yigal Kaufman, a spokesman for Elad, a Jewish settlement group, which has purchased properties and moved Jews into Silwan (a village outside Jerusalem) in recent years. Enraged Palestinians and Israeli peace advocates accused Prime Minister Benjamin Netanyahu and Mayor Ehud Olmert of Jerusalem of complicity in what they described as a calculated political provocation.

Egypt and Syria along with the Palestinians led eight other Arab nations in calling on the international community to put more pressure on Israel to reverse its policies on the issue of restoring peace in West Asia, failing which a separate Arab summit on the issue would be held. A summit, attended by Egyptian President Hosni Mubarak, President Arafat of Palestine and King Hussein of Jordan at Cairo a few days ago, also took stock of the deadlocked Arab-Israeli peace talks and warned Israel not to alter the status of Jerusalem.

Demonstrations are taking place continuously against Israel's occupation of South Lebanon, both in Tel Aviv and Beirut. Some of the Israeli's are calling it Israel's Vietnam. The South of Lebanon has remained tense since Israeli forces invaded the region in March 1978 and intensified their military aggression in June 1982. Israel established the so-called "Security Zone" in Southern Lebanon in 1985 to shield northern Israel from attacks. The zone is patrolled by Israeli soldiers and Israeli-backed South-Lebanon Army (SLA).

Israel's relations with the two countries with which it has signed treaties, Egypt and Jordan, are also rocky.

In his policy guidelines, the Israeli Prime Minister said he would expand the Jewish settlements in the West Bank and Gaza Strip and retain Israel's self-proclaimed and aggressive sovereignty over the occupied Golan Heights and all of Jerusalem. Netanyahu also pledged a get-touch campaign against the Palestinian demand for a state with Jerusalem as its capital. Hopes that the signing of accords between Israel and Arab-Palestinians would lead to a reduction in violent incidents in Israel and Arab-Palestinian territories were frustrated.

The killing of Hamas' senior military leader in Gaza in November 1996, the Israeli idea of building more Jewish settlements in Arab-East Jerusalem and the violent incidents that followed, including the Palestinian street demonstrations on May 14 this year to mark the 50th anniversary of the loss of Palestine to the Jews in 1948 and their subsequent dispersal as refugees, have brought the Arab-Palestinian and Israeli region to the brink of explosion.

The current crisis in the West Asian peace process were precipitated by changes in Israel's policy, following the formation of a new right wing coalition government there. This government relies on that part of Israeli society which cannot be described as being in the peace camp. The main obstacle to implementation of international legality and peace in West Asia has been the intransigence of the present Israeli government which had obstructed all avenues of negotiation while creating new Jewish settlements.

Simultaneously, the Israelis intensified oppression through confiscation of Arab-Palestinian territories marked by deportations of Palestinians. Instead of taking any confidence-building measures, Israel is bent upon increasing hostility, bitterness and distrust. The other was in which Israel has been derailing the peace process is by imposing impossible pre-conditions without calling them pre-conditions. Yet another tactic is to get the peace process bogged down in technicalities and details and semantics. If these Israeli delay tactics and intransigence continue it will further hinder the search for peace in West Asia.

The future of West Asia depends on how Israel sheds it's garb of occupation, exploitation, expansion, aggression and settlement. However, it should be remembered that a comprehensive settlement ensuring regional stability and security can be achieved only on the basis of resolutions 242, 338 and 425 of the UN Security Council and in accordance with the "Land for Peace" formula.

Securing complete Israeli withdrawal from Arab-Palestinian, Syrian and Lebanese territories and curtailing settlement-building in Jerusalem and other parts must be the top priorities for durable peace in West Asia.

27. The Wye River Peace Pact in West Asia

The post-cold war West Asia seems to be in the grip of dramatic changes. Perhaps no symbolic gesture, in recent times, has been as important as US President Bill Clinton's call for a new multi-billion dollar international aid package for the Palestinians. It is a necessary complement to the peace agreement that President Clinton put together in Maryland. This diplomatic deal remains significant to drive home the point that peace can deliver tangible economic and social gains to both the Palestinians and the Israelis. On the face of it, the Wye River Memorandum agreed to after nine days long of hectic parleys set out "steps to facilitate implementation" of an agreement on Palestinian self-rule signed more than three years ago. It was a major accomplishment for President Clinton. Written off as a victim of impeachment a few weeks ago, Clinton pulled off a mini Camp David that has proved to be the biggest foreign policy coup of his administration during his second tenure in office.

At the Wye conference centre on Maryland's eastern shore, all three main parties crossed important thresholds. Benjamin Netanyahu, the Israeli Prime Minister had always been sceptical about the 1993 peace agreement struck in Oslo between Israel and the Palestinians. The Oslo deal was forged by an Israeli government far more dovish than the one Netanyahu formed in 1996. But at the Wye, Netanyahu signalled that he is also committed to the Oslo framework. The Palestinian government-in-waiting all but declared war on its hardline opponents. "Your security is our security", Palestinian President Yasser Arafat declared during the White House ceremony. Washington formally becomes the guarantor of security arrangements aimed at breaking a 19-month deadlock over interim Israeli troops-withdrawals from the West Bank.

The Commitments

Under the US plans Israel would hand over an additional 13 per cent of West Bank land of which 3 per cent would be a "nature preserve" where no construction could take place. An additional 14.2 per cent will be passed on to the Palestinian authorities to remain under full Palestinian control. That would bring roughly 40 per cent of the territory under full or partial Palestinian control. President Arafat will also get an economic circulatory system: a two year-old airport in Gaza will be allowed to open and Israel will establish two "Safe Passage" corridors between the West Bank and Gaza. At the heart of the Wye agreement is a detailed American "working plan" on terrorism that had been under discussion for nearly a year. Its author: CIA Director George Tenet, who, along with the agency's Tel Aviv TV station chief, had become the de facto mediator between the two sides.

As part of the new Middle East profile, the agency will "facilitate the exchange of intelligence between the Palestinians and Israelis" over suspected terrorists and planned terrorist acts. The talks nearly broke down over security issues until the Israelis came out with concrete pledges to be carried out, in part, with CIA arbitration. Among them—a phased-in collection of illegal firearms; a reduction of the Palestinian police force, which the Israelis feared was turning into an army, from 43,000 to 30,000. President Clinton clearly relished his negotiating coup when he expressed to a gathering that the Wye agreements between the Israelis and the Palestinians was his "personal atonement". This December, President Clinton will visit Gaza to address a session of the Palestine National Council convened to strike of all references to the destruction of Israel from the Palestinian National Charter. He will be the first sitting US President to visit the Palestinian territory.

The Impediments

It is indisputable that the latest peace accord between the Israelis and the Palestinians represents a genuine breakthrough. However, it would be wrong to think that the potential of Peace has already been realised. There is even less cause to be optimistic about the developments taking into account the post-accord situation, particularly the toughening of the Israeli stance on applying the agreement and the mired Israeli Palestinian relations. The Israeli foreign minister, Mr. Ariel Sharon has gone back on draft agreements with the Palestinians concerning the opening of a sea port in Gaza and a safe passage corridor linking Gaza and the West Bank—both key elements of the Wye Land-for-Security Pact. Besides, Israeli Prime Minister, Netanyahu, refused to release Palestinian prisoners accused of attacks on Israelis to meet Israel's obligation under the Wye accord to free 750 detainees. The Wye accord also in no way restricts the Israeli construction and expansion of Jewish settlements.

The continued Israeli constructions in Jewish settlements in Arab-Palestinian territories violate all the Arab-Israeli Peace accords, including the Wye river land-for-security deal. Israel has authorised the construction of 480 homes in the Jewish settlement of Kochav Yaacov, more than triple the size of the West Bank Enclave. Palestinian negotiators warned that they would suspend the implementation of the Wye agreement, which would require the Palestinian Authority to crack down on armed anti-Israel militants, unless Israel frees the political prisoners and halts the construction works in the settlement area. "Things are still stalled. There seems to be not much change in Israel's colonial attitude", lamented Dr. Khalid el-Sheikh, Palestinian Ambassador to India.

Conclusion

The Palestinians have not even succeeded in obtaining a specific assurance on ending the Israeli occupation of Arab-Palestinian territories. The whole question of transition to autonomy is hedged in with numerous conditions, some of which project Palestinians as unequal so far as the agreement was concerned.

Ever since the 1996 elections that elevated Israeli Prime Minister Netanyahu to office, the political scene in West Asia has been overshadowed by his abuse of Israel's commitments under the Oslo Peace Accords. Instead of taking confidence-building measures, Israel is bent on expressing increasing hostility, bitterness and distrust towards the very idea of an independent Palestinian state. The future of West Asia depends on how Israel shed it's Zionist policy of occupation, exploitation, expansion and settlement. However, it should be remembered that a comprehensive peace settlement ensuring regional stability and security can be achieved only on the basis of UN resolutions 242, 338 and 425 and in accordance with the "Land for Peace" formula. Securing complete Israeli withdrawal from Arab-Palestinian, Syrian and Lebanese territories and curtailing settlement building in Jerusalem and other parts must be the top priorities for anybody working sincerely for durable peace in West Asia. It is hard to imagine the Israelis enjoying a peaceful future unless they can overcome all the obstacles and reach a just compromise with their Arab-Palestinian neighbours.

28. A Look Back in Anger

The current Arab-Israeli peace process is in a crisis and much of what we believed in, and were hoping for is not materialising. The Wye river accord is yet to be fully implemented. It is in a difficult phase now. From 1993-1998 there was a feeling that the Arab-Israeli conflict was progressing towards a settlement. However, the future agreements are not so certain. It has taken four years for the Oslo West Asia peace process to peel off its wrappings to reveal and stark truth hidden at its core. There was no positive peace agreement, only an agreement to keep Israeli hegemony over the Palestinian territories.

The Israeli-Syrian negotiations were suspended in March 1996 and have yet to be resumed. The election of Israel's hardline Prime Minister, Benjamin Netanyahu, sent shock waves throughout the Arab-Palestinian world. In his policy guidelines, the former Israeli Prime Minister had alarmed the Arab leaders by stating that he would expand the Jewish settlements in the West Bank and Gaza Strip and retain Israel's self-proclaimed sovereignty over the occupied Golan Heights and all of Jerusalem. Netanyahu had also pledged a get-tough campaign against the Palestinians struggle for independence and declined even to discuss the Palestinian demand for a State with Jerusalem as its capital.

Hopes that the signing of accords between the Israel and Arab-Palestinians would lead to a reduction in violent incidents in Israel and Arab-Palestinian territories were frustrated. The killing of Hamas' senior military leader in Gaza in November 1996, the Israeli idea of building more Jewish enclaves on Arab East Jerusalem and West Bank and the violent incidents that followed, the happenings in Hebron and the frequent arrests of Palestinians suspected of organising riots against Israeli occupation, the continuing clashes between Palestinian teenagers and Israeli troops, the plastering of caricatures by a Jewish extremist denigrating Prophet Mohammed in Arab shops in Hebron and the subsequent humiliations of the Muslims, the time-to-time Israeli missile attacks on Lebanon, the deliberate tax collection drive by Israel from the eastern sector of Jerusalem, claimed by the Palestinians as their future capital, the weakness of the American policy in West Asia, the suicidal bombings which killed 16 Israelis and left more than 150 others wounded and the (September 1997) Israeli attempt to kill a Palestinian Hamas polit bureau member, Khaled Mehal in Amman and the Israeli security restrictions at the holy city of Bethlehem brought the Arab-Palestinian and Israeli region to the brink of explosion.

Mr. Benjamin Netanyahu called off the political dialogue with the Palestinians and blamed the Palestinian leader Yasser Arafat for failing to work seriously against terrorist plans. He sent the army to seal off Israel's borders to all Palestinians, putting some 100,000 day labourers out to work. He ringed the seven self-ruled Palestinian cities with troops to prevent any movement in or out. Besides, for the first time the Israeli government warned it would stop paying several million dollars it owed to the Palestinian National Authority in tax refunds.

On alert for more suicide bombings, Israel also mounted a tough blockade on Palestinian areas and deployed soldiers, bomb squads and extra police in major cities. Long lines of cars waited at road blocks, including a bride stranded in her wedding dress, as soldiers checked identity cards and peered into trunks. The Israeli army not only barred travel into Israel but also prevented movement between Palestinian cities. The army detained 37 Palestinians suspected of "terrorist activity" in an overnight sweep in the West Bank following the tragic bombing in Jerusalem. That brought to 125 the number of Palestinians jailed since the bombing, with scores of others questioned and harassed.

Palestinians termed the Israeli measures as collective punishment. "Israel has not yet identified the suicide bombers ... but has rushed to blame the Palestinian Authority for the attack and imposed a series of collective punishment measures", an editorial in the Palestinian daily *Al-Quds* said. Palestinian President Yasser Arafat had to ask the United Nations to help force Israel to lift the reprisal measures it had imposed on Palestinians. Mr. Arafat accused Israel of "declaring war" on the Palestinians by sealing the borders of the Palestinian territories and blockading Palestinian-controlled towns. "I condemn completely these terrorist activities because it is against the peace process, against the Palestinians and against Israelis, and we will do all in our capability to face these terrorist activities", Mr. Arafat told Israeli television.

An urgent meeting of the 22-member Arab League was held on August 5, 1997, which discussed the harsh measures introduced by Israel against the Arab-Palestinians after the deadly suicide bombing in Israeli-occupied Jerusalem. UAE's Deputy Prime Minister, Sheikh Sultan bin Zayed, called for the resumption of West Asia peace talks which had been stalled because of Israel's hardline policies, especially its plans for Jewish settlements at Tebel Abou Ghneim in occupied Jerusalem. Mr. Zayed also called for the implementation of UN Security Council resolutions, the principle of Land for Peace and the Oslo agreements signed between the Palestinians and the Israelis.

An official Syrian newspaper said that US President Bill Clinton's policy in the middle east was leading the region to "explosion". The weakness of the American policy in the region had led the US venture to a hard peace, and consequently brought the region to the brink of explosion. "This particular situation has constituted a fertile soil to extreme trends and racism in the Israeli society", it said. In its editorial dated August 1, 1997 the *Syria Times* said, "the current explosion and other clashes in the occupied Palestinian territories are only one example of the difficult times through which the region is passing. Had just and comprehensive peace solution been implemented such sorrowful events would have not existed".

Sporadic Syrian-Israeli peace talks faced a new deadlock when Mr. Netanyahu ruled out withdrawal from the Golan Heights captured by Israel in 1967, in return for peace with Syria. The return to power of the Israeli right-wing was viewed in the region as little less than a disaster for the peace process. The former Israeli Prime Ministers Mr. Shimon Peres and the late Yitzhak Rabin had indicated that they would trace part or all of the Israeli captured Golan Heights for a peace agreement with Syria; Netanyahu ruled that out.

President Assad of Syria called Mr. Netanyahu "an enemy of peace" and praised the Left-leaning Israeli Opposition. Mr. Assad's remarks came during a three-hour meeting with 42 Arabs living in Israel, who were on a week-long visit to Syria to promote peace between the long-time foes. Mr. Saleh Tarif, Israeli member of

Knesset, also pointed out that Syria was interested in working with Israel's Left parties to push forward the peace process.

To quote Mr. Ahmad Mansour, former Syrian representative and diplomat in India, "Syria offered full peace for full Israeli withdrawal from Arab-Palestinian territories. It offered peace for land. As peace brings security it should be established on the principles of human rights, human dignity and justice. Peace should be just and comprehensive. No one can go for peace without getting back their own territories occupied by Israel. What Israel is looking for today is other than peace".

President Saddam Hussein of Iraq also called for unconditional Israeli withdrawal from all Arab-Palestinian territories which Israel occupied in 1967 and only then peace would be ensured. He appealed to the Arab states and their leaders to convene a special Arab meet on Palestine.

"We are insisting that the main issue is the political issue". Arafat's adviser Nabil Abu Rdainahh told Israel Radio. "Unless they understand there is a peace agreement signed by the Palestinian Authority and the Israeli authorities, unless it's implemented fully and accurately, the crisis will carry on".

Egyptian President Hosni Mubarak had warned Mr. Netanyahu that his hardline policies were sending peace "down the drain" and leading moderate Arab states to reassess their relations with Iran. Following a summit meeting in Cairo in the first week of September 1997 between Mr. Mubarak, Mr. Yasser Arafat and Jordan's late King Hussein, the Egyptian President sent messages to Mr. Netanyahu and other senior Israeli ministers expressing serious concern about the future of Arab-Israeli peace process. The Cairo summit was called after Mr. Netanyahu froze application of the Oslo peace accords with the Palestinians following two multiple suicide bombings in occupied Jerusalem and ahead of US Secretary of State, Ms. Madeleine Albright's official mission to the region.

The Egyptian government has once again called upon Israel to stop defaulting and take initiative for restoring the peace process in West Asia by honouring its commitments to the Palestinians and Arabs.

Leading Muslim leaders blasted Israel at the OIC summit at Teheran and Riyadh (December 1997 and August 1999 respectively) and also condemned terrorism in the name of Islam. Israel was sharply criticised for human rights violations and was branded as enemy and threat to peace in West Asia. Leading intellectual and former member of the Palestinian National Council, Prof. Edward W. Said, condemned the peace process pointing out that it was a "fraudulent" exercise. Fifty years of Israeli statehood, and a century of Zionist ideology have neither brought normalcy for Jewish citizens, nor a comparable lessening of insecurity". Denying any glimmer of hope, he said: "I foresee nothing but further misery, bloodshed and futile insecurity for Israelis and Arabs in the coming years".

For the Jewish refugees and pioneers who built Israel on the ashes of the Holocaust, theirs was a straight forward tale of justice, heroism and redemption. But half-a-century later, a so-called maturing nation is reassessing its violent birth, with Israeli historians angrily debating a long suppressed question with broad implications; was Israel born in sin? From Iian Pappe, among the most outspoken of Israel's new historians, the answer is resounding "yes". "The Jews came and took, by means of uprooting and expulsion; a land that was Arab", the Haifa University scholar said in an interview with the Associated Press. "We wanted to be a *colonialist occupier*, and yet to come across as moral at the same time".

The new Israeli historians claim that in many cases their predecessors dishonestly perpetuated national myths, especially surrounding the 1948-49 war that established Israel and created the Palestinian refugee problem. The Palestine issue is currently on the front-page headlines of world affairs. There are signs that a steady heat is bringing this perennial dish once more to the boil. The uncertainty in West Asia is increasing day-by-day.

For the Arab-Palestinian, the stagnation in the peace process for settling the Palestinian problem contributes to general political and social discontent. The inability of the US to generate progress in the peace process cannot but encourage the growth of militant opposition movements and violence. Mr. Netanyahu's term of office as Israeli Prime Minister witnessed only a stalemate in the West Asia peace process. Netanyahu was not the flexible Israeli politician that many had hoped he would be, but rather an ideologue, committed to the holding on to the maximum of occupied Arab-Palestinian land, irrespective of the impact on Israeli's Arab peace partners, the Palestinians, the Syrians, Jordanians, Lebanese and Egyptians.

A solution to the vicious circle of political violence and retaliation eluded the region. In order to achieve peace, both parties, the Arab-Palestinians and Israelis, have to come to terms with some basic realisations. The Israeli leadership and public have to end the physical occupation, the roadblocks, the settlements, the confiscation and demolition of Arab-Palestinian homes, curfews, military control and daily humiliations inflicted on Palestinians by Israeli soldiers. A durable peace is as much in the interest of Israel as of Palestine.

Moreover, to quote late King Hussein of Jordan, Washington should play a more active role in pressing Israel to abandon policies such as building settlements in the West Bank, that are pushing the region towards an "explosion". "The United States with its tremendous influence and impact on this area and all the people of the region, and its position in the world, should move from being a messenger to being actively involved", King Hussein had said in an interview. "It just cannot carry on continuing to deliver messages from one side to another".

The 1999 elections in Israel has provided an opportunity to the Israeli people to demonstrate their desire for peace. The defeat of Netanyahu and the emergence of Mr. Ehud Barak seemed to hold the promise for a breakthrough in the stalled peace process. But that was not to be under Ariel Sharon, the situation turned from bad to worst.

29. New Dangers in West Asia

The Arab African world enters the twenty-first century against a background of turmoil. A just resolution of the Palestinian problem hangs in the balance. The past few months have seen the potentially most decisive turning points in the confrontation between Israel and the Arab-Palestinians. The Arab-African world have, in recent times, ricocheted from dreams of peace to the possibility of a renewed Arab-Israeli conflict and perhaps even more widespread violence. The United Nations peacekeepers including troops from the Indian Army's Madras Regiment, deployed along the Israel-Lebanon border are grappling with an explosive situation. India's External Affairs Minister, Mr. Jaswant Singh during his recent trip to Algeria made it clear that India stood for the inalienable rights of the Palestinian people and said "all provocative acts" must stop to allow peace to return to violence-torn Palestinian areas. "We believe in the inalienable rights of the Palestinian people and the first requirement is restoration of peace", Mr. Singh said.

The Congress, the socialists and the Left opposition parties have criticised the BJP-led Indian government's Arab-Africa policy saying it had departed from the traditional "Pro-Palestine" and "Pro-Western Sahara" approach of the country and demanded that the government came out forthright in support of Palestine.

"The NDA government has departed from the traditional Indian policy of favouring the Palestinian cause. Even before Independence, India had supported Palestinians. We hope, the government will come out forthright in support of Palestine, chairman of the Congress' foreign affairs department K. Natwar Singh told reporters. He said the Vajpayee government, instead of coming out in favour of the Palestinian cause, has adopted the policy of maintaining "equidistance" between Israel and Palestine, that is, equating the aggressor with the sufferers. Pointing out that the situation in Palestine had deteriorated in the two weeks after the Sharm al-Sheikh (Cairo) agreement, Mr. Singh expressed surprise over NDA governments silence on the killings in the region.[1]

A war in Palestine today means a war on the whole Afro-Arab and Asian region. Leaders of this region assert that the defence of Palestine is important for the national security, peace and prosperity of the Afro-Arab-Asian region. If this momentum of Israeli bombings and attacks is allowed to continue in Palestine it would create problems for all of us in Developing World. What is happening today represents one long struggle for Independence in contemporary history. Israel under Prime Minister, Ehud Barak is at the moment against decolonisation, peace, stability, progress and against history. When evils like apartheid are eliminated in Africa, the Zionist mentality of Israel needs to be rooted out of its body-politic, if permanent peace to be achieved.

This is the first time since 1991 that a major Palestinian-Israeli conflict has occurred, re-kindling Arab-Israeli antagonism back to the levels which existed in the pre-1982 era. This is also the first time that India has to react to this conflict situation in the context of its equally balanced relations with Arab-African countries and Israel. The situation has been compounded further by violence between Israeli armed forces and the struggling Palestinian youth in all the Arab settlements within Israel. Palestinian President Yasser Arafat, at the end of the Arab League summit in Cairo (October, 2000) and the organisation of Islamic conference meet in Doha (November, 2000), announced that the Palestinian objective is to clear the road to Jerusalem which is the capital of the Palestinian state. What is most alarming is Israeli Prime Minister Barak's hardening stance of not negotiating sincerely with the Palestinians.

The Palestinians, the United Nations and the Leaders from the Afro-Arab-Asian world, have accused the Israelis of using excessive force in the daily confrontation. In almost twelve weeks of fighting that erupted after Ariel Sharon, (Israeli rightist Likud Party opposition leader) visited the wailing wall near the Al Aqsa mosque in Jerusalem on 28 September, 2000 accompanied by a huge number of Israeli security forces, leading to the escalation of tension.[2] About 450 people have been killed and several thousands wounded, most of them being Palestinians including children.

Many Palestinians and Arab-Islamic leaders voiced anger at President Arafat's agreement to attend an US sponsored emergency

Middle East summit, accusing him of wasting the sacrifices of more than 500 martyrs in clashes with Israel. To many Palestinians, the Sharm El-Sheikh summit, held in Cairo on 4th December, 1999, is an attempt to defang an Arab position on the thorny issue of Jerusalem. About 8,000 Palestinians, including intellectuals and law-makers, signed a petition, calling for the continuation of the new *Intifadeh*, that is, the resistance to Israel. The spiritual leader of *Hamas* (Islamic moderate party) Sheikh Ahmed Yassin has spoken out against the summit, in an interview with Russian newspaper, "We have two options: either we surrender or we continue the resistance. We chose the second path. We will fight because the enemy only understands the language of Force", Sheikh Yassin told the Vremia Novosti newspaper.[3] "We will fight until we have liberated all of Palestine, the land occupied by Israel in 1967 and 1948", he said.

Two Palestinian radical factions opposed to interim peace deals with Israel issued a joint statement criticising President Arafat's participation in Peace summit's with Israel. Syria and Iran also condemned Arafat's peace overtures and both vociferously opposed the recent US-brokered peace process.

"To have such meetings at a time when the Zionists continue their ruthless policies and brutal killings does not help the Palestinians", Iranian foreign ministry spokesman Hamid Reza Asefi said.

Syria bitterly opposed the peace summits with Israel aimed at stopping the *Intifadeh* in the Palestinian territories. In Syria's view, "the only true solution to the crisis is a complete withdrawal by Israel from the Arab-Palestinian land it captured in the 1967 Arab-Israeli war, including Syria's Golan Heights".

The Jordanian parliament accused the US House of Representatives of "total bias" towards Israel following a resolution that blamed the Palestinians for the ongoing violence.

"We have been profoundly surprised by the position of the American Congress concerning the dangerous political and security developments in the Palestinian territories", Jordanian Parliament Speaker Bassam Haddadin said.[4]

Saudi Arabia's crown prince Abdullah took his tough stance on the West Asia violence by partly blaming his country's main ally, the United States, for the collapse of the Peace process in Palestine. He warned the US administration and American companies with lucrative businesses in the Saudi Kingdom of unspecified action if Washington continues to support Israel at the expense of the struggling Palestinians.[5]

Iraq has called on Arabs to revolt against moderate rulers who "exposed themselves as representing zionist and American domination" during the October 2000 Arab summit in Cairo that fell short of cutting ties with Israel—the minimum demand of many Arabs who have demonstrated daily in the streets against Israeli military actions against Palestinians to quell violence.

Morocco said it had severed diplomatic ties with Israel in protest at Israeli violence against civilians in the Palestinian territories. In a statement in Rabat (24 October 2000) the official news agency said: "because of the failure of the peace process due to the Israeli violence against Palestinians, Morocco shuts the Israeli liaison bureau in Rabat".

The hurriedly called October Arab summit in Cairo demanded the setting up of an international commission of inquiry into the causes of the conflict and to try Israeli soldiers for their use of excessive force. The Arab Leaders also set up a fund of $1 billion for the aid of Palestinians.[6]

Continuing their tirade against Israel for committing war crimes on the Palestinians, Leaders of several Afro-Arab-Asian nations urged the 9th summit of Organisation of Islamic Conference (November 12-14, 2000) to give a call for *Jehad* (holy war) to liberate Palestine from the clutches of the Israeli occupation. The Iranian President, Mohammad Khatami, opened the summit with a tribute to Palestinians killed in violence that erupted on September 28. Speaking at the OIC summit, Leaders of Iraq, Sudan and Syria said that Jihad was the only way to liberate Palestine from the clutches of the Israeli occupation.

"No true believer is exempted from *Jehad*" and Iraq is ready to put its offspring in the forefront to seek liberation of Palestine, said the message of Iraqi President, Saddam Hussein, which was read out by Vice-President Izzat Ibrahim. The Iraqi President, Saddam Hussein, has called on Arab rulers to cut their ties with Israel, but urged Arab States to open their borders with the Jewish state to allow Arabs to "liberate Palestine". In response to Iraqi President's call and in protest against recent attacks by the Israel Defence Forces (IDF) on Palestinians, Egypt has recalled its ambassador from Israel, Mohammed Bassiouni.[7]

Sudanese President Colonel Omer Bashir said *Jehad* is the sole channel for restoring usurped rights of the Palestinians, especially in the face of incessant Israeli aggression. He also lashed out at the United States, stating it cannot be a mediator as it is not neutral in its approach towards the Arab-African problems.

Syrian President Bashar Assad also justified joint struggle against Israel and supported severing all kinds of relations with Tel Aviv. He said Jerusalem is the core of the Arab-Israeli conflict.

Saudi crown prince Abdullah Bin Abdul Aziz urged the 56-member OIC group to snap all ties with any country that shifts its diplomatic mission to Jerusalem. "It is our duty to break diplomatic relations with any nation which tries to change the status of Jerusalem.[8]

Bangladesh Prime Minister Sheikh Hasina Wajed said the Islamic countries should take a United stand on the question of Palestine and its "rightful cause".

Malaysian Prime Minister Dr. Mahathir Mohammad, while supporting the Palestinian *Intifadeh*, castigated the Islamic nations for helplessly watching Israeli brutalities in the occupied territories.

"Sadly, Muslim countries representing more than a third of membership of the United Nations watch helplessly as Israel continues with impunity and arrogance to kill innocent Palestinians".

UN Secretary-General Kofi Annan implicitly agreed that the World body had double standards in terms of its own resolutions. He said that the past eight weeks had made abundantly clear to all sides that the cause of peace could only be damaged by excessive use of force. A US-based medical rights group published a research paper on November 3, 2000 saying the Israeli Army violated international norms by using excessive force against Palestinian protesters. At least 450 people have been killed in more than four months of clashes in the West Bank and Gaza Strip, more than 400 of them Palestinians.

Physicians for Human Rights said it found two "disturbing patterns"—(Israeli) soldiers did not always fire in self-defence and aimed at times, at heads and thighs "to injure and kill, not to avoid loss of life and injury". PHR said it heard numerous independent eyewitness accounts and saw other reliable reports showing most of those shot with real ammunition or rubber or rubber-coated bullets were unarmed. Its team saw soldiers firing at civilians in Ramallah when they could see no sign of Palestinians using firearms. "The numerous high velocity wounds to the thigh are highly unlikely to be random events, but rather, suggest a policy on the part of the *IDF* (Israel Defence Force) that allows individual soldiers to shoot under very broad circumstances", the report added.[9]

Jamina Khan, wife of Pakistan's cricketer-turned-politician Imran Khan, daughter of Sir James Goldsmith in her recent article in the *Guardian* (London) November 1, 2000, argued that the American media was pro-Israel in its coverage of the Arab-Israeli crisis and questioned the impartiality of influence of American politicians over the peace process in the run up to the elections.

She wrote: "The media is largely controlled by the Jews as is Hollywood" and that comprises "more than half the top policy-making jobs in the Clinton administration". She continued: "Peace can only be achieved once the US acts as an honest broker and the US media as impartial commentators". As violent clashes continued between Israelis and Palestinians, the anger that these clashes churned across the Afro-Arab-Asian region since the violence began suggested that the polarisation of Arab-Muslim opinion may have sharply reduced prospects for an overall Arab-Israeli Settlement, even if the violence can be curbed. Not since the OSLO peace efforts began in 1993 has the region seen such widespread turmoil. The angry crowds that have marched in capitals like Amman, Baghdad, Beirut, Cairo, Damascus, Tripoli and Teheran, hotbeds of hostility toward Israel, have been matched by protests in nations that have moved in recent years towards an acceptance of Israel's existence, including oil-rich monarchies in the Gulf like Kuwait, Saudi Arabia and the United Arab Emirates, and Tunisia and Morocco in North Africa.[10]

The volatile situation in the Israeli occupied areas of Palestine is even having its serious impact on the local government elections in South Africa, scheduled for December 5. Posters went up over the weekend in some areas of Cape Town with a significant Muslim population with the message: "A vote for the DA (Democratic Alliance—whose leader Tony Leon, is Jewish) is a vote for Israel, with the picture of the Israeli flag, dripping with blood, at the bottom. The poster is simply attributed to "Friends of Palestine". A spokesperson for the Democratic Alliance accused the African National Congress (ANC) of putting up the posters, a charge hotly denied by the ANC.

Though there have been sporadic violence and wars since 1948 (the creation of the state of Israel on Palestinian soil), interaction between the PLO and the Israelis was continuing since their Madrid and OSLO meetings in the early 1990s. Arafat and his limited government returned to Gaza. The proponents of the OSLO agreement, including the Bill Clinton administration, never fully informed the Palestinian people that the accord did not offer any guarantee of Palestinian self-determination, full equality and an end to the military occupation of Israel. In 1994, the interim phase of the peace process began with Palestinians widely believing that by May 1999 the Israeli occupation of the West Bank and Gaza would be over. In reality, this stage of the accord provided only for the establishment of a Palestinian legislature and Palestinian Authority while keeping control of overall security and resources and commerce in the hands of the Israeli military occupation.

The transition to greater autonomy—not independence—was left to be negotiated with the goal of moving to the next stage by May 1999, a deadline that was not met. The agreement authorised the Israeli military to stop the movement of Palestinians and their immigration to the Israeli occupied territories and decide the location of their borders. Even new legislation issued by the Palestinian Authority had to bear an Israeli seal of approval. On this harsh ground of everyday reality in Gaza and the West Bank, the false optimism of OSLO quickly faded when the Palestinians realised that the interim agreement had not significantly changed the conditions of the occupation. Since 1994, Palestinians have witnessed the influx of 50,000 new Jewish settlers into the Israeli occupied Arab-Palestinian territories, the paving of more than 400 kilometres of roads on confiscated land, demolition of more than 850 Palestinian homes, a threefold increase in Palestinian unemployment and a 17 per cent decline in gross national product of the territories, the arrest of 13,000 Palestinians and complete curtailment of freedom of movement. According to a leading scholar, "the establishment of a Palestinian State truncated by a massive system of bypass roads, encircled by Israeli settlement blocs, subject to closures and restrictions on freedom of movement and commerce, with no control of its borders or natural resources, will only create a reality of apartheid, a Palestinian state as a Bantustan".[11]

Taking into account the war situation in Palestine it is very difficult to be optimistic about the prospects for peace and stability in the Arab-Israeli region. The future looks uncertain one could easily be misled if one failed to take into account the history of the Arab-Israeli conflict and the degree of compromise being offered by Arab-Palestinians, but so far rejected by Israel from time to time. The overwhelming majority of Palestinians feel strongly that they have already paid a heavy price for ending the conflict by conceding three quarters of their historic homeland to Israel and agreeing to confine their own state within the 1967 borders instead of 1948. As far as the vast majority of Arab Palestinians is concerned, a state on the territories occupied by Israel in 1967 is the non-negotiable bottom line, with full sovereignty over East Jerusalem. This is not simply because of the special historical, religious and cultural significance of Jerusalem, but also because creating a Palestinian state without Jerusalem as its capital is viewed by most Arab Palestinians as a Worthless enterprise.

There exists already great division on the simplest of issues among Palestinians who believe that the compromise agreed now and then, as an interim solution will never advance further. Israel has made no direct indication of yielding ground in negotiations with the Arab-Palestinians. The enlarging dimensions of conflict and violence in Israeli occupied Jerusalem and the Palestinian territories, which pits Israelis against Palestinians and threatens to unravel the OSLO peace process, cause Afro-Arab and Asian World deep concern. "To know what it means to live under occupation, you have to go through it. It means to be humiliated and harassed every minute like the Palestinians. Your water, your electricity, your economy, your freedom to express yourself and your land all are controlled by a foreign military force. You ingest the occupation in the oxygen that you breathe, the water that you drink, the food that you eat, and the news that you read or watch at the end of the day".[12]

It is the fundamental right of Palestinian people to resist Israeli colonial occupation. In the meantime the costs of the conflict and violence are mounting by the day. While the plight of Palestinians is of course worse,[13] the Israelis too are feeling the pinch. Israel's agriculture, construction, hotel and tourism industries are suffering because of the non-availability of Palestinian workers. The Arab-Israeli peace process is seriously threatened. Unless Israel goes back to the spirit of earlier agreements it will be difficult to reach at a permanent settlement. In the interest of peace the peace process must continue. The United Nations resolutions 242 and 338 must be implemented with the creation of an independent Palestinian state with East Jerusalem as its capital.

"It's not gun or Israeli air power but the peace diplomacy which would lead to a permanent and secure peace. If escalation continues it would lead to all around destruction of the Arab-Israeli region":[14] If the peace process in Palestine fails, it would lead to full scale conflict, destruction and insecurity. Israel with its heavy military arms and technology may be able to suppress the stone-throwing Arab-Palestinian kids but they will never have peace. The emergency conditions of the Arab-Israeli conflict will affect the normal life and socio-politico and economic life and all activities of the people of the Afro-Arab-Asian region. Continuing confrontation will not be a happy situation. Peace can be achieved only with a peaceful neighbourhood.

REFERENCES

1. *The Asian Age* (London, Delhi), October 25, 2000.
2. *UN News Letter* (New Delhi) Vol. 55, No. 41, 7th October, 2000, p. 1.
3. Quoted in *Khaleej Times* (Dubai) October 16, 2000.
4. *Jordan News* (Amman) October 28, 2000.
5. Saudi Arabia, the World's largest oil exporter, is a strong regional ally of the United States. US troops are based there and more than 200 US companies, including major oil, defence and construction firms, have contracts worth billions of dollars with Saudi Arabia. See *Asian Age*, Oct. 30, 2000.
6. *The Hindu* (Madras) October 23, 2000.
7. Egypt, Jordan, Syria and Lebanon have borders with Israel. Egypt (1979) and Jordan (1995) have already signed peace treaties with the Jewish state.
8. On 23 January 1950, Israel declared Jerusalem its capital and established government agencies in the western part of the city. As a result of the June 1967 Arab-Israeli war, Israel occupied East

Jerusalem, the West Bank, Sinai Peninsula, Golan Heights and other areas. Since then, Israel imposed demographic and physical changes in this area. For details see *The United Nations and the Question of Palestine*; United Nations: Department of Public Information, October 1994. Also see *Jerusalem: Historical, Legal and Political Facts*, New Delhi: League of Arab States Mission, 1995.

9. *The Asian Age*, 5 November 2000.
10. An Arab businessman in Dubai placed a newspaper advertisement to announce plans to ship 50 truckloads of stones and 500,000 slingshots overland to Jordan for use by Palestinian Intifadeh fighters. For details see *International Herald Tribune* (Bangkok) 9 October, 2000.
11. For details see Allegra Pacheeo, "The OSLO process, Unfair and unreal, was Never Going to Work", *International Herald Tribune*, 6 October, 2000.
12. Jumana Odeh, the director of the Palestinian Happy Child Centre, quoted in *International Herald Tribune*, Published in *Asian Age*, November 1, 2000.
13. The worsening of the situation on the ground in the past few weeks has had an extremely damaging effect on the Palestinian economy. As a result of the conflict, the unemployment and poverty rates have risen considerably after several years of improvement. There is a growing sense of despair, frustration and anger among Palestinians. This is why it is essential to restore calm as soon as possible, and to revive the peace negotiations in order also to restart the economy. See the text of the UN Secretary-General Kofi Annan's message on the occasion of *International Day of Solidarity With the Palestinian People* 29, November.
14. Dr. Khalid el-Sheikh, Ambassador of the State of Palestine in India quoted in a recent seminar in New Delhi.

30. Yasser Arafat: The Peace Maker

Some leaders around the Arab world and Israel have described the recently signed peace accord between the Palestine Liberation Organisation's Chairman Mr. Yasser Arafat and Premier of Israel Mr. Yitzhak Rabin as fruitless, a sell out and even a waste of time. But credit must be given where it is due. For when Israel and the Palestinians make peace in Washington it is not an ordinary event. Such an initiative is rightly pregnant with the possibility of putting an end to the age-old conflict between the followers of world's three leading religions: Christianity, Judaism and Islam. It marks a truly dramatic beginning to solve one of the long-lingering, bloodiest and most complex problems that has plagued international relations for close to half a century.

The Indian government has timely extended felicitations to Palestinian President Yasser Arafat and his negotiations and the Israeli Premier Mr. Yitzhak Rabin for the landmark understanding reached between them and hoped that this would lead to further positive steps in achieving the legitimate rights of the Arab-Palestinian People and also hoped that this initial agreement will lead to more comprehensive understanding on all major issues between the two countries and pave the way for establishment of a just and durable peace and stability in West Asia.

"By recognising the national legitimate rights of our people, the Palestine Liberation Organisation (PLO) as their representative and the necessity to conclude a political settlement, based on UN security council resolutions 242 and 338, the people of Palestine have good reasons to rejoice this historic moment", says Dr. Khalid El-Sheikh, Ambassador of the Palestine to India. The eminently Patient and repeatedly successful diplomacy in which Mr. Yasser Arafat, the Palestinian chief indulged, did not go waste. By bringing pressure in devious ways and on both Israelis, the Americans and the Arab powers, Mr. Arafat did accomplish a great part of his life aim, that is, Peace with Israel and recognition of the legitimate struggle and rights of the Arab Palestinian people.

The fact that such an agreement was indeed signed and the both Israelis and Arab-Palestinians attended it, is in itself regarded by experts on West Asian affairs as an achievement. The decades long war, fought with Israeli guns, tanks, bombs and Palestinian stones, has convinced all but the most rational among them that neither can Israel live in peace nor can the Arab-Palestinians have a homeland by wanting the other destroyed. In the end the credit for exploiting the opportunities provided by these developments must go to the uncommon statesmanship demonstrated by the Bill Clinton administration, the Norwegian Foreign Minister, Johan Jogen, moderate Israeli leadership represented by Yitzhak Rabin and Shimon Peres, the Egyptian Leadership and the great peace diplomat and charismatic leader Yasser Arafat and Mahmound Abbas, the leading PLO executive member.

President Arafat has rightly acclaimed in his speech that, "My people are hoping that this agreement which we are signing marks the beginning of the end of a chapter of pain and suffering which has lasted throughout this century ... this agreement will usher in an age of Peace, Coexistence and equal rights".

The beacon of light and love for the suffering Arab-Palestinian People has always been the Palestinian Chief Yasser Arafat (Abu Amar). In his olive uniform and scruffy beard, the commander-in chief of the Arab Palestinian People has consistently staked his life for his people. He has kindled hope amongst millions of Palestinians rendered homeless. His courageous leadership instilled new hope in them. His indomitable sacrifice, steadfastness, courage and determination have allowed him to forge ahead overcoming obstacles placed by other men and nations, more particularly Israel. Nothing has deterred him.

Yasser Arafat was born as Rahman Abdul Raouf Arafat al-Qudura al-Husseini in Jerusalem, Palestine, on 4 August 1929. Even as a young student in Cairo, he formed the League of Palestine Students in 1945 and led the same from 1952 to 1956. He participated in the first Arab-Israeli war in 1948. He was a second lieutenant in an Egyptian Army demolition squad during the 1956 Suez war. After his graduation in Engineering from Cairo university, he formed Fateh the Palestine Liberation movement. In February 1969 he was elected chairman of the 15 member Executive Committee of the PLO. President Arafat has played a key role in mobilising International Public Opinion for the Arab-Palestinian cause. He along with Late Khalil al-Wazir also known as Abu Jihad (the hero of the Arab-Palestinian movement, who was murdered by the Israelis in his Tunis home in 1988), Farooq Qaddomi (Head of Fatah Political Department), Dr. Mahmoud Abbas (Fatah, Head of Department of International Relations), George Habash, (Leader, Popular Front for the Liberation of Palestine), Naif Hawatmeh (Leader of the Popular Democratic Front for the Liberation of Palestine) and Yasir Abed Arboo (Head of Fatah, Department of Information led the Arab-Palestinian movement for peace, self-determination and freedom.

Arafat's movement for peace, self-determination and Palestinian independence had been recognised by the United Nations, the Non-Aligned Movement, the League of Arab states, the Organisation of Islamic Conference, the Organisation of African Unity and also by over one hundred and eighty-five countries including recently Israel and the United States. Among Arab-Palestinian People, there is indeed a deep affection for President Arafat. It is manifested throughout the struggle of the Arab-Palestinian People including in the recent times when the Arab-Palestinian and Jewish crowds spanned in a joyous dance. Arafat made his famous appearance at the United Nations in 1974, offering both the gun and the olive branch to the world. Loyalty and admiration to and for his friends was perhaps one of his most distinct characteristics. When his local commanders fled southern Lebanon during the Israeli invasion in 1982, he stood by them to the last moment and sustained the Israeli aggression. He felt quite amazed one-time at the attitude of Americans who expected the PLO to control all the acts of all Palestinians. He was presented by the Americans to the world as a Super Power, who should be held responsible for everything that happens anywhere in the world in which any Palestinian is involved. He was also worried about the US campaign against the PLO, which has been as full for the Arab-Palestinians. But he is patient and quite certain that the victory of the Arab-Palestinians will be a turning Point for the Afro-Asian world.

The recent Arab-Palestinian and Israeli accord, which ended President Arafat's four decades of "armed but legitimate struggle" against Israel, was only the end of what he calls the small Jihad, or holy war. The "big" Jihad, Mr. Arafat rightly feels, would be to build the new Palestinian entity. "I have fulfilled the promise we gave to our People to establish the Palestinian national authority on any land from which Israel withdraws or which was liberated", he said recently.

The Palestinian-Israeli Peace Accord will not make Arab-Palestinians and Israelis friends overnight, but it truly signals a common understanding of exactly what lies at the heart of their problems. The prospects for the socio-economic, political growth of Arab-Palestine are dependent on the Israeli commitment to peace. The peace in Palestine alone is not enough, says Dr. Ali Muhsen Hamid, Chief Representative of the League of Arab States in New Delhi.

"Total peace requires a comprehensive solution on all Arab fronts i.e. Israeli withdrawal from the Israeli occupied Arab-Palestinian territories must be followed by its complete withdrawal from the occupied territories of Lebanon, Syria and Jordan". Moreover, the solution to the West Asian impasse to a great extent lies in the early establishment of a Arab-Palestinian state in the West Bank and Gaza Strip with its capital at Jerusalem instead of granting limited Palestinian autonomy in the Gaza Strip and the West Bank town of Jericho. However, it can be concluded that the Palestinian-Israeli Peace Accord is the first and most significant step towards Peace in the Middle East region since the end of the second Gulf War.

31. Assad's Peace Strategy

Modern West Asia, particularly Syria, owes much to President Hafez Al-Assad (1930-2000) who died in Damascus recently. He brought remarkable stability, identity and pride to an ancient land that had remained as unstable as the desert sand. Assad carved for Syria and the Arab world a role far larger than its military power or state-dominated economy justified.

The history and politics of contemporary West Asia cannot be understood without reference to the role and contribution of President Assad. Among the important players in the West Asia peace process if there was one leader who was constantly courted and yet managed to remain aloof, he was the late Syrian President. He was an uncompromising Arab nationalist, unwilling to yield under pressure to the powerful Jewish state. He had staunchly opposed Egypt's decision to sign its own peace deal with Israel and was also critical of the Palestinians and Jordanians for their compromise with Israel at the instance of the United States considering it as a betrayal of the Arab-Palestine cause. He also demonstrated the courage to criticise Iraq for its intrusion into Kuwait. And to his people he promised a comprehensive peace with honour by his resolve to recover the Golan Heights and Arab-Palestinian territories lost to Israel in the 1967 Arab-Israeli war.

The death of President Assad brought expressions of both apprehension and cautious hope for stability from regional and world leaders. To the Western and the Israeli analysts, Mr. Assad's death and the resulting dose of political uncertainty in Damascus are likely to freeze the already dim chances of reviving peace talks between Syria and Israel in the short to medium term. Yet there are also cautious hopes that in the long term, once the dust of succession settles in Damascus, Mr. Assad's successor, Basher Assad could remove an obstacle to peace in West Asia and eventually prepare the ground for somewhat more modern and flexible leadership in Damascus. Rather than accepting an offer to make a partial peace in return for recovering all but a part of the Golan Heights and other land occupied by Israel in the 1967 Arab-Israeli war, the late Assad had dismissed the proposal presented on Israel's behalf by President Bill Clinton in Geneva in March this year, which is not to say that he did not seek peace.

"He will go down in Syrian history as the man who took the decision to explore the possibility of peace with Israel", said Shlomo Ben-Ami, the Public Security Minister of Israel and a leading peace negotiator. Cautious, cool-headed and shrewd, Mr. Assad was a focal point of international efforts to devise a durable and lasting peace in West Asia. No one else in Syria, according to Western officials, could make an agreement with Israel stick. This was also the view of Mr. Ehud Barak, the Israeli Prime Minister, who took office 11 months ago and recently lost majority support in Israeli parliament.

The US President, Mr. Bill Clinton, in a statement issued in Northfield, Minnesota, offered his condolences to the Assad family and to Syrians while adding his hope for a renewed peace effort. Over the past seven years, I have met him many times and got to know him very well", Mr. Clinton said. "We had our differences, but I always respected him".

In Russia, Mr. Assad was remembered as a "wise leader" by Mr. Evgeni Primakov, a former Prime Minister, who knew the Syrian President well. "I have known Hafez Assad since 1966", Mr. Primakov said. "I have great respect for him. He was a wise statesman who ran his country under the difficult conditions of confrontation with Israel and the West".

In Lebanon, where President Assad exercised great influence, leaders praised him effusively as the guardian of Arab pride and the man who helped Lebanon emerge from its long civil war. Here the recent withdrawal of Israeli troops after two decades of occupation was hailed as a great victory for the Arabs. The Arab League praised Assad as "one who devoted his life to serving the Arab and Islamic nations and fighting for the recovery of their land and for Arab right". In Gaza city, President Yasser Arafat called for a three-day period of mourning.

Known as the "Lion of Damascus"—his family name means lion in Arabic—Mr. Assad was the last surviving member of a generation of Arab leaders after the death of President Anwar al-Sadat of Egypt, King Hassan of Morocco, King Hussein of

Jordan and former President Habib Bourguiba of Tunisia. In much of the Arab world, Assad is seen as a purist who remained, until his death, one of the last few believers in Arab nationalism and Arab unity, one who disagreed with leaders of Egypt, Jordan, Morocco and lastly the Palestinian Authority, who negotiated individual peace treaties with Israel.

Syria was a young historic nation before Mr. Assad's rule. It was under the French colonial mandate till April 1946 when it got complete independence. But the political situation remained unsettled as military coups were staged there from time to time till 1970. It was when Lt. Gen. Hafez Al-Assad became Prime Minister on November 13, 1970 and assumed Presidency on February 22, 1971 that some semblance of stability was visible. Syria under President Assad witnessed relative economic development and the first modern construction of roads, schools and hospitals. Mr. Assad followed the Soviet model of a socialist state. Syria under Assad has long been a state of complex interest to major foreign or western powers.

It was in regional sphere, however, that Mr. Assad most sought to create a legacy, remaking Syria into a influential power among the Arabs. He was inspired by the Arab nationalism preached by President Abdel Gamal Nasser of Egypt. Like others of his generation, President Jaafar Numeiry of Sudan, Col Muammar Gaddafi of Libya, Chairman Yasser Arafat of Palestine Liberation Organisation and later President Saddam Hussein of Iraq, he sought to inherit Nasser's role as the voice of Arab nationalism, Arab unity, Arab identity and Arab pride.

From the beginning, Assad showed that he was a man of action. The Nasserite leanings of the Assad regime in foreign policy soon became apparent. Although Syria continued to reject the November 1967 UN Security Council resolutions 242 and 338, relations with Egypt (United Arab Republic) and Jordan improved and Syria's isolation in the Arab world was soon reduced. Syria's willingness to join a union with Egypt, Sudan and Libya almost became apparent and agreement on federation with Libya and Egypt was reached in April 1971. But the federation had little effect. A new constitution, approved by the plebiscite on March 12, 1973 confirmed the Arab Socialist Renaissance (Ba'ath) party as the leading party in the state and society.

It was under Assad, on the afternoon of October 6, 1973 that

Egyptian, Palestinian and Syrian forces launched a war against Israel in an effort to regain Arab-Palestinian territories lost in 1967. On the Egyptian and Syrian fronts, complete surprise was achieved, giving the Arabs a strong initial advantage, much of which they subsequently lost. Since the 1970s the Ba'ath party constituted the main ideological base of the Assad regime in Syria. The regime's projection of its "steadfast" policies in the wake of Israel's brutal invasion of Lebanon was an effort to regain the Arab legitimacy it had lost after February 1982.

As the leader of Arab Ba'ath Socialism, Assad aspired to liberate Syrians from all kinds of disabilities. His motive was to make Syria independent of foreign involvement and transform it into a modern Arab state. Since the last three decades, he managed to offer Syrians self-respect, national dignity, identity and purpose. With his death the political landscape of Syria as well as the region has changed.

Syria under Assad occupied an important position in the region and enjoyed considerable socio-political weight in the Arab world. The best tribute to President Assad is to aspire to fulfil his ideals of a comprehensive peace, that is, complete Israeli withdrawal from all occupied Arab-Palestinian territories including Golan Heights and the establishment of an independent Arab-Palestinian state with East Jerusalem as its capital.

32. The Arab-African Fraternity

The mere attempt at close regional cooperation between states is a difficult and remarkable consideration. There is no doubt that regional institutions play an important role in triggering off integrative potentialities. The recent cooperative effort among sovereign Arab States to which this article is devoted involves Egypt, Iraq, Jordan and North Yemen on one side and Algeria, Libya, Mauritania, Morocco and Tunisia on the other. In the recent times, the Arab world witnessed birth of two vigorous integration-oriented bodies when the leaders of the above mentioned Arab Economic Groupings met in Baghdad and Rabat on 16 and 17 February to mark the formal establishment of the organisations called the Arab Cooperation Council (ACC) and the Arab Maghreb Union (AMU) approved their status and by-laws. The ACC and AMU are the second and third of the three Arab economic organisations. The six member (Saudi Arabia, Kuwait, the United Arab Emirates (UAE), Oman, Bahrain and Qatar) Gulf Cooperation Council was formed in 1981.

The ACC and the AMU members have a natural affinity, sharing close proximity and a common language (that is Arabic) and a common religion (that is Islam). With combined economic resources and manpower perhaps significant in the world, they should be able to expect a bright future, socio-economic and political success. They are located, however, in an area where serious conflicts began in the distant past as well as those of contemporary origin continue to play themselves out, threatening the very economic security and socio-political stability of that region. Perhaps among the more important factors in the composition of the ACC and the AMU, the people of these nations (about 150 million, ten times that of the six member GCC) recognise and understand their fraternity in the wider implications of Arab nationality.

For ACC, President Hosni Mubarak of Egypt, King Hussein of Jordan, President Ali Abdullah Saleh of North Yemen and the four power Arab Summit host, President Saddam Hussein of Iraq signed the agreement forming this four-country economic trading Arab group. They expressed the hope that it would eventually lead to an Arab common market. The Baghdad ACC foundation meeting had been preceded by a meeting in Amman of the four above states' Prime Ministers who drew up the charter for this new Arab bloc.

For AMU, King Hassan of Morocco, Colonel Muammar Gaddafi of Libya, President Chadli Bendjadid of Algeria, President Zine el-ebidine Ben Ali of Tunisia and Colonel Maawiya Ould Sid'Ahmed Taya of Mauritania signed the agreement at Marrakech (Morocco).

The ACC and AMU aim at cementing economic ties between the member countries on the pattern of EEC (European Economic Community) and GCC but not at setting up a new Arab political and military or religious bloc. These organisations also aspire to achieve cooperation, solidarity and joint action in all fields to safeguard their security, to tend their legitimate integrity, to continue their efforts for progress and prosperity, and to strengthen their positive and constructive international role in serving the causes of peace, security, progress and equitable and fruitful co-operation amongst the peoples of the world.

The new ACC pact (consisting of seventeen articles) foresees achieving "complementary economy in the various fields of production, achieving economic integration in all production centres and coordination in the fields of economy, finance, industry, agriculture, transport, communications, education, culture, information, technology, health, tourism, residence, travel and labour and social affairs.

The ACC statutes, which were approved earlier by the Prime Ministers of the four member states in Amman on 14-15 February this year stressed "full adherence" to the Charter of the League of Arab States and the League's Defence Pact, which calls for solidarity with any of the member states in case of foreign attack. Besides, the ACC charter called for encouraging joint investment projects among the private and public sectors of the member states. However, the Charter made no mention of the petroleum sector and some of the oil ministers of the four member countries participated in the negotiations that led to the summit. The current oil production of the four member states is around 3.75 mn/bd.

From the point of the ACC organisation set-up (Art. V to XIV), the ACC will have three commissions: a Supreme Commission of the heads of states (Art, six) which will meet once a year; a ministerial commission headed by the Prime Ministers (Art. IX) that will meet twice a year; and a General Secretariat (Art. XIII) with its headquarters in Amman, headed by a Secretary-General and composed of a member of officials as necessary. Membership is open to all Arab states provided that there is unanimous agreement of the founders for each new applicant. A meeting of the ministerial commission was scheduled in Cairo this May. More ACC Summit conferences have been scheduled for this year and the leaders of the four member Arab States are expected to accord priority in their meet to such pressing and urgent problems as the Palestinian cause and Israel's oppressive practices against the Palestinians in the Israeli-occupied Arab-Palestinian territories.

Reacting to the birth of ACC, President Mubarak of Egypt affirmed that the ACC serves the interests of the Arab nation as much as it does its founding members. To President Saddam Hussein of Iraq, the economic relations among the four member Arab-states of the ACC were the base for the new Arab gathering because evaluating progress and prosperity of any country in the Third World was measured by the strength of its economy.

Before going into the theoretical sum-up of ACC, it is necessary to highlight some reasons which made the respective Arab states to come together. For Jordan, the reasons are basically economic. But in the cases of other three participants it is probably the political factors (to some extent) which motivated their decision to join the same. In the general sense, all of them could probably use a counterweight to the above mentioned six member GCC. Besides, taking into consideration, the Iraqi-GCC relations, Iraq's membership might be seen to reflect Baghdad's displeasure at Post-Gulf war overtures in Iran's direction by the GCC members.

Egypt's was at least in part an expression of its frustration at the Saudis' failure to mediate its membership to the Arab League, the negative attitude of the radical Arab states like Syria and Libya and at the successive postponements of the Arab summit at which this was (that is the Egyptian Readmission to Arab League) to have taken place. However, for North Yemen, the ACC probably represents an opportunity to expose the Saudi domination in that region.

followed it with a treaty of 'perpetual peace and friendship', on the lines of the one signed between India and Iran in March 1950. Besides, the cultural links between the two countries were sought to be revived by a cultural agreement of July 1954.

However, the friendship thus forged provided only a framework and not the substance of a partnership as visualised earlier. At least on political level India and Iraq were far from being close to each other. In the 1950s India encountered a two-fold challenge to its interests in the Persian Gulf region. First, it was the Western, particularly British and American, drive to bring about a military grouping of West Asian nations which would promote their imperial interests in the region and second, Pakistan's design to forge a Pan-Islamic alliance of Arab and Islamic States, while the former threatened to bring cold war between the East and West to India's doorsteps, the latter sought to isolate India from a region, vital to its security and economic well being. These two forces converged in 1955 giving birth to the Baghdad Pact[18] which constituted the states like Turkey, Iraq, Iran and Pakistan. India strongly opposed the creation of this military pact on the grounds that it aggravated tensions in the Arab world by provoking the super powers to enter the region in a big way. But most important of all, its opposition emanated from Pakistan's membership of the pact which posed a serious threat to India's security. Prime Minister Nehru had openly declared that the Baghdad Pact tended to "encircle India".

A new phase in Indo-Iraqi relations began with the revolution (1958)[19] in Iraq which transformed the West Asian situation. Monarchy in Iraq was abolished. It also constituted a serious setback to the Western policy of military bloc network around the world and at the same time gave a boost to the forces of Non-Alignment and secularism in West Asia. India welcomed the change of government in Iraq and Nehru expressed his satisfaction commenting that "the present system in Iraq is well-established, stable and popular". India's relations with Iraq took a turn for the better, although the major development in relations came between 1966 and 1976. By an agreement of 13 December 1962, the two countries had accorded a most favoured nation treatment to each other and Iraq, along with other West Asian states became an important market for tea, jute, textiles and spices.[20]

In 1962 when China attacked India, almost all Arab countries expressed their solidarity and support to India. Surprisingly, Iraq was the only West Asian state which did not come out in India's favour and remained neutral throughout the conflict. However, Indo-Iraqi relations reached greater heights during the regime of field Marshal Aref who became the President of Iraq after another military takeover in 1963. Thus before the Indo-Pak war of 1965, India had established close commercial and cultural contacts with all the Persian Gulf countries besides sharing intimate political relationship with Iraq. On the other hand, the Gulf States were also appreciative of India's constituent identification with the Arab-Palestinian cause. But when the Indo-Pak war began (1965), the government of Iraq, despite anti-India tirade in its press, did not take sides in the conflict.[21] The first Iraqi foreign minister to visit India was in March 1967. It is significant that Dr. Andra Al-Pachachi, the Iraqi foreign minister, expressed his belief that India and Iraq would strengthen their trade and economic relations and lauded India's role in the field of disarmament and her stand on the Arab-Palestine issue.[22]

In the 1970s India's political and economic relationship with Iraq continued to be strengthened. During the Bangladesh War (1971) although there was a general sympathy in the Gulf States on the question of refugees, yet most of the Gulf States including Shah of Iran blamed India as an aggressor. Iraq was not hostile although it did not adopt a vocally sympathetic standpoint. But the post-1971 era saw a major spurt in the relationship between India and Iraq. A high level delegation from the ruling Baa'th Socialist Party came to India on 1 October 1972 and during its 12-days visit established party to party relationship with the Indian National Congress, which laid the basis for a stronger politico-economic relationship between the two countries. In the mid-1970s two other notable developments were the visits of the then Vice-President of Iraq, Saddam Hussein, who subsequently became the President, and Indian Prime Minister Mrs. Indira Gandhi's visit to Baghdad in 1975. Both the leaders acknowledged the need to diversify and develop the politico-economic cooperation and called upon the developed countries to place their economic relations with developing countries on an equitable and just basis.[23]

In the 1980s economic relations with Iraq remained quite

satisfactory despite the difficulties caused by the continuation of the Iraq-Iran or Gulf War. Iraq continued to supply its quota of oil to India and in return imported Indian goods as per an earlier trade agreement. There were about 100 Indian companies executing projects worth over Rs.10,000 crore in Iraq and a number of Indian experts and workers were helping in various capacities. In the recent times, i.e. the post-Gulf war ceasefire period, Indo-Iraqi relations have developed with the identification of new areas of cooperation in trade, economy and technology.

The Iraq-Iran War

The Iraq-Iran or Gulf War, which started in September 1980,[24] posed a big challenge to the Non-Aligned Movement. It caused deep disappointment and dismay among the Non-Aligned members due to the division in the West Asian world with Syria and Libya sympathising with Islamic Iran, and Saudi Arabia, Kuwait, UAR, Jordan and Egypt strongly supporting Iraq.

India, as a leading member of the Non-Aligned Movement, was dismayed by the wasteful fratricidal conflict between the two Non-Aligned Islamic states. More significantly, Iraq and Iran, together, constituted its major oil suppliers. It led to the jeopardy in India's export of goods to this region and import of oil from them. Besides, the war disturbed the construction projects values at Rs.6,000 crore constituting over one-third of India's overseas contracts. In a meeting of the Non-Aligned countries at the United Nations (October 1980), a peace mission was set up with India and five other Non-Aligned nations, together with a representative from the PLO, to help restore peace in the region. The mission visited the two warring nations' capitals but could not succeed in stopping the war.[25] As the war grounded to a stalemate, another fruitless effort was made to end hostilities by the late Prime Minister Mrs. Indira Gandhi at the Seventh Non-Aligned Summit at New Delhi (1983). The Gulf War had raged on for about nine years (1980-1988) with no signs of cessation of hostilities from other side.

The Gulf War exposed the weaknesses as well as the limitations of the Non-Aligned Movement. The Non-Aligned countries watched helplessly while two of their members tore each other apart. However, this unending Gulf War came to an end when the Iranian government under the leadership of late Ayatollah Khomeini was finally persuaded to agree to a ceasefire and announced on July 18, 1988 of Islamic Republic of Iran's acceptance of the one-year old UN Security Council resolution 598 (1987).[26]

India and the Palestine Question

India's support to the Arab-Palestinian cause goes back to its own freedom struggle during which it had supported the emergence of an independent state for the Palestinians. But Mahatma Gandhi and Pandit Jawaharlal Nehru[27] had rightly said that Palestine was essentially an Arab country and must remain so and that the Arabs must not be crushed and suppressed in their homeland. The All-India Congress Committee meeting in October 1937 protested against the reign of terror that was being established in Palestine by British Imperialism.

India has always been against the formation of states like Israel on the basis of religion and in this context India had voted against the UN partition resolution establishing two separate states (1948).[28] India's unequivocal support to the Palestinian cause since the very beginning was not based on Islamic solidarity but on the principles of anti-colonialism, anti-imperialism and human justice. India has maintained a record of consistent support to the Palestinian cause which cannot be surpassed even by many of the Arab and Islamic States.[29]

Since its independence India has consistently supported the inalienable and legitimate rights of the Palestinian people for self-determination and for an independent homeland. Besides, India recognises the PLO (Palestine Liberation Organisation) under the leadership of President Yasser Arafat as the sole and legitimate representative of the Arab-Palestinian people. India's ties with the PLO became closer during the last fifteen years. In sum, India's policy was based on three premises, viz.: (a) Israel must withdraw from the Arab-Palestinian territory it had occupied by force, whether in Palestine, Egypt, Syria, Lebanon or elsewhere. (b) The right of the Arab-Palestinian people to a homeland must be recognised and given effect to. The exact boundaries of such a state (which has been declared recently with Yasser Arafat as President) and other details could be worked out through direct negotiations between PLO and the Israeli leadership. (c) Israeli's right to exist as a state in independence and security should be acknowledged.

India deplored Israel's obstruction of the UN efforts aimed at establishing peace based on justice in accordance with the Security Council resolution of November 22, 1967, and recommended to the UN to take adequate measures against Israel if it continues to disregard the UN efforts. During the Janata period, Atal Behari Vajpayee, the then External Affairs Minister, felt that a lasting solution to the Arab-Palestinian question could not be found or peace ensured in the region by keeping the PLO under Yasser Arafat out of any negotiations. He said that India was with them and was prepared to raise its voice wherever necessary and fight with them shoulder to shoulder.

India condemned the Camp David agreements[30] and the Egypt-Israel Treaty of March 26, 1979 which meant the total abandonment of the cause of the Arab countries and Palestine as an act of complicity with the sustained occupation of the Arab-Palestinian territories. It also condemned the threat by the United States to use the veto in the UN Security Council against any resolution concerning the Israeli atrocities on the Arab-Palestinian people and their inalienable national rights. In the early 1980s the late Prime Minister Mrs. Indira Gandhi, after her party's election (1980) victory had said that India considered the Arab-Palestinian question as "central to the West Asian situation". India during this period granted full diplomatic status to the Palestine Liberation Organisation (which opened its office in New Delhi ten years ago).

Moreover in the recent times (1989), India whole-heartedly welcomed the West Asian Peace Plan proposed by the PLO Chairman Yasser Arafat (at present Arafat is the President of the newly declared State of Palestine) before the UN General Assembly meeting in the special session at Geneva to discuss the question of Palestine. Prime Minister Rajiv Gandhi congratulated the PLO leader Yasser Arafat for declaring an independent State of Palestine in November 1988[31] and welcomed the proposal of the Palestine National Council (met in Algiers)[32] for an international conference on West Asia under the auspices of the United Nations. The Indian representative at the UN urged Israel to respond "adequately and constructively" to the PLO's new offer negotiating lasting peace in West Asia under the mediation of the United Nations and to take seriously the PLO's renunciation of terrorism. President R. Venkataraman said, "Mr. Arafat's bold and courageous initiatives for peace had entirely transformed the West Asian question and had most deservedly on universal acclaim". The President also emphasised that India was convinced that the most appropriate forum for durable peace in West Asia was UN sponsored peace conference with full participation of all concerned States including Palestine (PLO) and the permanent members of the Security Council.[33]

India and the Arab World in the 1990s

The story of India's relations with the West Asian States in the contemporary period is thus the part of the larger narrative of the quest of man for healthy, positive and friendly relations between diverse peoples inhabiting the many countries of our present times. The ongoing decade of 1990s, in sum, is going to be fraught with success and cooperation between these two regions. On the Palestine question, the Israeli repression of Palestinian uprising and Israeli invasion of Lebanon, Indian policy pronouncements had been closer to the stand of Arabs. This trend has been continued and would continue in future under the Prime Minister V.P. Singh's leadership.

India's attitude towards Israel and the Arab-Israeli conflict was influenced by her national interest. With Indian policy being essentially based on its experience of needing to condemn aggression of all kinds, condemning Israeli aggression was natural. Besides, the Israeli State is antithetical to the Indian State as India does not recognise the principle of states being created on the basis of religion. Therefore India's support for the secular Palestine Liberation Organisation under the leadership of President Yasser Arafat in its struggle against Israeli occupation of the Palestine homeland is obvious.

Moreover, Indian President R. Venkataraman (i.e. on 27 March 1990) presented the prestigious Jawaharlal Nehru Award for International Understanding to the Palestine President Yasser Arafat for his "steadfastness, valour and tireless devotion" to the Palestine cause.[34] Palestine President Yasser Arafat's leadership of the PLO had been recognised by India since late Prime Minister Indira

Gandhi's leadership and has been continued under Morarji Desai, Rajiv Gandhi and V.P. Singh. The future leadership, if any, is likely to continue the same policy.

India's relations with other West Asian States like Algeria, Tunisia, Morocco, Libya, Bahrain, Iran, Iraq, Saudi Arabia, Jordan, Kuwait, Lebanon, Oman, Qatar, UAE (United Arab Emirates), United Yemen, Turkey and Syria had also grown slowly and steadily, despite few ups and downs. India has had a long history of trade, commerce, navigation and movement of goods and personnel in this area. From the above analysis, it can be concluded that Indo-Arab friendship is deep rooted and strong and will continue to grow stronger.

However, it is being felt that India failed to play any significant role in the second Gulf crisis i.e. the Iraqi intrusion in Kuwait.[35] In the absence of Soviet Union playing a leading role it was but natural on the part of the Third World to expect India to play a bigger role in solving the Gulf crisis.

REFERENCES

1. For details see, the author's article titled, "Towards Arab Fraternity", in *Third Concept* (New Delhi), Vol. 3, No. 28, June 1989, pp. 48-9; and "Economic Security and the Arabs", in *Democratic World* (New Delhi), Vol. XVII, No. 25, 18 June 1989, pp. 11-12.
2. "Middle East" is an arbitrary term invented by the European naval historian, A.T. Mehan, in 1900 to divide the orient in three sections: The Near East, the Middle East, and the Far East. In a broader sense this area extends all the way from the Atlantic coast across North Africa through the Fertile Crescent to the eastern border of Iran.
3. The proclamation of the Sahrawi Arab Democratic Republic (SADR) was made on 27 February 1976. See *Basic Information About the Sahrawi Arab Democratic Republic*, edited by Asia-Oceania Department of the Polisario Front, pp. 49-50.
4. Lebanon has always been a microcosm of the Arab World because it reflects the rivalries and squabbles of the Arab powers (Iraq and Syria in the recent times) on the Lebanese stage. For details, see Marius Deeb, *The Lebanese Civil War* (New York: Praeger Publishers, 1980).
5. In March 1945 the League of Arab States came into existence. It was born out of Arab nationalism and a general Arab desire for unity. See Ahmed M. Gomma, *The Foundation of the League of Arab*

States: Wartime Diplomacy and Inter-Arab Politics, 1941 to 1945 (London, New York: Longman, 1977), pp. 235-264.

6. For details, see Peter Mangold, *Super Power Intervention in the Middle East* (London: Croom Helm, 1978).
7. Mohammed Hassan El-Zayyat, *India and Egypt: Modern Relations Between two Ancient Nations* (New Delhi: Indian Council for Cultural Relations, 1984), pp. 9-25.
8. Under the Fatimid rulers, Egypt enjoyed a golden age. The Fatimids in Cairo sometimes granted documents (*Sanads*) to certain Indian princes allowing them to rule in their names as Khalifa's representative. Muhammad Bin Tughlaq, the Sultan of Delhi, had requested for such a *Sanad* from Khalifa Al-Hakim of Cairo (A.D. 1339-1347).
9. Attar Chand, "Indo-Egyptian Relations: A Glorious Saga", *The Century*, 23 February 1974, p. 5.
10. V.P. Dutt, *India's Foreign Policy* (Delhi: Allied, 1984), p. 304.
11. See author's article titled, "The Rise of Arab Nationalism and Egypt", in *Patriot* (New Delhi), 1 October 1986.
12. Jean and Simonne Lacouture, *Egypt in Transition* (London: Methuenes Co., 1958), p. 86.
13. See author's article titled "Nasser and Non-Alignment", in *Third Concept* (New Delhi), April-May 1987.
14. G.S. Bhargava, *India and West Asia* (New Delhi: Popular Book Services, 1967), p. 10.
15. Jawaharlal Nehru, *India's Foreign Policy* (New Delhi: Publications Division, Government of India, 1961), p. 281.
16. Ghali Shoukri, *Egypt: Portrait of a President, 1971-1981* (London: Zed Press, 1981), p. IV.

    The death of President Nasser of Egypt in 1970 took away something definite though intangible from the special relationship that was evolving between Egypt and India. President Sadat's policy underwent an about-turn on Nasser's policy of Non-Alignment. It is interesting to note that Sadat's successor, President Hosni Mubarak is within the limitations imposed by Egypt by Sadat's policy, trying to revert back to some of the principles initiated by Nasser.
17. See author's article, titled "Challenges before Mubarak", *Third Concept*, July 1987, p. 29.
18. "Mubarak Lauds NAM efforts for peace", *National Herald* (New Delhi), 15 March 1988.
19. The Baghdad Pact was signed on 24 February 1955. For details, see Majid Khaddouri, *Independent Iraq 1932-1958: A Study in Iraqi Politics* (London, New York, Karachi: Oxford, 1960), p. 348.
20. For details, see K.R. Singh, "Party Politics in Iraq: Post Revolution Era", *International Studies* (New Delhi), Vol. 3, pp. 242-262. Also

see Singh, "Iraq Since 1945", *Foreign Affairs Reports*, Vol. IX, July 1960, pp. 75-83.

21. *Asian Recorder*, 8-14 January 1963, p. 4683.
22. *Ibid.*, 26 March-1 April 1966, p. 7002.
23. *Times of India*, 7 March 1967.
24. See author's article, titled "The never-ending Gulf War", *Democratic World* (New Delhi), Vol. XVI, no. 18, 3 May 1987, p. 13.

    The war started with the Iraqi abrogation of the 1975 agreement and invasion of Iraq of the newly born Islamic Republic of Iran on 22 September 1980.
25. V.P. Dutt, *India's Foreign Policy* (New Delhi: Vikas Publishing House, 1984), p. 341.
26. See author's article, titled "Ceasefire in the Gulf", *Democratic World*, vol. XVII, no. 33, 14 August 1988, pp. 12-13.
27. Dr. B.S.N. Murti, *Nehru's Foreign Policy* (New Delhi: The Beacon Information and Publications, 1953), p. 102.
28. For details, see Abdulla Frangi, *The PLO and Palestine* (London: Zed Books, 1983), pp. 81-85. Also see Mehmood Hussain, *The Palestine Liberation Organisation* (New Delhi: Univ. Publishers, 1975).
29. K.R. Singh, "India's Strategic and Economic Interests in West Asia", in Satish Kumar's *Year Book on India's Foreign Policy, 1983-84* (ed.) (New Delhi, London: Sage Publications, 1986), p. 122.
30. Late Mohammad Anwar el-Sadat, President of the Arab Republic of Egypt, and Menachem Begin, the then Prime Minister of Israel, met with Jimmy Carter, then President of the United States of America, at Camp David from 5 to 17 September 1978 and signed the Camp David Accords at the White House on 26 March 1979. Dor details, see Mohamed Ibrahim Kamel, *The Camp David Across—A Testimony* (London, Boston, Sydney: KPI Limited, 1986).
31. *Hindustan Times* (New Delhi), 25 November 1988.
32. See author's article, titled "PLO Victory at Algiers Summit", *Democratic World*, Vol. XVII, no. 28, 10 July 1988, p. 11.
33. *Hindustan Times*, 15 December 1988. Also see *Patriot*, 10 March 1989.
34. See author's article, titled "What India Owes to Palestine?", *Third Concept*, April-May 1990, p. 11.
35. The Iraqi intrusion into Kuwait shook the lakhs of Indian expatriates in Kuwait and the Gulf region. The Iraqi President Saddam Hussain and the Israeli leaders had spoiled the plans of any body who had brought into the idea that a new "Era of Universal Peace" was dawning. None of the world's leaders wanted to believe that Saddam would send his Army into Kuwait. So also no one expected Israel to be as repressive and inhuman as it is in the present times.

38. India and Israel

India's vote at the UN favouring rescinding of the 1957 resolution equating Zionism with racism and its sudden announcement of full diplomatic relations with Israel (29 January 1992) is generally seen as a major reversal and a deviation from the country's policy[1] of Non-Alignment and commitment to the Arab-Palestinian cause. A few days before, Madhav Singh Solanki, India's Ex-Minister of External Affairs, had linked restoration of full diplomatic ties with Israel to "genuine settlement of the Palestine issue".[2] He cited Israel's inflexibility as an obstacle in the way of upgrading diplomatic relations.

Prominent intellectuals, leaders and well-wishers felt that the Government should have awaited the outcome of the ongoing West Asia peace talks.[3] They criticised the Government's policy as a deviation from the country's long-standing, value-based policy of commitment to the Palestinian cause given by the great leaders like Mahatma Gandhi, Jawaharlal Nehru and Subhas Chandra Bose long before independence. The CPI (Communist Party of India) felt that the Palestinians had been let down by India which had championed their cause over the years. India had decided to upgrade its relations with Israel when the Palestinian issue was still unresolved.

The CPI(M) (Communist Party of India Marxist) said in a statement that India's decision must be seen in the context of Israel's continued occupation of Arab territories and as "endorsement" of the Israeli position. It was a departure from the policy framework adopted during the freedom struggle and after independence, said Mr. K.P. Unnikrishnan, Congress(S) leader. Prof. M.S. Agwani, once Vice-Chancellor of Jawaharlal Nehru University, felt that India had taken the decision "under pressure from the United States"[4] and expressed the hope that the pressure would stop somewhere. The far-reaching changes the world has witnessed in recent years may indeed necessitate a real appraisal of certain foreign policy assumptions and doctrines.

Prominent Muslim leaders and the former Prime Minister V.P. Singh of Janata Dal Party criticised the present Congress Government's decision to recognise Israel and alleged that it was a total sell out of the country's foreign policy under pressure from the International Monetary Fund.

About the most natural way of looking at India's "new diplomatic ties with Israel is to see it as not so well considered turn in its long-standing and balanced foreign policy. The Israeli factor has been a weighty determinant in India's West Asia policy. Initially there was considerable sympathy within our country for the Jewish State as the Jews had been oppressed not only by the Nazis but also more subtly in other European countries too. India recognised the new Jewish State[5] on September 17, 1950 but did not establish diplomatic relations. India voted against the UN Partition decision on Palestine of November 29, 1947. Again on May 11, 1949, India voted against the same resolution along with Afghanistan, Pakistan, Iran, Ethiopia and other six Arab states. M.C. Setalvad, India's chief delegate, pleaded that his government "could not recognise Israel which had been achieved through the use of force and not through negotiations".[6] At the Bandung Conference (1955), the then Prime Minister Nehru urged the Arabs not to rule out negotiations as a means of settling the Palestine issue and joined other Afro-Asian States in calling for implementation of UN resolutions on Palestine. An Israeli consulate was allowed to be set up in Bombay. But as Israel consolidated power, drove out large number of Arab-Palestinians from their homes and became an increasingly aggressive power, occupying larger chunks of Arab-Palestinian territory and colonising them with Jewish settlements, the initial sympathy waned and India became strongly opposed to Israeli policies.[7]

Since history Indians and Arabs have influenced each other deeply in various spheres of life—social, cultural and intellectual. The medieval Arab image of India was one of respect and deep regard for Indian philosophy, history, society, sciences and arts and for their valuable contribution to the progress of human civilisation. A new phase of India's relations with the Arab world began with the dawn of independence about the early part of this century. During the last five decades, India and many of the Arab states had forged a common political understanding and a similar outlook in the international political scene. The farsighted policies of Indian leaders like Jawaharlal Nehru, V.K. Krishna Menon, Lal Bahadur Shastri, Mrs. Indira Gandhi, Rajiv Gandhi and Arab leaders like Gamal Abdel Nasser, Indians and the Arabs along with other Non-Aligned nations have taken a common stand in the UN on many an important international question.

Both Mahatma Gandhi and Jawaharlal Nehru, the leaders of the Indian national movement, appreciated the Arab-Palestinian struggle against Zionism as the integral part of the Afro-Asian struggle against the forces of imperialism, racialism and colonialism. Pandit Nehru had sympathy even for Jews as victims of the Nazi holocaust but with the Arab-Palestinians, especially Nasser's Arab world, he shared the anti-imperialist sentiment.[8] Besides, Israel had persistently violated UN resolutions and had pursued policies which makes a West Asian peace impossible to attain.[9] Since its independence India has consistently supported the inalienable and legitimate rights of the Palestinian people for self-determination and for an independent homeland.[10] India's support to the Arab-Palestinian cause also became stronger and firmer over the years until it became one of principal aspects of her entire policy in the conflict in West Asia. Moreover, India recognised the PLO (Palestine Liberation Organisation) and its leader Yasser Arafat as the sole and legitimate representative of the Arab-Palestinian people. India's ties with the PLO became closer in the last twenty years. In sum, India's policy was based on three premises: Israel must withdraw from the territory it had occupied by force whether in Egypt, Syria, Palestine, Lebanon, Jordan or elsewhere, the right of the Arab-Palestinian people to a homeland must be recognised and given effect to and Israel's right to exist as a state in independence and security should be acknowledged. India also deplored Israel's obstruction of the UN efforts aimed at establishing peace.[11] Besides India condemned the Camp David Agreement and the Egypt-Israel treaty of March 26, 1979 which meant the total abandonment of the cause of the Arab countries, i.e. Palestine. It also condemned the threat by the United States to use veto in the Security Council against any resolution concerning the implementation of the Palestinian people's inalienable national rights.

In 1982, the Indian Government expelled Mr. Yosef Hasseen the Israeli Consul in Bombay and declared him *persona non-grata* for making objectionable statements in a Press interview. In his interview to a Bombay weekly newspaper *Sunday Observer* in its July 3 issue, Mr. Hasseen had said 'there was a strong Muslim-Arab lobby against Israel in Delhi. Several Arab diplomats put pressure on the Indian Government and used local Muslims. No Hindu wanted the closure of the Israeli consulate in Bombay'. Also he had said the press in India was very bad. Mr. Hasseen's remarks constituted an 'unacceptable interference' in India's domestic affairs. At a time when the whole world was appalled by the unspeakable Israeli atrocities in Lebanon and Palestine, he had the intolerable impertinence to use Indian soil to insult this country's government, the ruling party and the press—all because they refuse to go along with him in applauding nauseating Israeli genocide and condemn it instead. To make matters worse, he had tried to sow communal discord in this country.[12]

The then Prime Minister Mrs. Indira Gandhi felt that for centuries, European countries persecuted Jews, and India, then represented by the Indian National Congress, condemned this persecution and sided with the Jews. Yet, instead of solving this problem by granting human rights to the Jews in the countries in which they lived, the European powers with the assistance of the United States transplanted them to Palestine where Jews, Christians and Muslims had lived in peace and goodwill for generations. As Mrs. Gandhi said, the hatred and bitterness which had been accumulated by the Jews were transplanted to West Asia. Expansionism, lack of tolerance, and flexing of Israeli military muscle are part of life in West Asia. The attack on Lebanon and the bid to exterminate the Arab-Palestinians were only to be expected. At the same time, Mrs. Gandhi felt, the world has a duty to the Arab-Palestinians, the Lebanese and all others who are the victims of Israeli state terrorism. Peace and goodwill cannot be extorted from neighbours at the point of gun.[13] She concluded that India has consistently maintained that the Arab-Palestinians have a right to have their own nation-state and without that there can be no peace in the sensitive and strategic West Asian region.

There is a rationale and logic behind India's consistent stand that an aggressor like Israel should not be allowed by the world community to enjoy the fruits of aggression. When people are denied their right for equality, independence and homeland, they cannot but struggle for that. Israel which had itself indulged in acts of gross terrorism and repression when Israel as a state was still a dream, cannot today accuse the Arab-Palestinians of indulging in violence. India is against all kinds of violence. But it does make a distinction between blatant aggression in which thousands of civilians become war victims and the Arab-Palestinians fight for their own homeland. This policy of support to freedom struggle of oppressed Arab-Palestinians had nothing to do with India's relations with other Arab countries.

Permanent peace and security would elude West Asia until the Arab-Palestinians' just and legitimate rights to the creation of an independent state were recognised, commented P.V. Narasimha Rao, the then India's Minister for External Affairs. Talking to the APN correspondent in Geneva, where he attended the International Conference on Palestine, Rao stressed that it was necessary to stop the creation of new Jewish settlements on the West Bank. As Chairman of the Non-aligned movement (1983), Rao said, India tried its best to create an atmosphere of peace, stability and mutual understanding in West Asia.[14] Speaking in the debate on the question of Palestine in UN General Assembly (1983), Indian delegate Najma Heptullah said the Israeli aggression in Lebanon and occupied Arab-Palestine area had cast a shadow over the glimmer of hope and peace in the international sphere. India urged UN member states to strive for the discontinuation of the Jewish policy of settlements and called for an immediate freeze on new Israeli settlements in Lebanon and occupied Arab-Palestine and dismantling of those already established. She warned that the unresolved crisis in West Asia was assuming critical dimension and posed a great threat to international peace and security.[15]

In 1985, India had told Israel that its "patrons and collaborators" will not be able to deny the inalienable rights of the Arab-Palestinian people, including their homeland. The Indian delegate to the Special UN Political Committee, K.K. Tewary rebuked the Israeli representative, Joel Barromi, for 'conveniently forgetting' what the Israelis had been doing to the Arab-Palestinian people. In his speech condemning the Israeli practices in Israeli occupied territories, Tewary had quoted Mahatma Gandhi and said that, "Palestine belongs to the Arab-Palestinians in the same sense that England belongs to the English, or France to the French' and that, 'it is wrong and inhuman to impose the Jews on the Arabs'.[16] In 1985, India urged Israel and her "allies" to shed their inhibitions and their erroneous perceived interests and summon the necessary political will to join in giving a start to the peace process in West Asia. One can not settle the question of Palestine without the Palestinians and one cannot even begin to settle the question without engaging with the accepted interlocutor of the Palestinians that has sustained the struggle, i.e. the Palestine Liberation Organisation under the able leadership of Yasser Arafat.

During an unprecedented and bitter clash at the UN Security Council session in December 1987, a visibly angry ambassador of India to the United Nations, Chinmoy R. Gharekhan asked, "how dare Israel compare the atrocities it continues to perpetrate in the Israeli-occupied Arab territories with the events in sovereign and democratic India?"[17] Strongly protesting against the 'unwarranted' and 'untenable analogy' Mr. Gharekhan accused his Israeli counterpart, Mr. Banjamin Netanyahu, of seeking to use the events in an integral part of India (Punjab) in an attempt to justify Israeli brutalities against a defenceless people in an occupied territory. He condemned the atrocities by Israeli occupation forces in the occupied Arab territories of West Bank and Gaza, which constituted one aspect of the "Iron-fist and expansionist" policy that Israel had been practising with a view to enforcing its annexation of Palestinian and other occupied territories.[18]

In 1988, late Prime Minister Rajiv Gandhi denied reports that Israel and India would establish full diplomatic ties. He committed India's full support to the Palestinian struggle for freedom. "We want the Palestine Liberation Organisation (PLO) to have a homeland and all countries of West Asia should be secure in their borders. The best solution in the matter was the convening of an international peace meet on the subject with all the parties represented in their own rights and have powers to implement its decision", Mr. Rajiv Gandhi added.[19] However, Israelis were willing to bend over heels to seek cooperation, exchange, trade, business and collaboration with India for they believed that both countries were confronted with the same problems when they attained independence.

In the ongoing debate in early 1990s whether or not India should open diplomatic relations with Israel many aspects have been dealt with: the political, social, economic, industrial, the diplomatic—but one very important aspect had not been considered, i.e. the moral. In reality, is the Jewish state an entity that is worth having contact with? For one thing it was brought into existence by the United Nations which created it as a new entity where no Jewish entity had existed before. Besides, the UN's child has had a strange relationship with its parent body. The UN has rightly passed more resolutions condemning Israeli actions than all the condemnatory resolutions passed against all other member-states put together. Moreover, as of today, Israel is in violation of more UN resolutions than any other UN member.[20]

India during the 1980s granted full diplomatic status to the Palestine Liberation Organisation and reaffirmed India's unequivocal and unflinching support to the people of Arab-Palestine. India also appreciated the *Intifadeh* movement of the young Palestinian Arabs. Again, the Indian President R. Venkataraman, presented the prestigious Jawaharlal Nehru Award for International Understanding to the Palestinian leader Yasser Arafat. Even the former Prime Minister P.V. Narasimha Rao had reiterated that India's policy has been to render whatever help and support it could to achieve peace and also consistent and unequivocal support for the Arab-Palestinian people. However, it should be remembered that the policy just announced does in every way presage an anti-Palestinian posture. Furthermore, there is nothing special on which India could cooperate with Israel. Realism and flexibility are important, no doubt, in the conduct of a nation's foreign policy. But it should not be at the cost of India's inherent socio-political, moral and cultural foreign policy realities. It is argued that in concrete terms there are distinct advantages for India in establishing contacts with Israel in specific areas like military modernisation, agricultural improvement and investments of capitalist Jewish establishment.[21] In the field of agriculture and defence even US and former USSR had to seek technology from it itself had borrowed from the West particularly the US.[22] It is said that India could also benefit in countering terrorism. In the sphere of countering terrorism even UK and US have failed in checking Irish terrorists. Then, how can Israel provide India super technology to counter terrorism?

The argument that closer ties with Israel could give New Delhi much greater leverage in the West Asia peace process[23] is difficult to digest taking into consideration the day-to-day Israeli brutalities in the Israeli-occupied Arab territories. The atrocities inflicted on the Palestinian protagonists of the *Intifadeh*[24] have been documented by impartial Western observers. The democratic character of the State of Israel has not come in the way of draconian conduct. It is ironical that the successors of the victims of Hitler's persecution do not hesitate to adopt similar policies towards the Arab-Palestinians. The present decision of establishing ties with Israel is an "endorsement of Israel's aggressive policies in the illegally occupied Arab-Palestinian territories". Had India still insisted on genuine progress[25] in the Palestinian question as the sole criterion, it would have certainly raised India's prestige in the Afro-Asian and Arab world.[26]

Because Israel (sometimes) is known as the 51st state of the US (economic, military, political reasons) therefore only US can possibly alter Israel's current rigid stance. The UN's acceptance of PLO on observer's status was taken against Western policy which has a very powerful Jewish lobby. India does not have any extraordinary role in West Asian peace talks. After recognition of Israel, India's relations with that country have improved markedly under the Vajpayee government.

REFERENCES

1. India's image among Arab countries suffered as a result of the secret visit to India of former Israeli foreign minister Moshe Dayan in 1977 during Janata Party government period. *Patriot* (Delhi), 13 June 1980; *Statesman* (Delhi), 13 June 1980. Also, *New India* (New York), 27 April 1979.
2. As a nation Israel has evoked different shades of international opinion. It has been openly condemned for its oppressive policies. A few have supported it. India recognised Israel formally on 18 September 1950. It permitted Israel to open a consulate in Bombay to serve the needs of more than 50,000 Indian Jews who migrated to India. However, it chose not to have a consulate of its own in Tel Aviv and had not established full diplomatic relations till this year (1992). See *Indian Express* (Delhi), 27 January 1992.
3. The Arab-Palestinians want an Israeli withdrawal from the West Bank and Gaza Strip, seized from Jordan and Egypt in 1967 where they wish to establish an independent homeland. Israeli's are only willing to discuss limited self-rule for Palestinians. *Patriot* (Delhi), 22 September 1992.
4. M.S. Agwani, "US Cannot Determine our W. Asia Policy", *The Times of India* (Delhi), 14 February 1992.

5. India was one of the first countries to recognise Israel. See *India and Palestine: A Reply* (Delhi: Society for Parliamentary Studies, n.d.).
6. Quoted in *The Hindu* (Madras), 13 May 1949.
7. V.P. Dutt, *India's Foreign Policy* (Delhi: Vikas Publishing House, 1984), p. 329.
8. India has maintained a record of consistent support to the Arab-Palestinian cause which cannot be surpassed even by many of the Arab and Islamic states.
9. India supports the Arab-Palestinian cause not because it is an Arab cause but because it is a just one. Besides, Palestine the usual factors governing Indo-Arab relations, where the Indo-Pak confrontation, the cold war and its regional ramifications, and the concept of Islamic solidarity. See K.R. Singh, "Indian Strategic and Economic Interests in West Asia", in Satish Kumar, *Yearbook on India's Foreign Policy, 1983-84* (Delhi, Beverley Hills, New York, London: Sage Publications, 1986), p. 122.
10. Hundreds of thousands of Arab-Palestinians had been driven out of, or had fled their homes because of Israeli repression. For details see *Question of Palestine: Legal Aspects* (New York: United Nations, 1992). Also see Har Govind Pant, *India's Foreign Policy* (Jaipur: Panchsheel Prakashan, 1971), pp. 82-83.
11. G.S. Bhargava, *India and West Asia: A Survey of Public Opinion* (ed.) (Delhi: Popular Book Service, 1967), pp. 58-60.
12. *Indian Express*, 9 July 1982, *National Herald*, 12 July 1982, *Ceylon Daily News*, 10 July 1982, *The Hindu*, 9 July 1982.
13. *National Herald*, 12 July 1982.
14. *Patriot*, 9 September 1983.
15. *Patriot*, 3 December 1983 and *The Times of India*, 1 September 1984.
16. *Hindustan Times*, 6 November 1985.
17. Israeli ambassador Mr. Benjamin Netanyahu compared the atrocities by his country's troops in Israeli-occupied Arab-Palestinian territories with the "heavy toll of casualties" in the Golden Temple. See *Hindustan Times*, 18 December 1987.
18. *The Times of India*, 18 December 1987.
19. *National Herald*, 11 June 1988; 13 June 1988.
20. Indeed so bad are Israel's relations with the world organisation that Israel had tried its best to exclude the UN from the ongoing West Asian Peace Process. See *The Times of India*, 9 September 1991.
21. India and Israel had their first ministerial level meeting in New York on 23rd September 1992 (Wednesday) between the Minister of State for External Affairs Eduardo Faleiro and his Israeli counterpart Shimon Peres. At the meeting, the two sides discussed detailed agendas for cooperation in agriculture, technology, water management

and other economic areas. See *The Observer of Business and Politics* (Delhi), 25 September 1992, p. 16.

22. India and Israel signed their first industrial cooperation agreement, the *BBC* said quoting the Israeli defence forces radio.

    A permanent body would be set up for the exchange of information between industrialists' associations to increase trade and technological cooperation between the two countries. Quoted from *BBC* (London), 21 September 1992.

23. *Hindustan Times* (Delhi), 18 May 1980; and *Tribune* (Chandigarh), 12 June 1980.
24. See Yusif A. Sayigh, "The Intifada and the Balance of Power in the Region", *The International Spectator* (Rome), Vol. XXIII, No. 4, Oct.-Dec. 1988, pp. 203-214. Also see Franco Reyles, "Israel and the PLO: The Impact of the Intifeda", *International Spectator*, Oct.-Dec. 1988, pp. 215-229.
25. Palestinians in the Israeli occupied Arab-Palestinian territories are not openly optimistic about prospects for progress on the ongoing Arab-Israeli peace talks in Washington. See *The Middle East* (London), September 1992, p. 10.
26. In spite of raising relations up to full diplomatic level India still holds the view that premier Yitzhak Rabin's Israel must vacate occupied Arab-Palestinian lands and restore the inalienable rights of Arab-Palestinians.

39. India's Foreign Policy: Continuity and Some Change

Though the BJP-led Vajpayee Government has declared that continuity will be basic to the country's foreign policy, the changing political equations round the world, nevertheless, call for a fresh look.

Relations with neighbours on equal footing have always remained central to India's foreign policy, as have been relations with Afro-Asian countries.

The Bandung Conference of 1955 brought the countries of Asia and Africa together which had emerged as free nations from colonialism and imperialism and some in Afro-Asia, particularly the Palestinians who are still struggling for total independence.

Prime Minister Atal Behari Vajpayee has been fairly vocal on India's foreign policy, particularly on continuing the dialogue with Pakistan.

Vajpayee has said that the two countries must not remain mired in the past. The aid to terrorists in Kashmir, though disavowed by Pakistan, has caused tension in Indo-Pak relations. Pakistan should find a way of ending such interference.

Improving relations with Bangladesh, Nepal, Bhutan and Sri Lanka remain an important objective of Vajpayee's foreign policy. Some of these countries have become a safe sanctuary for anti-India terrorists and intelligence agencies.

On Afghanistan, India's largely inactive role in recent times may soon come to an end. India, which is not among the six nations invited to a UN-sponsored conference on Afghanistan being held in Turkmenistan's capital, Ashgabat, is watching the proceedings with more than detached interest.

"Till the previous government, there has been some shortfall in India's role in finding a political settlement to the conflict in Afghanistan. The BJP will certainly watch the outcome of the conference with interest to find out the implications for our security concerns and to see what role India can play in this regard", according to a member of the ruling BJP National Executive N.N. Jha.

Crisis-ridden Afghanistan has increasingly become a leading source of religious fundamentalism in various parts of the world in general and Kashmir in particular.

Speculations that India might change its Tibet policy were also set at rest by Vajpayee's first foreign policy announcement of there being "no change" in the country's China policy.

With faith in Panchsheel, India under Jawaharlal Nehru advocated, promoted and established close relations with China but India suffered at the very hands which it had been shaking for a long time.

There is also not much change in the Chinese attitude so far as its policy towards India is concerned.

In February 1996, armed Chinese intruders were seen deep in Indian territory in the central sector of the Indo-Tibetan border. They are still in occupation of India's territory in Aksaichin in Ladakh and the eastern region.

However, India's efforts to develop relations with the US in many fields have been successful and given rise to new hopes for the future.

US President Bill Clinton had taken an early initiative to establish a rapport between his administration and the BJP-led Government by deputing his permanent representative to the United Nations, Bill Richardson, who visited New Delhi for discussion with new Indian leaders.

President Clinton sent a congratulatory letter to Vajpayee through the US Embassy and followed it up with a phone call on March 20.

Clinton did not raise the issue of the new Government's decision to keep the nuclear option open. Clinton's gestures are being interpreted as his administration's policy to give greater importance to South Asia, particularly India and carry forward the "strategic dialogue" initiated by the two countries.

Clinton was also the first US President to visit India in two decades.

The new BJP-led Government has also called for expanding ties with Russia in all spheres. While the relations between the two countries have steadily improved in post-cold war era over the last decade, there is an urgent need to give a fresh political vigour to them.

As far as West Asian and African regions are concerned, India's decision to open full scale diplomatic relations with Israel did not surprise many since demand for the same had been made a number of times.

But India had been delaying the decision for the fear of annoying the friendly countries of people of West Asia and Arab-Africa, particularly the Palestinians.

With the recognition of the Palestine Liberation Organisation (PLO) by Israel and the signing of peace accords between some Arab States, Palestinians and Israel, India had also readjusted its policy and established diplomatic relations with Israel.

India has also tried to improve relations with Iran, Iraq, the Gulf region and Central Asian countries in recent years.

India has always worked for peace in the Arab-African world even while conflicts and wars have continued between the Arabs and the Israelis, besides the Gulf War of 1991.

India had sent its military and other missions of Korea, Laos, Vietnam, Congo, Somalia, South Africa, Maldives, Sri Lanka, Bangladesh and in other Afro-Asian states.

However, there is a concern in the Arab-African world about the new BJP-led government's close defence ties with Israel.

India has had increasingly close economic and political relations with the South-East Asian nations and Japan. Senior Indian diplomats in the region want the new government to keep the focus on the east and work out individual initiatives for each country.

Singapore is perhaps the largest trading partner for India and probably the least affected economy in the South East Asian region.

Japan, Korea and member countries of the Association of South East Asian Nations (ASEAN) are still the major markets and sources of foreign direct investments for India.

With Europe, economic, political and cultural relations, particularly with England, France, Germany have been consistent. In the economic field Britain had colonial ties with India, but after independence the economic relationship has remained intimate.

Britain still remains one of the leading trading partners of India.

The European economic community's participation in investments in India is quite encouraging. Efforts are afoot to encourage joint ventures and partnership between the European Union and India.

Reiterating India's commitment to rapid and sustainable development, Vajpayee has indicated that he will continue with the economic reforms process, strengthen macro-economic stability and harmonise demands of development and environment.

Vajpayee placed the country's total foreign policy in its broad perspective when he said in his reply to the confidence vote debate in the Lok Sabha that "A change in the Government does not mean a change in the country's foreign policy. Only the Minister has changed, the policy is the same".

40. Globalisation: A Case Study of Suez

Recent years have seen a sharp swing towards more liberal trade policies in the world economy. In the Afro-Asian world, the performance of socialist-oriented developing countries has not generally been outstanding. Excessively hasty, heavy industry-centred industrialisation drives have had, as their consequences, large accumulated foreign debts and trade deficits. The socialist economies demonstrated the ability to grow rapidly with massive mobilisation of human and material resources, an experience which also influenced policies in many developing countries of the Afro-Asian world. However, during the last two decades, there has occurred a serious deterioration in performance forcing a fundamental revaluation of comparative merits of different systems and an intensive search for an alternative and a good way of reaching it.[1] Political and economic changes that would have been dismissed as inconceivable only a few years ago have hastened economic transformation. That transformation has brought more radical changes in science and latest technology, in production methods and life-styles. Advances in telecommunications and data processing have helped to make the global village and global market a reality.[2] This paper examines the globalisation process in its historical perspective with special reference to Egypt. It also deals with the socio-politico and economic impact of the process on the Egyptian society.

Since the last two decades, the global economy has been going through several changes, the most pervasive of which have been in the realm of trade, technology and commerce. The essential feature of these changes has been the marked opening up of their economies by developing countries. Economic liberalisation was the distinct objective that was pursued and was indeed considered as the panacea for developing countries in economic crisis. Globalisation has been talked of in a large number of studies since the eighties. Globalisation, for the purpose of the present scenario, is inseparable from 'liberalisation' or 'privatisation' structural adjustment, or restructuring, or infitah.

They are the similar sides of a unified process. It is this unification, which distinguishes the present stage of globalisation from all earlier ones in the history of capitalism. Globalisation is not a new word. Recently it has become very popular and well-known term. It is a comprehensive term covering a wide variety of reforms. It means any capital outflow and inflow, frequent movement of trade and technology. It involves removal of various forms of regulation and control such as licences and permits as well as other barriers to investment. Globalisation covers a wide range of ideas, programmes and policies, both as economic theory and political practice. It has to be seen as an approach towards economic policy in a given political system, rather than a policy in itself.[3] Globalisation refers to the global dimension of every problem particularly the evolving world economy in all walks of life conceived as a large scale project, globalisation is the pivot of economic reforms being carried out by countries throughout the world. It envisages closer all-round integration of a developing economy with the international market. Such integration is sought not only through expanding trade and foreign direct investment, but also by way of free mobility of finance capital. With that target in view, it seeks a 'structural change' in the International Monetary Fund (IMF)-World Bank (IBRD) sense of it—in which the state is excluded from ownership of directly productive capital or from regulating private ownership and use of capital.

History, which until recently looked like repeating itself may, after all have taken a different turn. The fifty years from the end of the Second World War to the mid-1990s bear an uncanny resemblance to the five decades from the mid-1840s to the mid-1890s. At that time Europe had witnessed a generalised movement towards free trade from the repeal of Britain's Corn laws in 1846 to the depression of the 1870s and then an equally generalised return to protectionism.[4] Globalisation philosophy thus emerges from a historical perspective. This process has existed since the dawn of the "modern era". Globalisation began about five hundred years ago with the conquest of America by the colonial or Imperial empires of Europe. The process began as a result of the growth of the first colonial empires, such as those of England, Spain, France, and Portugal; the worldwide establishment of colonial and commercial networks controlled, more or less, by political or military powers; the opening up of new markets in peripheral areas; and the exploitation and extraction of raw materials for various purposes, including industrialisation and mechanisation.[5] The development of steamboats, trains and the telegraph during the nineteenth century facilitated the globalisation trend. Later, the invention, discovery and spread of new telecommunications systems such as the telephone, the radio, and more recently, television and computer—permitted a quantum leap towards a more unified planet. These developments led to profound changes with widespread socio-economic effects concerning local and global environment.[6]

In the historical and theoretical context, Adam Smith is said to be the author of the present policy of economic liberalisation. He was the greatest of the economic liberals. In his famous book *The Wealth of Nations*, Smith advocated a "system of natural liberty", in which each individual would be left free to pursue and advance his own interests. This system, Smith argued, would result in the greatest wealth both for the individual and for society. The greatest hindrance to economic progress was government, in Adam Smith's view. The "progress of opulence", according to Smith, is the direct result of three factors: division of labour, widening markets, and accumulation of capital. Accumulation of capital was seen as the key to economic and political expansion. Liberalisation in the nineteenth century began with intra-country trade (through such initiatives as the 1834 Italian customs unions). It then spread to international trade from the 1850s, through widespread tariff reductions embedded in a dense network of bilateral treaties. Revenue raising was an imperialist consideration as strengthening European nationalism required military expenditure.[7] Though the foundation of liberal economic policy was laid by Adam Smith, it reached the acme of its development with the writings of David Hume, James Mill and David Ricardo who in 1815 advocated free trade in grain. Their explanations of the international trade process have shaped the international economic policies of many countries.

Even in the Darwinian evolutionary theory of man, the essential message is one of gradual movement from imperfections to perfections, or from untruth to semi-truth. By the early years of the eighteenth century the political philosophers had developed a theory of liberal political democracy based on natural law precepts. An analysis of the economy in similar terms was next followed and culminated in the above Smithian writing i.e., *The Wealth of Nations*. The early period beginning from Torrens, Richardo and others of the early nineteenth century goes up to the second decade of the twentieth century when the work of Hecksher and Ohlin made an innovative breakthrough in the analytical approach to the understanding of international trade phenomena. Viewed in a broad setting, the extension of economic science to the phenomena of exchange between two nations in this early period implies an attempt to integrate the economic space into geographical space with location of production recognised as an important factor determining the nature of exchange. Ricardian framework was essentially his Labour of Value applied to international trade. It recognises the differences in technologies and demands conditions, as determinants of trade. It considers only one factor of production viz: Labour and assumes constant returns everywhere. Heckscher-Ohlin Theory or commonly known as Factor Proportions Theory—which came on the scene almost a century later after Richardo, essentially singles out differences between factor-endowments and factor-proportions as the determinants of the patterns of liberal trade.[8]

The last decade of the eighteenth century was significant for England. That fateful decade marked the beginning of a period, spanning nearly half a century of epochal significance for the British monetary system. The wars with France, which continued sporadically till Nepoleon's decisive defeat in 1815, the second half was characterised by economic and commercial changes. The system underwent a series of transformations culminating in the Bank Charter Act of 1644, which can be regarded as having firmly set the course for the globalisation system to evolve into its present form.[9] The British empire in the eighteenth century was extended politically, economically and territorically by the acquisition of Canada, Gibraltar, Malta, and Ceylon. Robert Clive and Warren Hastings achieved supremacy in India for the British. Captain James Cook explored the Pacific from Australia and New Zealand to California and Hawaii—for more than a decade. George Vancouver explored the northwest coast of America. James Bruce penetrated Africa in a daring expedition and found the source of the Egyptian Blue Nile. By 1900, all Africa was mapped, explored, estimated, divided and exploited between and by the European powers including Great Britain. Great Britain got possession of Egypt in 1882 and remained there in spite of the fact that Egypt was technically a part of the Turkish empire. The scramble for slaves, resources and territories led to war between France and Britain in 1898, when Colonel Marchand, while crossing Central Africa from the west coast, tried at Fashoda to seize the upper Nile. The British occupation of Egypt also embittered relations with France.

The western impact upon the modern Afro-Arab world, however, may be said to begin on the day in 1798 when Napoleon Bonaparte landed in Egypt with his army of invasion. Napoleon's real objective had been to strike at Britain's position in the East. His expedition had a lasting effect on Egypt, for it was more than a military affair. It was also a cultural incursion by the West into the heart of the Afro-Arab world. Napoleon also crushed the power of the established ruling class in Egypt during his brief campaign in that country. This paved the way for the rise to power of an Albanian Turkish military adventurer, Mehmet Ali. The historical significance of Mehmet Ali, the founder of modern Egypt, is that he was the first Afro-Arab potentate who sensed the significance of western technology and used it effectively to serve his purposes. Ali's accomplishments transformed Egypt into a formidable modern power. His plan was to create an Arab empire out of the Ottoman provinces. But this was not acceptable to Britain, which preferred the weak Ottoman empire rather than a strong Arab empire en route to India.

Mehmet Ali died in 1849 at the age of eighty and was succeeded by his incompetent and extravagant son, Ismail Pasha. Ismail's period in Egypt witnessed western military domination of that country and economic bankruptcy. During the sixteen years of Ismail's reign the European funded debt rose from 3 million to 68 million pounds. Another factor during this period was the opening up of the Suez Canal in 1869. This contributed more than any single factor to doom Egypt to western intervention, as also the fact that Egypt was in no position to repay its debts to these western nations. Yet the Suez Canal was not the immediate cause of the first intervention of the Europeans in Egypt's government since 1798. It came about because of actions and policies of Ismail during whose period Egypt was the happy hunting ground for the vampire-like financiers of Europe. Having spent 4 million pounds on the Suez Canal, the British government naturally took greatest interest in Egypt than ever before. When Ismail Pasha became ruler, in 1863, the price of cotton, Egypt's main export, was high because of the American Civil War. Ismail's financial prospects, therefore, looked good. Unfortunately, his financial management left plenty to desire. The results were to be seen in the rise in the Egyptian national debt; 700,000 pounds at Ismail Pasha's accession, it stood at nearly 100,000,000 pounds thirteen years later. The interest charges amounted to 5,000,000 pounds a year in an age when such sums still mattered. In 1876 the Egyptian government was bankrupt and ceased to pay its debts.

The outcome was that Egypt was forced to accept an international Public Debt Commission, headed by two foreign controllers, one British, one French. This body was installed to make sure that Egypt was governed by Ismail's son with the priority of keeping up revenue and paying off the debt. The above body saw to it that all obligations were promptly met, but the country and its people were bled white in the process. The total revenue in 1877 amounted to 9,543,000 pounds of which 7,473,000 pounds had to be paid out for the service of the debt, and other amounts, for fixed obligation such as the annual tribute to the Sultan. Only a little over 1 million was left for the administration of the country, a sum that was patently inadequate. Under these circumstances a nationalist revolt broke out in 1882 under the leadership of an Egyptian army officer, Ahmad Arabi. The British became the prime targets of nationalist hatred in Egypt. It was also directed against the ruling Khedive and the Turkish oligarchy that monopolised all the senior posts in both the army and the bureaucracy. After some rioting and loss of life in Alexandria, a British fleet bombarded the fortifications of Alexandria in July 1882, and two months later an expeditionary force landed in Egypt and defeated Arabi. The British expeditionary force remained there to become an army of occupation. No British statesman, liberal or conservative, at that time contemplated a permanent occupation of Egypt which was still a Turkish province; but, on the other hand, Britain was determined to secure an absolute guarantee of the security of the Suez Canal, which implied the non-interference of any other power in Egypt and the restoration of administrative and financial order in that country. Six years after the British occupation of Egypt, the maritime powers of Europe (in 1888) signed a convention securing the conditions for free transit through the Suez Canal in peace and war.[10] The Suez Canal was 'the jugular vein' of the British empire, as Ernest Bevin, British Labour Party's foreign secretary (1945-51) later described it. Great Britain not only occupied Egypt but seemed likely to make its occupation permanent despite frequent promises to withdraw. Indeed, from the opening of the waterway in 1869, British-flagged vessels passing through the Suez accounted on an average for 70 per cent or more of the total, tying the metropole to India, East Africa, Gulf region and Australia. At present the Suez Canal is the main source of Egyptian foreign currency, the third after the petroleum revenue and savings of Egyptians working abroad. In 1982, the Suez Canal revenues amounted to 956 million pounds. The canal has got a vital strategic position.

It is one of the geographical, political and informational landmarks of Egypt. The idea of creating a canal linking the Mediterranean to the Red Sea is a very old one that dates back to 4000 years when the Ancient Egyptians thought of linking the two seas using the river Nile and its branches.[11] Dug by Ferdinand De Lesseps in 1854, Suez is the first man-made canal in the service of European global trade and at present is the biggest navigation canal between East and West. The Suez Canal is a sea level canal and is a great commercial bridge. The banks of this canal are protected against the great wash generated by the transit of ships by rivetments of hard stones and steel piles corresponding to the nature of soil in every area. On both sides of the canal there are mooring bollards every 125 miles for the mooring of vessels in case of emergency and kilometric sign posts helping locate the position of ships in the waterway. There are eleven signal stations along the western bank of the canal, each of which is about 10 kilometre apart from the other in addition to a traffic office in Port-Said and Port Taw Fik and the main office in Ismalia. These offices are to control traffic and facilitate pilotage operations.

The opening of Suez Canal in 1869 was of immense importance to world trade. The geographical position of the Suez Canal has made it the shortest navigable route between the East and West as compared with the route of the Cape of Good Hope. It shortens the distance between countries situated to the north of the canal and those situated to South, thus offering considerable economic benefits in cost operations, time and fuel oil. The canal is run in a convoy system to transit at a fixed speed and a fixed distance between every two passing ships. The Suez Canal pilots are credited with piloting ships from the time they arrive at the roadsteads till they exit at the other end of the canal to the open sea. It takes the ship from 12 to 16 hours to transit the canal. The numerical capacity of the canal is about 76 ships per day.[12] It is the third longest international waterway, following the Lawrence passage in North America and the Baltic Sea canal in the former Soviet Union. It is also considered the main artery connecting the production centres in Western Europe to the consumer markets in South and East Asia. As mentioned above, passage through the Suez Canal saves 17 to 66 per cent of the distance and 58 to 75 per cent of fuel, all to the advantage of international trade. It becomes the fourth tributary in the Egyptian balance of payment and is considered as a cash pump, gives around 5.5 million dollars every day to the Egyptian economic system.[13] And so Britain came to control Egypt in every respect—economically, politically and militarily.

In the pursuit of its colonial and imperial aims, Britain was led by the hard logic of facts to gradually establish a veiled protectorate which, after the outbreak of the First World War in December 1914, it converted by proclamation into a 'de jure' protectorate. Egypt was placed under British colonial marital law right through the war. British officials were thus virtually running the administration of the country while, to the South, Anglo-Egyptian rule had been pushed deep into the Sudan. With the growth of foreign trade a new nationalist middle class arose in Egypt and this class became the backbone of new Egyptian nationalism. Out of this emerged Saad Zaghlul Pasha, arguably the greatest of modern Egyptian leaders. Zaghlul Pasha had served under Arabi Pasha and worked for Egyptian independence till his death in 1927. Zaghlul Pasha demanded autonomy for Egypt from the British and wanted to lead a big delegation to London and Paris to plead for Egyptian independence but permission was refused and he was arrested in March 1919. This led to a bloody nationalist revolt. Though this revolt was contained by the Britain it was far from suppressed. In 1922 Britain proclaimed Egypt "an independent sovereign state" but reserved for itself control of foreign affairs and of external security, as well as protection of minorities and of foreign interests and Suez Canal.[14] The nationalists under Zaghlul's leadership rejected this fake independence and continued the struggle. Finally in 1936 a compromise settlement was reached with the signing of a twenty-years alliance treaty. Britain undertook to end its military occupation of the country and to arrange for Egypt's admission to the League of Nations. In return, Egypt agreed to stand by British in time of war, to accept the British garrison stationed for the defence of the Suez Canal; and also to continue the joint British-Egyptian administration of Sudan. Nationalist leaders were far from satisfied with this settlement. But they accepted it as the best available under the circumstances, but they waited for the first opportunity to abolish the hated remnants of foreign control.

In the 1936 treaty on Suez, the British retained the right to maintain up to 10,000 troops in the canal zone. At the end of a period of twenty years after the signing of the treaty i.e., after 1956, there had to be agreement on the future shape of the Suez Canal zone. Although Egypt strove to remain neutral in the Second World War it became a battle ground between British and Axis forces. On 23 September 1945 the Egyptian government demanded that British military occupation of Egypt and Suez be terminated and that the Sudan be transferred to full Egyptian control. In face of growing anti-British agitation, the British government announced its readiness to withdraw its forces from Egypt. However, after breaking off negotiations with Great Britain for revision of the 1936 treaty, the then Egyptian government decided to refer the question to the newly born world organisation—the United Nations. But the Egyptian effort in 1947 failed to accomplish any positive result.[15] At the end of the Second World War, Egypt was moving steadily towards a nationalist revolution. British had maintained a presence in Egypt primarily because of the Suez Canal. Since London's interest in Egypt had seemed to Egyptians essentially exploitative, many Egyptian nationalists including Nasser and other young army officers who were to become so important after the end of this war, hoped that the Germans would be successful in driving the

British from Cairo, Suez and eventually from all of Egypt. Consequently, when the war ended, many Egyptians felt a disappointment akin to that experienced by nationalists among the undefeated powers. Every effort made by the Egyptian government to secure a compromise with the British was criticized violently. This criticism developed in spite of the fact that such compromises were aimed at lessening the British hold on Egyptian affairs. Apparently nothing short of the exodus of all foreign forces would satisfy the average Egyptian. By the end of 1948 Egypt was in turmoil.

The Wafd Party, which had been the spearhead of mass revolt against the British since the 1920s, won the election in 1950. Then, in a desperate attempt to gain the backing of a majority of Egyptian people, the Wafd turned guerrilla forces against the British troops in the Suez zone and in 1951 denounced the Anglo-Egyptian agreement of 1986. Nationalists revolts now flared up throughout Egypt and merged with protests against an anachronistic social system. The British cruiser *Liverpool* fired on Port Said as British troops clashed with Egyptian nationalist guerrillas on 18 January 1952. This was followed by riots in Cairo, which brought death to over twenty people and wholesale destruction of foreign properties. Thus the mob turned against the upper starts of pro-West Egyptian society and at the same time it lashed out at foreign control. After Cairo riots in January 1952, King Farouk's regime of Egypt appeared to be disintegrating rapidly. Urged to action by the prospect of a tottering government, Lieutenant Colonel Gamal Abdel Nasser (1918-1970), organized a *Free Officer's Committee*. In the early hours of 23 July 1952, the above committee became active as the Farouk regime seemed to be disintegrating. Tanks were moved to strategic locations in Cairo and the centres of civil administration were taken over. There was virtually no opposition to *Free Officer's* seizure of power. King Farouk was forced into exile. In June 1953, the Egyptian monarchy was abolished and General Mohammad Naguib became the President and Prime Minister of the newly born Republic. By 1954, Nasser obtained, subject to certain rights of re-entry, British evacuation of the Suez Canal zone.[16]

The fear of communism in the 1950s forced Washington to pressurize London to reach a settlement on the basis of the Suez Canal zone that would be acceptable to Egypt. Under the new

Anglo-Egyptian agreement, which was signed on 19 October 1954, Britain agreed to evacuate the canal zone.

The successful outbreak of Egyptian revolution in 1952 and emergence of a young nationalist, Gamal Abdel Nasser provided the historic opportunity in throwing off the remnants of British colonialism. The year 1956 saw the ascendancy of Egypt in the Afro-Arab world. Nasser's programme of social reform and Afro-Arab nationalism looked like a model for wide acceptance among emerging and revolutionary Afro-Arab nations. Nasser urged the Afro-Arab masses to oppose the stooges of imperialism and warned pro-western regimes to stay away from imperialist military pacts. He became increasingly convinced that Afro-Asian countries must avoid alignments with great powers. Nasser's prestigious arms deal with the Soviets after the western bluff, endorsed Egypt's proclaimed independence from western influence. The deal signified the elimination of the western arms monopoly and the manifestation of Afro-Arab independence. An Egyptian arms deal with Czechoslovakia on the security of the cotton crop and the Egyptian recognition of communist China prompted serious thoughts in the West and in the US about Nasser. By way of indicating displeasure, an American and British initial offer to finance the cherished project of the construction of a high dam on the Nile, was withdrawn. As a riposte, Nasser seized the assets of the private western company which owned and ran the Suez Canal, saying its profits should finance the dam. On 13 June 1956 the 74-year British occupation of the Suez Canal ended, with the withdrawal of the last British forces from the Suez Canal zones, leaving Egypt with full responsibility for the defence of the canal. On 26 July 1956, Egyptian President Nasser's nationalization of the Suez Canal immediately led to feverish attempts by western colonial powers to thwart him.[17] After talks in London, Britain, France and the US called a conference of most interested nations to discuss Egypt's action on the Suez Canal. Egypt refused to attend the same. British Prime Minister Eden announced a British-French-US agreement to establish an association to operate the canal, but Nasser dubbed this as an attempt to provoke war. On 31 October 1956 France and Britain vetoed UN Security Council resolution to refrain from the use of force and opened bombardments of Cairo and the Suez Canal area. From Nasser's perspective, the nationalization had two objectives: to provide foreign exchange for Egypt to build the dam and pursue its developmental plans; and to demonstrate that small countries need no longer accept open insults and degradation from great powers. The British and French protected over the seizure of the Suez Canal. They, in collaboration with Israel, attacked Egypt in October 1956. The Suez affair was disastrous for western interests in the Afro-Arab world. When Egypt was invaded, the entire Afro-Arab-Asian world, including India, felt and acted in unison. The Soviet Union threatened action to end the Suez fighting and the US President Eisenhower ordered a global alert of the US armed forces. The British government accepted the UN ceasefire, followed by Israel and France, and the UN created an emergency force (UNEF) to supervise the ceasefire and the withdrawal of the invaders.[18] The support that Nasser received during the Suez crisis from the Afro-Arab-Asian world was considerable and this gave credibility to his policies, not only in his country but throughout the world.

The nationalisation of Suez Canal by President Nasser made him the anti-colonialist hero of the Afro-Asian continent. Nasser emerged as one of the greatest leaders of the modern period in the Third World. His policies made the Afro-Arabs in general and Egyptians in particular, an important factor in international politics. Nasser's policy gave new impetus to the anti-colonial drive in which Egypt has since participated more actively and effectively.[19] By regaining the Suez Canal the Egyptian people dealt a stunning blow to European imperialism and their global monopolies. By their admirable steadfastness and their bitter fighting against the colonial invaders, the Egyptian people managed to shake the conscience of the world and stir it in a manner unprecedented in modern history.[20] The outstanding Suez battle marked a decisive turn in the history of liberation movements. The striving people, who had been facing the mighty tyrants alone, became no longer alone. The bitter defeat of imperialism in the Suez war has put an end to the age of armed imperialist adventures. The Suez crisis had also brought about a 'close friendship and understanding' between Nehru and Nasser. A testimony of Nehru's goodwill towards Egypt is provided by a letter written by him to Nasser shortly before the ceasefire came into effect, "Recent developments indicate definitely that the tide has turned in favour of Egypt. I am sure that this process will continue and not only bring relief to Egypt but ultimate removal of all aggression wherever it may come from. I shall like to congratulate you on this turn of events and to assure you that we shall stand by the independence of Egypt".[21]

REFERENCES

1. Stalislaw Gomulks, Young-chool Ha, Cae-one Kim, *Economic Reforms in the Socialist World* (Hampshire: The Macmillan Press, 1986), p. 2.
2. Hari Shankar Singhania, *Economic Issues Global and National: A Business Perspective* (New Delhi: Vikas Publishing House (Pvt.) Ltd., 1995), p. 9.
3. Asha Gupta, 'Privatisation: An economic device or a political strategy', *The Journal of Institute of Public Enterprises*, April-June 1996, p. 38.
4. Andre Bolthe, 'The return of free trade?, *International Affairs* (London), Vol. 72, No. 2, April 1996, p. 247.
5. H.G. Wells, *A Short History of the World* (New York: Penguin Books), p. 295. Also see Jagdish P. Sharma, *World History: New Horizons* (New Delhi: Low Price Publications, 1993), p. 62.
6. Danilo J. Anton, *Diversity, Globalisation and the Ways of Nature* (Singapore: International Development Research Centre, 1995), p. 3.
7. Andre Bolthe, *op. cit.*, pp. 249 and 253.
8. Devendre Thakur (ed.), *Globalisation and International Business* (New Delhi: Deep and Deep Publications, 1995), p. 173.
9. *Economic and Political Weekly* (Mumbai), 27 July 1996.
10. T.W. Riker, *A Short History of Modern Europe* (New York: The Macmillan Co., 1935), p. 609.
11. Mahmoud Fawzi, *Suez 1956: An Egyptian Perspective* (London: Shorouk International, 1986), p. 9.
12. *The Suez Canal* (Arab Republic of Egypt: Ministry of Information, State Information Service).
13. *Arab Republic of Egypt Year Book 1995* (Ministry of Information, State Information Service), p. 149.
14. Michael Adams, *The Middle East—A Handbook* (London, 1971), p. 324.
15. William L. Langer (ed.), *An Encyclopaedia of World History* (London: Harrap Limited, 1987), p. 1293.
16. Walter C. Lansam, Otis C. Mitchell, *The World Since 1919* (New York: The Macmillan Co.), p. 673.
17. Mohamed H. Heikal, *Cutting the Lion's Tail: Suez Through Egyptian Eyes* (London: Andre Deutsch, 1986), p. 121.

18. William L. Langer, *op. cit.*, p. 1283.
19. Jagdish P. Sharma, *The Arab Mind: A Study of Egypt, Arab Unity and the World* (New Delhi: H.K. Publishers, 1990), p. 148.
20. *Nasser Speaks: Basic Documents* (London: The Morssett Press, 1972), p. 147.
21. S. Gopal, *Jawaharlal Nehru: A Biography, 1947-1956*, Vol. II (New Delhi: Oxford University Press, 1979), p. 287.

APPENDIX I: Influence of Suez Canal in Shortening the Distance between Countries

From	To	Distance in miles		
		Round Africa	Through canal	Diff.
Rotterdam (north west Europe)	Bombay (India)	10850	6337	4513
Piracus (Greece) ...	Jeddah (Red Sea)	11410	1320	10090
New York (USA) ...	Singapore	12430	10169	2261

Source: The Suez Canal, Ministry of Information, State Information Service, p. 7.

APPENDIX II: Net Tonnage of Transiting Ships in 1993 as Compared to 1992

Category	1992			1993			Diff.
	Number	Net ton (000) tons	%	Number	Net ton (000) tons	%	
Tankers	3153	118154	32.0	3193	137879	34.8	+19725
Bulk carriers	2829	55885	15.1	3329	65698	16.6	+9813
Combined carners	307	15959	4.3	224	10982	2.8	+4977
General cargo ships	4104	30971	8.4	4335	31044	7.8	+73
Container ships	3482	93152	25.1	3656	100913	25.4	+7761
Lash ships	83	2724	0.7	73	2353	0.6	-371
Ro/Ro ships	604	12537	3.4	465	9635	2.4	+2905
Car carners	816	34290	9.3	752	31250	7.9	+3040
Passenger ships	45	519	0.4	66	799	0.2	+280
War ships	188	1666	0.5	177	1934	0.5	+268
Others	1018	3922	1.1	1047	4063	1.0	+141
Total	16629	369779	100	17317	396550	100	+141

New Challenges in Arab-Africa

41. Is Religious Fundamentalism on the Rise?

The recent car bomb explosions in Algeria killing 12 and injuring more than 30, assassination attempt on President Hosni Mubarak of Egypt and statements from a splinter group of Jihad urging Egyptian army to join extremists in toppling Mubarak's government—all these indicate that religious fundamentalism in the Arab-Maghreb region is on a rising trend.

Over the past decade, governments throughout the world, especially in the north African region, have been increasingly challenged by the fundamentalist forces based on Islamic propaganda.

Prime Minister Narasimha Rao at a special UN session categorised terrorism in the name of religion as the "world's great danger". After the collapse of communism, religious or Islamic fundamentalism is viewed as a major threat to world peace and security.

Dr. Esposito of the College of the Holy Cross, USA, says Islamic fundamentalism is most forceful in Algeria, Egypt, Tunisia, Sudan, Jordan, Bahrain and Iran as it has moved from the periphery of Islamic life to the centre. It is no longer marginal but a part of the Islamic mainstream.

Various social, economic and political factors contribute to the rise of traditionalist sentiments in the world. The most important of these, which appears to be relevant to both industrialised and developing countries, is the increased search for communal solidarity and identification.

In western industrialised countries, the problem stems from the growing feeling that socio-economic changes, represented by capitalist market economy and technological developments, have led to a growing abstraction of socio-political institutions that mediate between individuals and society.

The development of a radical Islamist movement has been a major feature of Algerian socio-political life since the mid-1970s and especially since the death of President Houari Boumediene in December, 1978.

A central element of the Islamists' project has been the re-conquest of the religious sphere and its reconstitution as a sphere autonomous of the state. An equally central element of the 'Islamist mission' has been the notion, "To command that which is proper and forbid that which is reprehensible to Islam".

Robbed of its election victory in Algeria (1990), the Islamic Salvation Front (FIS) has been banned and suppressed. In January, 1992, the then governing high state council of Algeria cancelled the elections on the eve of victory for the Islamic forces, saying that the radicalists would never allow another election if they won.

Since then, fighting between the Algerian authorities and the Islamic Salvation Front has taken 65,000 lives including the assassination of President Boudiaf and other leaders, intellectuals and journalists.

It was only on January 25 this year the leadership of the outlawed Islamic Salvation Front sent a letter to the newly elected President Liamine Zeroual proposing a dialogue without pre-conditions.

Islam's appeal in Algeria has grown because of economic hardships, political failure and social unrest that the country underwent after independence.

The urban riots of October, 1988 were a spontaneous reaction to the rising unemployment among the youth and the shattering of social and political expectations.

Unemployment rose up to 30 per cent of working population in 1933. Inflation rose from 9.9 per cent in 1990 to 16.5 per cent in 1991. The per capita income declined from 2,752 dollars in 1987 to 1,607 dollars in 1991.

The atrocities and violence which rocked the country are not only the outcome of the clandestine groups acting in the name of Islam. The strength of the fundamentalist appeal in Algeria owes much to the French colonial legacy which has resulted in a number of unsolved problems and independent Algeria's authoritarian Arab-Islamic socialism.

Many leading observers also trace the origin of Algerian

extremism to the decade and half long Afghan civil war where the American CIA and the Pakistani ISI assembled a large number of motivated volunteers to fight in Afghanistan.

Algeria was one of the countries that gained from the oil boom. The hardened and conditioned veterans of the Afghan war who went back, formed the core of the militants in Algeria.

Since the botched 1990 elections, Algeria has been in a state of low intensity civil war between the FIS, now underground and the security forces. Scores have been killed on both sides. 'It is simply for Algerians to say what kind of society they want', said Malik Ait-Aoudia, an official of the assembly for culture and democracy, a secularist political party.

"The Islamists and their political programmes don't represent merely an insurrection. Islamism is an assault on Algerian society, with its shock troops in the past three years busy killing women, intellectuals, artists, pupils and professors, journalists and artisans", Ait-Aoudia said.

But the situation in Algeria is only illustrative of a worldwide trend. Forces of religious fundamentalism seem to be increasingly challenging lawful governments, particularly North Africa. It's for the people now to stem the tide.

42. Algeria: Emerging Trends

Poised on the brink of major socio-politico-economic transformations, governments and societies in the West Asian and North African region are facing critical decisions that will have significant national and international reverberations. Reflecting upon the past month's pre-occupations and flashpoints of the Algerian scene, the picture that emerges is one of socio-politico-economic uprising that has dominated the regional scene since the 1980s.

The current crisis in Algeria (where a spontaneous outburst of rage and protest left a shocking toll of about 500 people dead) becomes clearer when we view it in its Third World context. Over thirty years after decolonisation and independence most of the Third World countries including Algeria have failed to build strong and stable socio-economic systems. Most of them have dictatorial, autocratic or theocratic governments, based on tribal or ethnic or religious foundations. In the case of Algeria, Ahmed Ben Bella emerged as the head of Algeria's first government after Algeria's exhausting war for independence from France, which came to an end on July 5, 1962.

After a legendary career of sacrifice as a freedom-fighter, Ben Bella emerged as the greatest hero of his day and was close to President Gamal Abdel Nasser of Egypt. However, his government which was committed to the Nasserist socialist policies was unable to bring order to the post-independence chaos. The economic plight of the country was severe. A few years later, the scene changed. In June 1965, Ben Bella was toppled in a Palace coup by the then Minister of Defence, Colonel Houari Boumediene, who ruled Algeria until his unexpected death, on December 27, 1978. Boumediene tried his best to establish a disciplined and effective government and to put the country on the road to economic development financed by oil and gas revenues.

Boumediene's Algeria went on along the non-aligned, socialist course within the Third World. After Boumediene's death, Colonel Chadli Benjedid, the military commander of the Oran region, succeeded as President in independent Algeria's first Peaceful succession. He declared that he would continue to uphold the policies of Boumediene, that is, the option of 'socialism' and 'national independence' in both the political and economic sphere. For a time, Benjedid, enjoyed a period of stable rule. In course of time he began to reverse the rigorously socialist and ambitious economic policies pursued by his predecessor.

He released Ben Bella and other opponents of the Boumediene regime and allowed them to go abroad (October 1980). He also gradually steered the country along a more pragmatic and less ideological course, by cautiously liberalising the political life, reorganising the country's only political party, the National Liberation Front (NLF) to make it more responsive to popular needs, encouraging private enterprise and loosening the regime of austerity imposed by his predecessor. But the years that followed have been somewhat sterile so far as the economic development of the country is concerned. Slowly, it has started dawning that Algeria is not able to cope with the day-to-day problems of development.

Today, the bright promise that Algeria holds has been greatly dimmed by a complex web of social and economic ills. The country is very much in the grip of the classic Third World syndrome, namely, sharply rising prices, the scarce supply and mobilisation of goods, high unemployment, rampant corruption, payment of kickbacks, bribery, wide gap between rich and poor and a flourishing black market besides the scourge of drought and invasions by locusts. The decaying infrastructure, the housing crisis and the population explosion are also some of Algeria's most pressing problems. A majority of its population is without adequate accommodation, sanitation facilities, drinking water, or electricity.

Further, it is estimated that Algeria like other Third World countries is dependent on foreign aid to an extent of 60 per cent of its basic needs including food, military equipment, oil drilling, refining and infrastructure of modernisation. Algeria's debt problem is particularly on the rise in the economic and military fields. This represents a three to four-fold increase compared with the amounts raised in the 1970s. Again, the industrial production has been reduced by about one half, resulting in the emigration of Algerians to the West and the Gulf in search of employment.

In the case of energy policy, there are two different styles—one for oil, the other for natural gas. The gas is not that expensive in Algeria. But the cost is driven up by the elaborate process of liquifying it, carrying it to the West and converting it back into gas. Unfortunately, the two are inconsistent with each other. Coupled with this, the politics of super power's aid particularly the US aid and the US government delays in approving projects and enormous development problems have also contributed to the present sad state of economic affairs.

In the agricultural sector and elsewhere, the progress remains negative. It is due to the inefficiency of the state-run distribution and marketing systems. The government agencies involved have shown a distressing disregard for both consumer and producer and the system has worked very poorly. Meanwhile, Algeria, like other Third World countries, continues to maintain a 3.2 per cent annual increase in its birth rate, already one of the highest in the world, which accounts for youth unemployment of more than 40 per cent. The young men in the poor districts have little to do but lounge against walls during the day, watching the world go by.

The high cost of living with demand exceeding supply, and the lack of future prospects, make a fertile breeding ground for insurrection. It was not surprising here that Islamic fundamentalists played a leading role in fomenting trouble in different towns and gave the riots a politico-religious orientation by calling for sweeping socio-political-economic reforms in the existing system.

Today, a state of immobilisation rather than one of stability prevails in Algeria. The Government, by the sheer force of coercion and repression will no longer be able to cope with the situation. Socio-economic change and natural erosion of power at the end of each and every recent generation coupled with the aspirations of the masses for political freedom, social justice and economic equality, all contributed to ripen the conditions for a change in the state.

The proposed reforms can be materialised into reality provided the following objectives are taken into account by the rulers of Algeria, namely, on the *political front* by dismantling the system of internal oppression and acknowledging the basic human political rights. On the *economic front*, by rationalising the economic behaviour through treating the national wealth as a social and not as a family or clan possession. At the *national level*, establishing a minimum basis of inter-state cooperation and collective action by ending inter-state rivalries through negotiation and compromise. On the level of *international relations* by maintaining a common United Arab Front in all international dealings.

43. Islamic Fundamentalism in Africa

The post-Cold War period witnessed significant changes throughout the world. Historic changes have overtaken the past. The mind boggling developments of the recent decades are all pervasive, engulfing science, technology, literature, art, politics, international relations and above all, human concepts, values and standards. The ongoing transformation has the potential to change the face of the plant. Threats and challenges equally bedevil the achievements. Military and economic globalisation, bilateral conflicts and frictions, trans-border terrorism, ethnic violence, political suppression, overt and covert support to religious fanaticism, all divert energy of Afro-Asian states and create conditions for destabilisation by developed nations. Events in the last two decades like the Islamic revolution in Iran, the Rushdie affair, the Gulf War, an attempt to assassinate President Hosni Mubarak of Egypt in Ethiopia while he was at Addis Ababa to attend a meeting of the Organisation of African Unity (OAU) and the recent Hamas bombings in West Asia followed by counter-Israeli violence and other incidents, including the terrorist violence and killings in the name of religion in Kashmir and Afghanistan and in other regions, have threatened the very fabric of world society. Opposition groups, articulating themselves in Islamic terms, have, recent years, created havoc with political structures and economies of most North and East African countries, notably Algeria, Egypt, Sudan, Morocco, to a great extent, and Tunisia, Libya, Somalia, Eritrea and Ethiopia, to some extent.

With a total population of over 680 million, Africa is the second largest continent in the world. The continent comprises 54 independent countries—nearly one-third of the membership of the United Nations. A new chapter in the history of Africa began to unfold in 1991 with the dismantling of the *apartheid* system in South Africa. It had special significance for India as South African Indians had been in the forefront of the struggle against *apartheid*. Eritrea won its independence after Africa's longest war; the regime of Mengistu Haile Mariam collapsed in Ethiopia giving way to the adoption of the constitution of the Federal Democratic Republic of Ethiopia by the Ethiopian constituent assembly on 8 December 1994, which has brought country into the democratic framework;[1] and Siyad Barre's over in Somalia was followed by extremely violent inter-clan co lawlessness and foreign intervention. The year 1991 also marked decline of the strategic value of the region to the major powers. American military intervention in Somalia was an interlude. It was partly caused by the creation of a Somali Islamic Organisation *Al-Ithad* which, in June 1992, occupied many towns including the important port of Basaco.[2]

In fact, after the collapse of communism, religious or Islamic fundamentalism is viewed as a major threat to world peace security. The world media, particularly the western or American have shown great interest in the events, especially the development in West Asia and Africa. The western media is largely seen by Muslim as a negative influence. Very often the news that we read about Muslim centres gives negative projections. It is such negative images that portray the image of Islam as the new enemy after Communism. It is hardly surprising Israel, and Pro-Israeli intellectuals and publicists like Samuel Hunting in the West, are in the forefront of the scare campaign against "green" or "Islamic peril", because for almost a century now the western attempt to create and protect an intrusive zionist state in the human of the Arab-African world is one of the prime causes of misunderstanding between Islam and Christianity.[3] Unfortunately, the above theoretical postulation continues to dominate US foreign policy *vis-a-vis* Africa. Washington fears that Sudan, backed by Islamic Iran, might became a 'new Lebanon' using militant groups to export Islamic revolution across Africa. Thus, the Clinton administration was reported to be braced itself to provide help to Ethiopia and Eritrea.[4] Sudan is seen as a heaven and a launching pad for radical Islamic groups across Africa. Sudan is constantly branded as a state aiding and abetting "international terrorism", and it is even listed by the US State Department, together with Iran, Iraq, Syria, Libya, North Korea and Cuba, as a "terrorist state", although Sudan has fully cooperated with France and the US in the extradition of the famous extremist Carlos.[5] The US has launched a clandestine campaign against Iran and the US

Congress has appropriated $25 million for the purpose presumably as a part of psychological warfare against Iran. They also dismissed Iran's condemnation of terrorism as false. President Clinton went to the extent of pledging $100 million to Israel to fight terrorism but not to put an end to the Israeli oppression, blockade collective punishment and occupation of the Palestinian land and resources.

In 1993, a group called *Jihad Eritrea* launched an attack against the Eritrean government soldiers in an area close to the Sudanese-Eritrean Border. On 22 February 1995, at least 11 people were killed and more than 150 wounded when Muslim factions opened fire on each other outside Addis Ababa's Grand Anwar Mosque. At the beginning of 1995, Islamic law was enforced in northern Mogadishu (Somalia), nominally controlled by the Somali warlord, Ali Mahdi Mohammed. In Djibouti, more and more women are being forced to wear the veil.[6] In the case of Algeria, the development of a radical Islamic movement has been a major feature of Algerian socio-political life since the mid-1970s, and especially since the death of President Houari Boumediene in December 1978. The resort to violence has been an inevitable corollary of the Islamists in Algeria. A central element of the Islamists' project has been carrying out the injunction which is notionally binding on every Muslim, 'to command that which is proper and forbids that which is reprehensible to Islam'. They frequently behaved as self-appointed censors of public morals, notably in relation to women deemed to be immodestly dressed. Their tendency to employ violence expresses the absolutist character of the Islamist movement itself in so far as it conceives of itself as the nucleus of the true *Umma* engaged in an unrelenting struggle against the anti-Islamic tendencies. Algeria has experienced dramatic consequences as a result of the army's decision to break up the political process which began with the legislative elections in 1991, thus forcing the departure of President Chadli Benjedid and overturning the results of the first ballot, which would have given the conservative Islamic Salvation Front (FIS) the majority of seats in the next Algerian Parliament.[7] Since then, fighting between the Algerian authorities and the Islamic Salvation Front has taken 80,000 lives including the assassination of President Boudiaf, and other leading leaders and intellectuals and journalists.

The newly chosen leader of Egypt's most powerful Islamic

movement, *The Muslim Brotherhood*, predicted that his group would establish an Islamic mega-state within the next 30 years. "The goal of the Brotherhood is simple", the groups Supreme Guide Mostafa Mashour was quoted recently as saying in an interview with the London-based *Al-Hayat* daily. "We are working for the establishment of an international Islamic State before a century has passed since the group was set up 70 years ago", he added.[8] The radicalist threat took a serious shape in Egypt in 1992 when a small war broke out between the state and the *Gamaat Islamiya*, the Islamic groups, as the loosely organised underground forces of political Islam call themselves. The armed Islamic bands treated the country to a season of wrath and troubles,[9] but the Egyptian authorities fought back, jailing its leaders. The state showed little mercy towards the insurgents. It pushed their challenge to remote, marginal parts of the country, provincial towns in middle and upper Egypt, the country's poorest areas. The state apparatus was given a green light to root out armed Islamic groups and to do it without the kind of restraints a lawful society honours and expects. The crackdown came after President Hosni Mubarak accused the Islamic militants of backing a campaign of violence and terror which left more than 940 people dead in Egypt.[10]

Unlike Algeria and Egypt, the Islamic fundamentalists remain on the fringe of society in Libya, Tunisia and Morocco. The revolutionary regime of Colonel Muammar Gaddafi in Libya looks immune to the Islamist challenge. It is from Islamic radicals or 'alternative Islam' who have created such havoc with the political order in Algeria and Egypt that many expected the most serious threat to the Gaddafi regime. Fundamentalist Islamic groups have operated in Libya for many years. They have, however, failed to become more than a nuisance to the revolutionary Libyan leadership. In March 1993, the Libyan leader lashed out at Islamic activists, inciting his followers to assassinate Muslim militants. Gaddafi was no less excoriated by Islamic opposition movements than other African leaders both for his secular military socialist economic model and for his repression of fundamentalists whom he likened in one of his speeches to AIDS victims.

In Morocco, where the colonial impact was less profound, continuity with the past is not merely a fact of life but an instrument of the monarchy. The King appoints all the religious officials. Prayers are said for him and his family every Friday in the mosques. While a token secular opposition is permitted, all attempts to create an Islamic party have been suppressed. As in other *Maghreb* countries, many of the unemployed in Morocco see their salvation in Islamic fundamentalism. Some of the leaders of the banned Islamic group, *Al-adl wa-'l Ihsan* including Sheikh Yassin, remained in detention, and in April 1991 eight other members were arrested (although subsequently released). In May 1991, *Al-Adl* and other opposition groups participated in a demonstration in Casablanca, in which an estimated 1,00,000 people demanded measures to enshrine the sovereignty of the people and reduce the powers of the King.

The accession of President Zine El Abidin Ben Ali in Tunisia in 1987 ushered in an era of marked political relaxation. Unlike King Hassan II of Morocco, President Ben Ali of Tunisia has attempted to seek popular mandate through both economic and political reforms.[11] "The arrival of Ben Ali and his containment of Islamic extremists through socio-economic and political achievement has left no room for the Islamic radicals to exploit the common frustration of the people, that is, poverty. The women's revolution has left no room for fundamentalism in Tunisia".[12] 'While aiming for progress and development, the Tunisian leaders have not forgotten social obligations to their people, laying stress on health, education and the elderly and deprived sections of the society', says Chabane Abdelaziz, Ambassador of Tunisia to India.

The emergence of religious Islamic fundamentalism can be attributed to both internal and external factors. In the Algerian and Egyptian societies there is a terrible sense of disappointment. The dismal results are all around the poverty of the underprivileged, the bleak political landscape, the sinking of these countries into sectarian strife between Muslims and non-Muslims and among Muslims themselves and the dreary state of socio-economic, cultural and educational lives. Islam's appeal in Algeria has grown because of economic hardship, social unrest and a combination of all the three that Algeria underwent after independence. By the mid-1980s, Algeria's economic crisis was probably the acutest. The urban riots of October 1988 were a spontaneous reaction to the deprivations suffered by people under economic reforms and Algerian government's abandonment of its historical commitment to the simultaneous pursuit of social welfare and economic development. Besides, much of the support to the *Islamic Salvation Front* (FIS) was to a great extent, a protest vote against 30 years of single-party rule by the National Liberation Front (FLN) which had grown old and corrupt. The party's tenure in office had become associated not only with economic failure but with widespread corruption among the army and FLN elites who had been the first, and often the only, beneficiaries of the economy.[13]

Because of the size of its population which is more than 60 million, Egypt seems to be vulnerable to this new radical Islamic movement. Egypt, under President Nasser's model, on the whole, experienced lot of social and economic development. However, during the post-Nasser era, there has been a sharp decline in the socio-economic sphere. Post-Nasser Egypt is marked by corruption and intrusion of private interests. The 1980s proved to be a difficult decade for Egypt's economy. The rate of annual growth plummeted. Egypt fell from the World Bank Group of lower-middle income countries to its lower-income category. Inflation rose and the real income of industrial workers eroded. No less a figure than the great novelist, Naguib Mahfouz, has spoken with sorrow and despair about this state of affairs. "Egypt's culture is declining fast", he wrote. "The state of education in our country is in crisis. Classrooms are more like warehouses to cramp children in for a few hours than places of education. The arts and literature are barely taught in these institutions, which are run more like army barracks than places where cultural awareness and appreciations can be nurtured".[14]

Unlike Algeria and Egypt, the increasing influence of fanaticism in other parts of Africa, particularly the Horn region, due to a religious renaissance in reaction to the process westernisation. Islamic activism in the region is only secondarised response of traditional societies to the forces of modernisation of western materialism. In Ethiopia and Eritrea, as in many country of Eastern Europe, the Islamic resurgence is not so much a consequence of the confusion and anxiety produced by modernity, as a react to religious repression by a totalitarian regime. Marxism-Leninism in Ethiopia under Mengistu moved against both Christianity and Islam. In 1977, the head of the Ethiopian Orthodox Church removed from office and arrested. Later, other religious leader both orthodox copts (Christian minority) and Sunni Muslims, arrested or assassinated. Since the collapse of the Ethic Communist state, and after decades of anti-religious propagation churches and mosques in Ethiopia and Eritrea are full of people practising their religion. From this perspective, what is happening the Horn of Africa is not so much as Islamic 'resurgence' as an Islam 'reassertion'.

As in the *Maghreb* region, the collapse of socialism and communism in the Horn of Africa has created an ideological vacuum. Young people in particular, are looking for answers in an era of economic development and political disillusionment and find in the *Koran*, or in the Economic and intellectual and sentimental refuge. In an era characterised by political apathy, political forces tend to look for new sources ideological legitimacy. Muslims in all the four countries of the Horn form significant constituencies. Almost all of Djibouti's and Soma inhabitants, the majority of Eritreans and about 45 per cent Ethiopians are Muslims. In sharp contrast to Libya and Iran, where fundamentalism is a product of material wealth, Islamic militancy in the Horn is, to some extent, the product of hardships. Desperate people seek a sense of direction in the strict Muslim morality.

However, no source of frustration is more fundamental than limited participation of the Afro-Arab people in deciding their own future. Many believe that even if Afro-Arab governments agree on joint policies on social justice, development and defence, policies will have limited popular support because of a consistent failure of the regimes to involve and consult the people. The solution to the economic and social problems of the Afro-Arab countries, for them to follow the example of South-East Asian Muslim nation including Malaysia and Indonesia, clean up their policies, develop and compete with the rest of the world. Islamic values should be viewed as being compatible with development and progress.

REFERENCES

1. *Ethioscope* (Ministry of Foreign Affairs, Ethiopia), vol. 1, (2): January 1995, p. 2.
2. Asteris C. Huliards, "Islam: Promise or Peril"?, *The World Today* (London), December 1995, p. 243.
3. For more details see the latest book by Graham Fuller, and Ian Lesser,

A Sense of Siege: The Geopolitics of Islam and the West (Oxford, Westview Press, 1995).

4. The Economic Intelligence Unit, *Country Report: Ethiopia, Eritrea, Somalia, Djibouti*, 2nd quarter, 1995, p. 21.
5. Musahid Hussain, "America's quest for an Islam Policy", *Middle East International* (London), No. 495: 3 March 1995, p. 17.
6. Jean-Pierre Tuquoi, "Djibouti Survives on French handouts", *The Guardian Weekly* (London), 20 August 1995, p. 16.
7. Ahmed Ben Bella, "A time for peace in Algeria", *The World Today*, November 1995, pp. 208-10.
8. Jagdish P. Sharma, "Religious and Social factors at work in North African Society", paper presented at the international seminar on *Contemporary Africa* in Delhi, February 1996.
9. Fouad Ajami, "The Sorrows of Egypt", *Foreign Affairs* (New York), vol. 74 (5): September/October 1995, p. 76.
10. *The Asian Age* (Delhi and London), 25 January 1996.
11. Jagdish P. Sharma, "Tunisia under Ben Ali", *National Herald* (Delhi), 5 July 1995.
12. Interview with former Tunisian Ambassador, *Mr. Ben Rejdab*, to India, 1 June 1995.
13. Lisa Anderson, "North Africa: The Limits of Liberalisation", *Current History* (Philadelphia), April 1995, p. 168.
14. Fouad Ajami, "The Sorrows of Egypt", *Foreign Affairs*, 1995, pp. 79-80.

44. India-Algeria: Trading Ties

Arab-Africa on the eve of the 21st century is at the crossroads of its socio-politico and economic history. To be able to understand Arab-Africa we need to acknowledge the vital economic and strategic importance of this region, which is undergoing rapid and traumatic socio-political, economic and scientific changes.

This great region which includes countries like Algeria, Egypt, Libya, Mauritania, Morocco, Saharawi Arab Republic (recognised by several Third World countries) Sudan and Tunisia, is of major importance because of the skills, abilities and achievements of its inhabitants. It is also of great significance for its natural resources, especially oil. Exploration and discovery of oil resources has brought about startling and highly visible changes in the lifestyle of the people of this area.

The exchange of visits between the leaders of India and the Arab-African region have provided opportunities for discussions on ways and means of promoting closer cooperation in various fields. Algeria is one country in Arab-Africa with which India has had cordial relations throughout. It is undeniable that India has contributed in great part to the development of Arab-Islamic sciences which characterised the 19th and 20th centuries. The printing presses of Delhi, Lahore, Hyderabad, Bombay and Calcutta have rendered great services to Arab scholars and have helped in spreading knowledge of Arab culture by publishing numerous works of great importance.

The Algerian scholars found in the Indian editions abundant material capable of satisfying their passion for Islamic studies, specially with regard to the sources of these studies, the Hadith and the Fiqh. India has contributed not only to safeguard the common heritage of all Muslims and all Arabs but also to its development and its enrichment.

During the modern period, the movement of Mahatma Gandhi was known and followed by a marked interest by the Algerian people. In 1930, on the occasion of the Round Table Conference held in London, a review in the Algerian Arabic daily *Al-Shihab* devoted extensively to the sacred fight of India. India has appreciated Algerian war of liberation against the French as a heroic saga of a valiant people's struggle. When France was facing its waterloo in North Africa, the government of India allowed the National Liberation Front (FLN) of Algeria to open its office in New Delhi.

Apart from providing financial, material and medical help to the FLN, India's advocacy in the United Nations in Algeria's right to freedom helped to forge Afro-Asian and Arab unity on this issue. Indian policy on the question of Algeria's struggle for independence in those days was guided by the following considerations:

India had sympathy and support for the FLN. This support was expressed in the United Nations as well as outside of it. Alongside, India followed a moderate approach of non-antagonism towards France. As in the case of other anti-colonial struggles, India avoided sending arms or men to Algeria, but its tangible support was demonstrated by shipping medical supplies to the country. Outside the United Nations, India sought to resolve the Algerian issue through peaceful negotiations between Algeria and France.

After the ceasefire agreement had been arrived at between the FLN and the French Government, Nehru welcomed the settlement and told Indian Parliament on March 12, 1962, that it was an intensive struggle unparalleled in history". Describing the agreement as a "long-hoped-for one", Nehru said: "I doubt if we can find from the records of history such an intensive struggle as the Algerian people have lived through during the past seven years and more such intense suffering, such as large number of killings and casualties. Surely no one can deny that if a price has to be paid for freedom, the Algerian people have paid much more than any price that could have been paid.

India granted de jure recognition to the government of Algeria soon after its independence in June 1962 and friendly relations developed between the two states. There is complete identity of views between the two countries at the political level. Peace, freedom and development are the goals cherished by both India and Algeria. At the official level friendship and mutual understanding mark the work of the two countries in the UN, the NAM, G-15, and the group of 77. Both countries follow the policy of non-alignment in their external relations. Algeria's membership of the Africa Fund under Indian chairmanship is considered a great asset. Both believe that the developing countries should cooperate and promote self-reliance amongst themselves. On the question of Palestine and Western Sahara, both reaffirm their full support and solidarity with the Palestinian and Western Sahara people for their right to self-determination.

In the economic sphere, Indo-Algerian ties are poised to become a model of South-South cooperation. During the last decade, a considerable increase in economic cooperation and commercial relations between the two countries has been noticed. Exchange of high-level delegations, as also the Indo-Algerian Joint Commission meetings have enhanced the range and scope of industrial and technical cooperation. Construction activity, power, irrigation, roads, railways, airports, machine-tools and petrochemicals are major fields of cooperation between the two countries.

In March (1993) the Indian Oil Corporation (IOC) finalised agreements with Sonatrach, the national oil company of Algeria, for supply of over one million tonnes of high speed diesel (HSD). The value of the contract was around $200 million. This was the first time that India had imported petroleum products from Algeria. This contract with Algeria comes in the wake of India's attempts to diversify its sources so as to enlarge its basket of supplies.

During the 5th session of the Indo-Algerian Joint Commission held in 1993 in Algeria, new objectives were fixed in various fields such as finance, commerce, industrial development, agriculture, transport and energy. The 6th session of the Indo-Algerian Joint Commission for economic and commercial cooperation was held at New Delhi from March 3 to 6, 1997. Mr. B.B. Ramaiah, Indian Minister of Commerce, led the Indian delegation while Mr. Essaid Bendakir, Algerian Minister of Transport led the Algerian delegation.

The solidarity between these two developing societies was reflected in the various joint communique and collaborative efforts launched by these two countries. Though the stress of joint communique has also been envisaged at the cultural and political level giving boost and impetus to the Indo-Algerian relations.

Mrs. Kamala Sinha, Indian Minister of State for Foreign Affairs, visited Algeria from 12-13 September 1997. During her visit, Mrs. Sinha called on Algerian Prime Minister, Ahmed Ouyahia; Foreign Minister, Ahmed Attaf; Finance Minister, Abdelkrim Harchaoui and Minister of Energy and Mines, Mr. Youcef Yousfi. In the official discussions held during the visit, both sides recalled their excellent bilateral political exchanges and consultations.

They also affirmed their commitment to upgrade and revitalise the economic and commercial exchanges between the two countries. They expressed their determination to work with the international community to combat terrorism in all its forms. Algeria has been at the throes of extremist violence unleashed by Islamic insurgents for nearly six years. At least 80,000 people are estimated to have been killed since the extremist violence began. Even as the violence continues. Algeria has been in the midst of an oil and natural gas boom that has kept the economy growing.

"We have excellent understanding on terrorism and its international connection and ramifications. We are working together to revitalise the Non-Aligned Movement which is still very relevant. It (NAM) still represents our vision and our will. What we need now is to implement political relations into economic relations. The last Indo-Algerian Joint Commission has laid stress on different sectors. Algeria is inviting India to invest in the hydrocarbon sector in order to secure its supplies. Others are taking advantage of the same", says Mr. Abdelhamid J. Bereksi, Algerian Ambassador to India.

Thus, there are plenty of opportunities and mutually beneficial trade areas which can add to the good Indo-Algerian relations and South-South cooperation.

The visit of President Abdel Aziz Boutaflika to India as the guest of honour at the Republic Day parade in 2001 testified to the closeness of Indo-Algerian relations.

45. The Algerian Trauma

Terrorism in the name of religion has given a new and dangerous dimension to world disorder. Today's world is different in fundamental ways from the one we knew for 50 years. The world in the post-Cold War era seems to be terribly complex. It is both safer and dangerous in terms of technology and human relations. It seems to be difficult for the States and the people to determine whether and how to act in a world of threats internal and external, to their security.

Different forms of terrorist threats in the name of religion, ethnicity and along caste lines—long restricted by the Cold War—have erupted with increasing ferocity. Bullets killings, maimings and bloodshed cast their shadows over states like Afghanistan, Pakistan, Algeria, Egypt, Rwanda and Burundi among others over the edge of the twenty-first century. The questions arise even more insistently as the body count of Algerian Islamist horror mounts. During this holy month of Ramzan, nearly 1,900 people were killed in Algeria, mostly in the western provinces and there is no respite yet.

Hardly a day passes without reports of innocent people living in villages at the outskirts of Algeria being massacred in cold blood allegedly by the Armed Islamic Group and other Islamic militant outfit. The toll of killings since early 1990s is believed to be more than 80,000, though official figures are much less. Officially, a growing list of countries have denounced the ghastly massacres of innocent people, including women and children.

For the first time, the secretariat of the Organisation of Islamic States has condemned the killings as un-Islamic. This followed a meeting of the foreign ministers of 21 Islamic states in Teheran who concluded an agreement to counter extremist terrorism. The 24-hour visit by the European Union envoys recently condemned the widespread fundamentalist violence in Algeria and urged the country to allow unhindered access to international bodies.

"I would stress that Europe is very willing to do everything it can to try and bring an end to the suffering of the Algerian people". British Foreign Secretary Robin Cook told reporters. "We need to explore to what extent we are able to get the willing cooperation of the government of Algeria in this objective".

The European Union has also asked the Algerian government to show "greater transparency" over the wave of fundamentalist violence. Most other governments, including India, have generally supported the Algerian government and the democratic elections last year. However, that spirit has begun to erode amid the continuing violence. The European government with the longest closest and deepest ties with Algeria, namely France, is also disposed to respond to the Algerian killings because of the long and bitter colonial past. The French, scorched by Algerian official reaction and fearful of the threat of terrorism on their own soil as well as the respect of an increasing flow of Algerian immigrants have been wary of taking any initiative.

Recent democratic multi-party elections held in Algeria have resulted in a certain show of support to the present Zeroul government there. France is a strong supporter of the present government. The southern European states are also dependent on Algeria's oil, gas and other energy resources.

The inhuman killings by the Islamic fundamentalists in Algeria defy all rationale, logic and analysis. A long war of attrition between Algerian secular government and Islamic fundamentalists has cost this North African country of 29 million people dearly in terms of social stability, political administration, economy, transportation, education, industry and market investment.

Algerian President Liamine Zeroul in a speech vowed to crush what he termed a conspiracy manipulated from outside. In his 2-minute nationwide broadcast on television. Mr. Zeroul vowed: "I confirm to the dear Algerian people the determination of the Algerian state to battle against the terrorist groups until their final eradication". He accused the Algerian legal opposition of having a hidden agenda of surrendering the country to Muslim fanatic guerrillas who are responsible for bombings and massacres of unarmed common people, intellectuals journalists, foreigners, political leaders, artists, women and innocent children in Algeria. He said that Algeria would pursue its course through pluralism, constitution and democracy.

However, Algeria's secular opposition leader Hocine Ait-Ahmed warned that if the six-year-old violence continued, there would be a danger of creating "a Somalia in Algeria". To many older Algerians it is almost as if the clock had been put back four decades to the period of terrible violence orchestrated by the *Organisation de l' Armee Secrete* (QAS), the French terrorist group which opposed Algerian independence. History for them seems to be repeating itself with a completely different cast of characters.

Islamic Iran recently has condemned the terrorist killings in Algeria and called upon the Islamic world not to remain "indifferent towards such shocking events". The Algerian government has time and again accused Islamic Iran of propping up terrorist militant groups in Algeria. During the last three decades the Muslim world has seen a marked increase in Islamic violence. Increasingly, religion, particularly Islam, has come to play a dominant role in the present day Muslim world through its ever-increasing militant proclivities.

With its extensive critique of Western and nationalist goals and values. Islamic fundamentalism has mounted an increasingly dangerous challenge to Arab nationalism. Marxism, socialism, and secularism as the dominant ideologies of the regime and opposition movements in various Arab, African and Asian countries. The fall of Shah of Iran in 1979 and the triumph of Islamic revolution led by late Ayatollah Khomeini was seen by many in West and the Arab world as the prelude to a worldwide movement of Islamic fundamentalism. In fact, after the collapse of Communism in East Europe and the former Soviet Union, Islamic militantism is being viewed as a major threat to world, civilisation, peace and security.

The neo-Islamists or militants try to re-Islamise society at the grassroots level. Preaching aims to encourage individuals to agree to return to the practice of Islam in daily life and fear of God. In this process, women are pushed to wear veils, alcohol is banned, co-education is condemned and attempts are made to promote the moralisation of society. They claim spiritual and inspirational inheritance from the early days of Islam. They are aggressive and fanatic in their approach and do not shy away from violence in their total rejection of the existing socio-politico, economic system. The Islamists desire legitimacy for violence from the fact that they see themselves to be at war with anti-Islamic forces.

In the colonial period Islam was the rallying cry of Algerian national struggle. When independence came, Islam was recognised as the state religion and a good deal of lip service was later paid to Boumediene's slogan that there could be no real Algerian independence without socialism and no socialism without Islam. In Boumediene's time, mosque attendance in Algeria was like church attendance in former Soviet Union. This has changed since the late 1980s. There is marked increase in the number of young unemployed men congregating at mosques. On occasions in the early 1980s, members of the congregation raided hotels and other establishments, smashing liquor bottles and throwing acid on women they thought were improperly dressed.

Another focus of such activity has been the universities, where students have demanded that rooms in dormitories be set aside as mosques. Similar demands for mosque-rooms have been made in factories and government office and have been met. The Algerian government has also undertaken a morality campaign of its own and a number of senior officials and political figures have been dismissed or arrested for corruption. Between 1988 and 1991, the Algerians attempted a political transformation without parallel in the Arab-African world.

After violent riots in October 1988, President Chadli Bendjedid responded to popular protests by proposing a broad set of political reforms. The Algerian constitution was amended by popular referendum to allow free political parties ending the National supremacy. This was followed by the Algerian government's 1989 decision to legalise the controversial Islamic Salvation Front (FIS), an umbrella organisation of Islamist opposition, broad freedoms of expression and progress in replacing the Algerian army from day-to-day politics.

However, Algeria's evolving experiment with democracy quickly deteriorated into violence as Islamist militants took up arms against the people and the regime after January 1992 legislative elections. By spring 1995, the Algerian government had secured, to some extent, impressive military and politico-economic gains over the Islamist militants. The November 1995 Presidential election with a majority voter turnout, despite militant threats, lent President Liamine Zeroul a degree of popular legitimacy. But the bloodshed of common Algerians by the Islamic fundamentalists still persists with daily bombings and assassinations and gruesome killings and slashing of throats and limbs of Algerians and foreigners.

The latter part of 1996, the whole of 1997 and till February 1998 has witnessed some of the most horrifying attacks on civilians. Thousands died in a series of massacres and bombings and are still dying. These killings and bloody massacres of Algerians by the Islamic terrorist organisations like Groups Islamique Armee (GIA) are a chilling testimony to the evolving and enduring values of democracy and secularism to a civilised society. Despite 30 years of independence and five years of democratic transition, the country still lies in ruins and at the mercy of Islamic terrorists. A fertile and beautiful country, well endowed with natural resources washed by the Mediterranean, Algeria is steadily sinking into an era of terrible chaos, anarchy, darkness and death.

The Algerian government has been unable to contain the current Islamist carnage. The recent violent killings have pushed Algeria into international spotlight and a violence-stricken nation has called for increased cooperation among Arab countries to fight terrorism. At a closed-door meeting of Arab ministers in Tunis (January 1998). Algeria's Interior Minister Mustapha Benmansour said, "we must more than ever mobilise our forces and capacity and unify our efforts to establish greater cooperation to combat this calamity and master it in all its forms.

"Terrorism would not have developed without the leniency or rather the indulgence of certain countries which do not want to see our Arab world stabilise and our people develop and progress" he emphasised.

The Algerian crisis embodies several long-term issues at stake in the Arab-African world and raises deeper questions about political, economic and social systems and their future prospects. Social and political reforms which allow for a degree of transparency and accountability to the people are critical to the Arab-African region's future economic growth. Only these can rescue the region from its dire problems. The demands of Algeria's deeply alienated and disproportionately young population underscores the limitations of the current system.

Cold-blooded violence on fellow human beings should not be justified. Something which is justified against foreign aggressors or colonialists, cannot be justified against fellow innocent human beings. The militant approach either on the part of fundamentalist radicals or the Algerian state needs to be strongly condemned. The long-term solution to the Algerian trauma still lies in peaceful dialogue, socio-economic justice and people's participation.

Algeria will have to sort out its crisis with its own people by adopting sincere social, political and economic measures with a human touch. Besides, the big powers should not fuel conflicts in various parts of the world including Algeria by selling deadliest weaponry to the terrorists and by furthering their economic and military interests without concern for humanity.

46. Libya and Afro-Arab Unity

Colonel Muammar Gaddafi, who celebrated the 31st anniversary of the Great September First Revolution recently, is a man to watch in the Afro-Arab world. In fact, his is a story of high ideals, of revolutionary ambitions and of vast oil wealth; but is ultimately a story of success and survival. Despite the Imperialist powers', particularly America's, tireless conspiracy against Gaddafi and its aggressive and brutal raids on his territory in April 1986—Gaddafi had succeeded to achieve a stature of his own.

Colonel Gaddafi's Great Socialist People's Libyan Arab Jamahiriya (as Libya has been known since April 1986) is a small state emerging to play a leading role in the Arab-African and Asian world. The last two decades have witnessed Gaddafi's ardent commitment to Arab nationalism and Arab unity, his 'holy war' against Zionism and Imperialism, his efforts for Arab unity and his contributing role in the world of oil.

Colonel Gaddafi came to power as the head of the revolutionary junta (calling themselves the Free Unionist Officers' movement) on September 1, 1969. He executed a successful transition against an aging conservative and corrupt monarchy and initiated a radical reorientation of the Libyan role in both regional and international affairs. He terminated the colonial association which the then Libyan monarchy maintained with the imperialist alliance system established by the United States, and initiated an intense, often radical, association with the existing revolutionary Nasserite Pan Arab system. Thereafter, the Libyan leader pursued a strategic and increasingly radical foreign policy, remarkable for the broad scope of its objectives and activities. He tried to establish a meaningful relationship between revolutionary Libya's aspirations and accomplishments.

During his visit to Libya (June 1970) the great Egyptian leader Nasser, said of Gaddafi: "I shall be leaving you tomorrow ... I feel a new strength, a new blood in me ... I feel that the Arab people recognise themselves in you, and that they have rediscovered their determination. In leaving you, I say to you: 'My brother Muammar el-Gaddafi is the representative of Arab nationalism, of Arab revolution, and of Arab unity ... May God keep you".

To start with, he created on the Nasserite model, an Arab Socialist Union as the sole political organisation in the country. Again, two years later, in 1973, he launched Libya's cultural revolution. The "direction" is based on his belief that there is a path of socialism opposed both to capitalism and communism, especially suitable to the Arab world. His sense of mission as a reformer is directed not only to the Libyans, but also to the Arab world as a whole. He has called his ideas the "Third Universal Theory", which rightly bears the theological foundation of Arab nationalism by drawing its inspiration from Islam. To quote Gaddafi: "The Arab nation is apt to play the role of the bearer of a third theory because it is a nation of age-old civilisation and is endowed with a heavenly and universal message, namely Islam".

Gaddafi was the Arab nationalist *par excellence*, owing his allegiance to the Arab socialist component of Nasserism. Freely acknowledging his debt to Nasser, Gaddafi described the Libyan revolution as a continuation of the Arab revolution best epitomised by the Egyptian revolution of 1952. He had sought by persuasion and through successive attempts at unity with Egypt and Syria, with Sudan, Morocco, Algeria and more recently with Tunisia, to put his ideas over directly to the Arab people. His ideas serve as a constant reminder of the concepts of Arab unity and Arab socialism, whether based on Islam or not, which are common to almost all the republican regimes of the Arab world.

Gaddafi founded his Arab nationalism on a glorification of Arab history and culture which conceived of the Arabic speaking world as the Arab nation, and thus as the custodian of Nasserist Pan-Arab nationalism. He blamed the backwardness of the Arab nation on four centuries of stagnation under the Ottoman oppressive rule, the subjugation and exploitation of first European colonialism and then imperialism, and the corruption and repression of reactionary, monarchical rule.

He gave stress on the liberation of the individual from poverty, ignorance and injustice, the liberation of the homeland (i.e. Libya) from imperialist and reactionary elements; and the political, economic and social emancipation of the entire Arab world.

Within Libya, Gaddafi's ideas have had practical effect in the formation throughout the country of "popular committees" to act not only as watchdogs, but also as executants of government policy.

Gaddafi modelled his Arab Nationalism on a wide range of Arab and Islamic thinkers, but the influence of Nasser was paramount. He also revived Islam as a key component of Arab nationalism. He believed that Arab and Islamic identities were inextricably linked. Besides, he saw himself as a revolutionary leader and thinker.

On Israel, he believes in the concept of launching a holy war for the sake of God, the Almighty. He rejects totally the concept of a political settlement with Israel and believes that the issue can be settled only by an armed struggle, one that the Arabs win. They (the Arabs) must keep on struggling until they do.

On Palestine, Gaddafi moved Libya from its sympathy to active support to Palestinians. The Palestinian cause was placed in the forefront of all Arab causes with the road to Palestine as the path to the liberation of Arabs everywhere. Palestine was seen as an integral part of the Arab nation. The Zionist presence in Palestine is said to be the latest bridgehead of military base to protect the interests of imperialism and neo-colonialism in the Third World. His policy with other states had been strongly influenced by their position on the Palestinian issue. The Palestine question still remains a focal point of Libyan foreign policy and Gaddafi's ideology. Recently Gaddafi has offered to host a Palestinian Government-in-exile.

A rather more successful outcome of his policy has been Libya's rapprochement with its neighbours, Chad, Egypt, Algeria and Tunisia. Anxiety over Libya's relations with Chad appears to have ended with Gaddafi's wish to have a peaceful neighbour in Chad. Besides, on March 28 this year the Libyan leader announced that he had withdrawn his troops stationed along the Egyptian-Libyan borders and that he had reopened the border posts closed since the late Egyptian President Anwar Sadat visited the Zionist entity in occupied Jerusalem in 1977, so that "any Egyptian can henceforth enter Libya freely, through the border post of his choice, and that any Libyan is free to go to Egypt". These moves followed a decision by the Libyan leader to apparently release 400 prisoners and destroy prisons.

Can anyone guess what will emerge from recently revived Libya-Algeria-Tunisia-PLO friendship. Certainly the Arab leaders need Gaddafi as much as Gaddafi needs his Arab brothers. Libya had very timely rejected what is known as a fundamental inequality of the imperialist system. Gaddafi pursued a new world order in which Afro-Arab nations in general and Libya in particular would have a more constructive role. He embarked on a broad range of all-round reforms and objectives. Moreover, he created new friends, institutions and organisations, to accomplish his just policies. On the Palestine issue, Gaddafi not only moved Libya from sympathy to active support, but also placed the issue in the forefront of Arab policy. Coming events will certainly prove Gaddafi's mettle.

47. Gaddafi and the United States

"I shall be leaving you tomorrow ... I feel a new strength, a new blood in me ... I feel that the Arab people recognise themselves in you, and that they have rediscovered their determination.

"In leaving you, I say to you: 'My brother Muammar el-Gaddafi is the representative of Arab nationalism, of the Arab Revolution, and of Arab unity", rightly spoke former Egyptian president Gamai Abdel Nasser, in Benghazi in June 1970.

Well before Colonel Muammar el-Gaddafi celebrated the thirty-first anniversary of the great Libyan Revolution that brought him to power in Libya on September 1, 1969, his revolution had really provided a distinct alternative to tackle the Afro-Asian issues. Although Gaddafi's views on some aspects of policy are either misunderstood or insufficiently known, his views on the Afro-Asian movement and its problems are, on the other hand, considered almost everywhere to be as clear and as simple as they can well be.

To Gaddafi, we sincerely believe that it is high time we reviewed our methods and renewed our means. We the member countries in the Afro-Asian movement should totally drop the method of courtesy speeches and rhetorical statements from the agenda of our periodical meetings. We should strive to ensure active and effective role for the movement at the international level and positive result for its members. It can be realised only through reflecting upon and addressing the basic issues confronting the Afro-Asian world and to find out their positive solutions by taking finding decisions followed by their implementation.

Our movement which is committed to the ideals of peace and justice and calls for a new political and economic order which may ensure equality, freedom and progress for all peoples must work seriously for translating these noble ideas into action and tackle all factors hindering the achievement of its goals. The irrational exercise of veto right enjoyed by the permanent members of the UN Security Council is one of the major issues which have been causing harm to many other member countries. The continuous exploitation of this right by certain countries to serve their political ends has virtually resulted in the paralysation of the Council in preserving international security and peace. For, and permanent member country can veto any unanimous decision of the world community. We should take decisions which may restore to the UN General Assembly their power and credibility and to the Security Council its effectiveness so that it could play its assigned role. We should also take such decisions which may ensure for the International Court of Justice its due place, prestige and power to implement its rulings. To ensure effectiveness, prestige and respect for the international law is a question of vital importance for all of us. To strive for restoration of power, credibility and effectiveness of these international institutions is inevitable if their existence is to be guaranteed. Otherwise, these institutions will tend to extinct and the world peace will be endangered once again.

It is different to achieve peace in the absence of justice. Both are interlinked. In our effort to achieve justice it is important that we pass decisions to pay compensation to those countries which were colonised and were subject to destruction by those power which were responsible for their colonisation. The passing of such decisions and insistence on its implementation will serve to achieve two important aims. It will be a strong deterrent before the imperialist countries and will force them ultimately to abjure their colonial policies. At the same time it will be consistent with the requirements of justice. The imperialist countries are in fact responsible, legally and morally for the consequences of their crimes. The principles which made the basis of our movement and which were accepted by all of us determine the stands of the member nations towards military alliances and foreign military bases. As per our commitment to these principles we should not allow any military bases in any member country. This commitment is a necessary prerequisite for obtaining membership and its continuation is of high significance due to our collective realisation that the presence of foreign bases in a member country does not only strip that country of its non-aligned character but constitutes serious threat to other member nations and creates congenial atmosphere for the return of neo-colonialism to our countries. Moreover, the presence of such forces constitutes flagrant violation of the Afro-Asian principles and the commitment made by the concerned member country while joining the Movement. Work for eviction of these forces is imperative for ensuring security and stability within the Non-aligned countries, protection of international peace and security and removal of the spectre of colonialism. Any member country which refuses to evacuate foreign forces stationed on its soil should be expelled from the Movement".

Since they came to office, the administration of President's Ronald Reagan and George Bush have made no secret of their desire to see Gaddafi ousted. Indeed, the very openness of their opposition served to focus attention on the American Imperialist and militarist campaign against the Afro-Asian world. Throughout the 1980s and 90s Gaddafi was portrayed by government officials and the mass media in the United States and Europe as a dangerous fanatic, supporter of extremists and a hostile opponent of American and European interests. The West and the US has found it difficult to come to terms with Colonel Gaddafi. They dismissed him very often as a mad man. The American administration had imposed diplomatic and commercial sanctions on Libya as early as 1981. By July 1985 top American officials met and agreed that while Iran and Syria had probably been more heavily involved in acts of extremism, Libya was the most defiant symbol of hostility to the United States. It was in this atmosphere that the US Central Intelligence Agency (CIA) drew up a plan to topple the Gaddafi regime by encouraging Libyan dissident elements. The Egyptians were approached with the idea of a joint military action that might provoke Gaddafi into response that would either prompt Libyan domestic upheavals or justify a massive American retaliation.

As the year ended, the US charged that Libya had supported the radical extremist groups that carried out terrorist attacks at Rome and Vienna airports in which five Americans were killed, although Americans conceded that the evidence was circumstantial and the Europeans also refused to go along with the American call for military action and further sanctions against Libya. Toward the end of March 1986, the US began naval exercises in the Gulf of Sidra, deliberately crossing what Gaddafi called "the line of death", the latitude that he claimed marked Libyan territorial waters. The above exercises were designed to lure Gaddafi into a deliberate foreign entanglement that would induce dissident army factions to launch a coup against the Libyan government. Subsequently, after an exchange of gunfire on March 22, the US sank two Libyan patrol boats, bombed a missile site killing more than 40 Libyan sailors.

These series of American interventions finally culminated in an US announcement during the seven o'clock evening news on April 14, 1986. 16 US Air Force F-III bombers had flown from England to attack three important targets near Tripoli under cover of darkness-Tripoli air port, a port facility as Sidi Bilal and military barracks at Bam al-Azizyyah, where Gaddafi was known to stay. Simultaneously, 15 A-16 and A-17 aircrafts from US Navy aircraft carriers in the Mediterranean attacked military facilities near Benghazi. Several civilian areas were damaged including the French embassy in the centre of Benghazi town. At least 100 Libyan civilians including children were killed and many were wounded including two of Gaddafi's little sons. Gaddafi escaped the attacks on his barracks uninjured, although he was badly shaken by America's mischievous attempt on his life. By the fall of 1986, American claims about Libya's role in terrorism had come under suspicion. In early October, *The Washington Post* reported that the US administration had undertaken a "disinformation campaign", deliberately planting false stories in the international press to frighten Gaddafi.

The ghastly inhuman US air strike was followed by another conspiracy against Gaddafi's Libya. By 1988, the US leaked misinformation about what it claimed was a chemical warfare plant at Rabta, building up pressure on Libya. After the destruction through sabotage of Pan-Am airliner over Lockerbie, the Americans tried to link Gaddafi to that outrage as well. The basic causes of tension between Gaddafi's Libya and the US are many To start with, Gaddafi is a strong supporter of, and a source of great inspiration to the struggling liberation movements. He has provided enormous economic and material aid to the Liberation movements in the Afro-Asian and Latin American World to enable them to wipe out remnants of Colonialism and racialism. The US and the West are unable to tolerate this. Besides, Gaddafi is a staunch opponent of neo-American Imperialist order which has assumed gigantic proportions in recent times. He is opposed to US Imperialism because it is continuing the political, military and economic exploitation of the Afro-Asian and Latin American countries in the same way as they were being exploited during the colonial era. Gaddafi wants that the new international order should be based on the principles of mutual respect, respect for the sovereignty of peoples, non-interference in the internal affairs of the States, fraternity and justice.

There have been reports that the US is cooperating with Israel in training the forces of Libyan dissidents to overthrow Gaddafi. This Libyan "contra" force has been trained in Chad, Cameroun, Gabon, the Central African Republic and the US, and is said to be operating out of Western Sudan. Moreover, the US, Britain and France indicted the Libyans for the Lockerbie air disaster which carries as much mystery as the bombings themselves. Now the question arises as to exactly why Libya has been singled out. Clearly the Europeans, particularly France, made a complete about-turn from their position at the Mediterranean nations meeting at the end of October 1991. There is very little that they know that they did not know before. Surprisingly, in spite of their declarations are continuing, the American and British governments have gone a long way towards implicating Syria and Iran. However, the deliberate Lockerbie indictments followed by international sanctions have hurt Libya to a great extent. They have forced Libya to confront its dependence on its oil industry, which in turn, is vulnerable to US sanctions because it badly needs to update its equipment. They have also resulted in throttling Libya's oil projects etc.

While the Americans have reservations about the Libyan regime a good number of Western diplomats argue Gaddafi is better than an alternative, particularly since, they say, no-one else can control this tribally organised North African country. They also argue that Gaddafi has been ferociously opposing the ongoing religious fundamentalism and that he has rationalised support for worldwide nationalist revolutionaries. He had displayed considerable restraint towards the West, not attacking them during the Gulf war or during West Asian peace negotiations. It was noticeable that despite his unflinching rejection of negotiations with Israel over the Palestine question, he did not see fit to condemn Yasser Arafat's peace initiative, and even apparently promised the PLO that he would restrain Arafat's critics from undertaking revolutionary actions. They fear that any

US, inspired violent change in Libya—with no obvious successor to Gaddafi could lead to a dangerous power vacuum, unleash violent socio-religious and tribal vendettas and an anarchic situation that would favour the incursion of fundamentalist forces and could produce a "ripple effect" throughout the Afro-Asian region. However, to the common people of the Afro-Asian-Arab world, Gaddafi, the man who likes to live in a tent, is a visionary of Arab unity and an example of defiance against Western domination. In the post-cold war scenario, Gaddafi has adopted a realistic approach to international developments.

48. Tunisia in Modern Times

More than any other country, with the exception of Lebanon, Tunisia is at the meeting point of the Arab and French cultures. It also finds itself at the turning point of Islam and secular modernism. Of all the North African states, Tunisia singles itself out as politically stable, socially cohesive and economically prosperous. November 7, 1987 marked a turning point in the contemporary history of Tunisia. Questions were raised as to what would happen after Bourguiba?

What happened in Tunisia on November 7 night was that the previous president Bourguiba voted for the new incumbent president Zine El Abidine Ben Ali. The new successor paid homage to the former leader. "We will never forget that Bourguiba was the man who established our modern state. In a family, when a father reaches an advanced age he can no longer rule. But Bourguiba will remain the reference and the symbol". It was the best tribute paid to the former president by his successor Ben Ali.

The failure of the socialist experiment of the sixties had created a credibility gap between the sayings and the actions of the then Tunisian government. Seemingly, insensitive to this gap, this dissonance, the Tunisian government did not tolerate any opposition and attempted to prevent any political discourse but its own.

The 'modernisation' experiment in Tunisia had not succeeded either in fulfilling its promises of economic independence and social equality or in the creation of a new equality or in the creation of a new coherent system of values. Questions were raised since 1967 about the efficacy of the Bourguibist model of development in providing national stability and prosperity. The period between 1967 and 1986 was characterised by a decline in popular political participation, especially amongst the youth, leading to the emergence of the Islamic protest movements and the virtual disappearance of that revolutionary nationalist spirit which had characterised the early years of Bourguiba's rule.

This popular protest led to the emergence of a parallel society which rejected the lifestyle and values of Tunisia's Frenchified elite in favour of Islamic alternative. This was visualised by a general increase in piety, the more frequent wearing of the *hijab* (veil), and by a proliferation of Islamic literature and music. Many were worried about what may come. They were worried that the example of puritanical Islamic radicalism in neighbouring Egypt and Algeria may prove infectious. The optimists counted on the moderate and easy-going nature of the Tunisians and the progress already achieved during Bourguiba's long reign to pull the country along the middle road.

However, the transition was smooth and significant in the sense that President Ben Ali had shown some political astuteness in dealing with the socio-economic and religious problems. He undertook, significant socio-economic and political reforms. He sought to control the deteriorating security situation in Tunisia, also caused by economic crisis and by the increasing activism of the local Islamic movements.

While paying tribute to Mr. Bourguiba's achievements in building this West-oriented country, Mr. Ben Ali promised to introduce new laws to broaden political participation and "put an end to chaos and laxity—political favouritism and indifference which hurts the public good". He said constitutional reform was imperative on matters such as the presidential succession and stressed the importance of democratic institutions.

A national pact supported by various political parties, student organisations, workers and other socio-professional organisations had been promulgated which laid emphasis on the spirit of reconciliation i.e. *Maan min Azlie Tunis* or "Together for Tunisia". The law on political parties was promulgated. Legal approval was granted to three parties in 1988, bringing the number of recognised parties to seven viz: the Democratic Constitutional Rally (RCD), the Movement of Socialist Democrats (MDS), the At Tajdid movement, the Party of the People's Unity (PUP), the Liberal Social Party (PSL), the Progressive Socialist Party (PSP) and the Unionist Democratic Union (UDU).

The electoral code was revised to modify the voting system for legislative elections and to give concrete expression to the political plurality of the Chamber of Deputies. Multiparty representation in the Chamber of Deputies was established by the election of opposition party candidates. All those who took part in Tunisia's independence struggle, like Salah Ben Youssef, Mahmoud Materi, Abdelaziz Thaalbi and many others were rehabilitated and honoured. The Tunisian chapter of Amnesty International was given official approval and a higher committee of human rights was established.

"We have a very mature society, politically and economically. Nowhere in the Arab world is women's condition better than in Tunisia", said Mr. Ben Redjeb, former Tunisian Ambassador to India. The rights of women, children and the family have been reinforced. A new law was also regulated on May 18, 1992 to combat the narcotics phenomenon, including provisions intended to protect children and youth from this curse.

In the social sphere, a new law had been promulgated pertaining to the promotion and protection of the handicapped. It had been made mandatory for economic enterprises employing more than 160 staff to reserve one per cent of the positions for the physically handicapped. A programme of social protection was being implemented to safeguard citizens from the negative effects of social, economic and cultural change, and to strengthen the cohesiveness and stability of the family.

In the religious sphere, law had been promulgated pertaining to the legal status of mosques and their protection from any influence that might turn them away from their cultural function. Public campaigns were made to safeguard moral values and eliminate manifestations that are contrary to Islamic ethics. Attempts have been made to create an awareness about the values of Islam, toleration and moderation and to expose the extremists who hide behind the mask of religion.

Development measures were undertaken to eradicate poverty through the scheme of 26 : 26. This project is meant to provide energy and education and to improve the living condition of the general public. What makes this project viable is its full transparency. This project is conducted on a limited time-frame basis. Students, soldiers and businessmen, all contribute to this project.

A total of 30 integrated urban development projects figure in the Eighth Plan (1992-1996) for all regions of the country. These projects are to provide direct benefits to a population of 150,000 to 200,000 inhabitants of lower-income group and would create over 10,000 new jobs.

In the economic sphere, a set of new measures have been adopted to further economic liberalisation and financial and monetary reforms. Business is being actively promoted; a bill has been drafted pertaining to the rescue of firms which are experiencing economic hardship; industrial zones have been developed; broad reforms have been carried out in the banking sector.

Important measures have also been adopted to accompany execution of the price control programme and import liberalisation, with a view to create a favourable climate. The private sector is being encouraged to create consultancy firms. Measures have been adopted to project the industrial sector from imbalanced foreign competition. Industrial restructuring has been encouraged, and additional resources mobilised to give new impetus to private investment and to finance operations of structural adjustment. A national energy strategy has been adopted to improve the yield of resources. A coherent programme of pollution control and environmental conservation has been adopted for mining regions and industrial zones.

Foreign trade has also staged a significant comeback since 1994. With a 20 per cent increase in exports and a 5 per cent decrease in imports, important steps have been adopted to liberalise domestic trade and prices. Serious thought has been given to rationalise the tax services. The income tax structure has been simplified and reduced. The maximum income tax, rate is now 35 per cent instead of 68 per cent for individuals; for legal entities the rates have been reduced to 35 per cent and 10 per cent instead of 54 per cent and 48 per cent.

New set of measures have been adopted to allow the capital market to grow into profitable investments. The system of credit control has also been eased. Customs tariffs have been readjusted. Plans have been made to achieve a customs union in stages among the countries of Arab Maghreb.

On the international front (in April 1994) Tunisia became a founding member of the World Trade Organisation (WTO) following the Marrakesh Economic Summit Conference. The aim was to give Tunisia a greater role in the region's productive activities.

There is also a determination to endow Tunisian diplomacy with greater vitality and effectiveness so as to broaden Tunisia's influence abroad. President Ben Ali has restored Tunisia's international standing and has gone far towards healing the breach with other neighbouring, Arab-African States. Steps have been taken to improve inter-Arab relations and to restore cohesiveness and solidarity within the Arab family. Tunisia and its neighbours like Libya, Egypt, Morocco, Algeria and Mauritania, all face similar socio-economic problems like demographic explosion, drought and falling oil prices with their resultant effects on food and jobs.

Moves among these countries to settle their considerable disagreements in favour of unity have been partly spurred by the burden of trying to ensure a stable future for the 70 per cent of their people aged under 25. For Tunis, the renewed ties with Libya, which had been broken since 1985, are a welcome blessing. Trade is in Tunisia's favour and Tunisian workers contribute significantly by taking up jobs in Libya and other Arab-African States.

The establishment of Arab Maghreb Union (AMU) in 1989, comprising Tunisia, Morocco, Algeria, Libya and Mauritania brought in a new era of regional economic unity. A number of Maghreb institutions have been set up in Tunisia including the Maghreb Bank for Investment and Foreign Trade and the Maghreb Trade Union.

Tunisians are proud of their reputation of being peaceful people. The country has been supporting the Palestinian people at all levels and has contributed to revitalising the West Asia peace process by participating in multilateral negotiations and contributing to the success of negotiations on Palestinian autonomy. It was within this framework that Tunisia met unofficially with the Israeli during the United Nations General Assembly session in New York in October 1994 and opened an office of Tunisian representation in Gaza and Ariha.

Tunisia supported the United Nations peace keeping efforts notably by sending Tunisian military contingents to Cambodia, Somalia, Rwanda and Burundi. Besides, Tunisia hosted the 30th African summit meet in 1994 and President Ben Ali was elected Chairman of the OAU for the period 1994-95. This 30th African summit adopted a "code of conduct" proposed by Tunisia to govern relations among African countries and combat all forms of extremism and fanaticism.

Tunisia was also chosen to represent Africa on the preparatory commissions of many international conferences such as the World Summit on Social Development (Copenhagen), the World Conference on Women (Beijing) and the International Year of the

Family. Tunisia has also been advocating to hold a special African summit to deal with the economic problems of the region.

In the domestic sphere, President Ben Ali has succeeded in containing the Islamic extremists through his balanced policy of socio-economic, political and international achievements. This has left no room for the Islamic radicals to exploit the common frustration of the people i.e. poverty. Besides, the reforms for women in Tunisia have left little room for fundamentalists.

"If you have very good soil, it is bound to give good growth, if a bad seed is put, it wouldn't grow. For fanaticism to grow it requires the soil and the seed. Tunisia has got neither of these", says the Tunisian Ambassador to India. Tunisia under Ben Ali thus projects a secular model of developed society in the Arab-Maghreb region.

49. Western Saharan Politics

It is disheartening to learn that a referendum on the future of the disputed Western Sahara Scheduled for July 31, 2000 is likely to be delayed by at least several months. The peace process in Western Sahara is about to collapse as Morocco shows no signs of following Indonesia's example in East Timor. The identification process for voters in the referendum in Western Sahara is still creeping forward, but one cannot help wondering where the next obstacle will come from. Observers are still studying the new Moroccan King's pronouncement that he is committed to defending Morocco's territorial integrity by holding the "confirmative" referendum in Western Sahara.

The United Nations proposed plebiscite in Western Sahara, which has been put off repeatedly since 1991, and was recently scheduled by the UN for July 31, 2000. Voters in the former Spanish colony are to choose between independence and being part of Morocco, which annexed the territory in 1975. It is interesting to note the publication of the second part of the provisional list of voters by the UN mission on Western Sahara, MINURSO (Mission d' Observation des nations Unies pour le referendum au Sahara occidentale). Of the 51,220 applicants from three contesting tribes, 2,130 individuals were recognised as having the right to vote. Added to the first list of 84,251 voters, the total number of voters is 86,381 out of about 200,000 auditioned applicants. The most contentious issue is the identity of 65,000 applicants who Morocco claims are indigenous people with the right to vote. The pro-independence Polisario Liberation Front says these people are immigrants sent to swing the referendum Morocco's way.

The long planned UN sponsored referendum for Western Sahara had to be postponed frequently owing to the stonewalling tactics adopted by the Moroccan government in the last five years.

Western Sahara represents one of the last problems of decolonisation in the world today. Originally this territory was known as Spanish Sahara on account of it being a colony of Spain since 1884. This phosphate-rich patch of desert covers 102,700 square miles. Spain had promised the country independence, but pressure from Morocco and the US forced the Spanish government, in the midst of its own delicate transition to democratic rule, to capitulate. On November 14, 1975, Spain entered into a tripartite agreement with Morocco and Mauritania, the northern and southern neighbours of this economically prosperous desert region, to partition this territory between Morocco and Mauritania, though within three years, the whole territory came under exclusive Moroccan control. This occurred despite the landmark October 1975 decision by the International Court of Justice that upheld the right of the people of Western Sahara to self-determination.

The conflict raging there is a dispute over sovereignty between indigenous Western Saharans are 'Saharawis' and their powerful neighbours to the north, that is, the Moroccans. The US sided with Morocco due to its Cold War calculations and concern about the likely prospects of an independent Western Sahara under the Left-leaning Polisario Liberation Front and also a wish to boost the political fortunes of Morocco's pro-Western monarch, late King Hassan II.

Moroccan forces invaded the territory, but initially suffered heavy losses to the Polisario Front. Unable to occupy the country by force, in 1980 the Moroccan army built the Hassan wall to keep out Polisario and the Saharawis generally. However, the Saharawis found refuge in Algeria from where their leaders declared independence of the Saharawi Arab Democratic Republic (SADR). The Organisation of African Unity (OAU) and a total of 70 countries had recognised SADR by 1990. The Moroccan army has never been effectively able to restrict Polisario's activities, despite a Hassan wall garrison of 110,000 and advanced surveillance systems. Some 80,000 troops are in the area, several encounters between the Polisario forces and Moroccan army took place during the early 1990s. In December 1990 Amnesty International reported to the UN that several hundred people had 'disappeared' after being arrested by the Moroccan security forces since 1975. Many of the victims came from the south of Morocco and from Western Sahara, and were suspected as supporting Polisario.

Mauritania was defeated outright and withdraw. Morocco succeeded in conquering virtually two-thirds of territory, including the former Mauritanian sector. The US blocked enforcement of the 1975 UN Security Council resolution demanding Morocco's withdrawal and recognising Western Sahara's right to national self-determination. The region remains occupied today, with most of the indigenous population known as Saharawis, exiled in refugee camps in neighbouring Algeria.

Late King Hassan II of Morocco had made the conquest of Western Sahara an issue of national pride. Besides, this region contains some of world's richest phosphate deposits, uranium and oil off its 1,200 km of coastline, and finest fishing grounds. In 1996, the two parties did reach a ceasefire agreement in Western Sahara. According to the then UN Plan, a referendum was to be held in the following year on the future of the former Spanish colony. But it could not be accomplished owing to the conflicting postures on who should be entitled to vote in the proposed referendum on the total independence of the Western Sahara or integration of the territory into Morocco. The Polisario or the Western Sahara Liberation Front defended the last Spanish colonial census of 1974 counting 73,000 Saharawis and objected to the participation in the referendum of Moroccan citizens who had been "transferred" into the territory as a result of the Moroccan sponsored famous "Green March" of 1975 and 1991. Over 145,000 potential voters have been identified, but the Moroccans insist on pressing the claims of another 65,000.

They have apparently started their referendum campaign and anticipated the voting to take place in July 2000. Others are less sanguine, which puts the ball in the court of James Baker, the former US-Secretary of State. In fact, during the debate, former President of South Africa, Mr. Nelson Mandela, linked Western Sahara and East Timor as two issues long overdue for resolution and Ghana's Jarry Rawlings expressed the unacceptability of an African country behaving in a colonialist way. Moroccan Foreign Minister Abdellatif Filali had another way of looking at it. He referred to "Saharawi brothers who have been waiting for more than 20 years to return to their homeland, Morocco".

Although Algeria seems to hold the key to peace in the Western Sahara conflict it could not succeed in persuading the late King Hassan of Morocco to change his mind. To the Algerians, the latest UN initiative under Mr. Kofi Annan was meant to give impetus to the delayed peace process signed between the Polisario Front and the Moroccan government. A UN brokered ceasefire has been in place for the last seven years with the UN peace keepers (MINURSO) ensuring that it is not violated. Morocco, along with the government of the Saharawi Arab Democratic Republic (SADR), which is a member of the Organisation of African Unity (OAU), and is recognised by about 80 countries including India, had agreed to a referendum to be held under UN auspices. Many deadlines for the referendum have come and gone and the latest one that had been set for July 31, 2000 has been postponed to the end of 2000. Morocco is already trying to wriggle out of its commitment. However, this time it may not succeed owing to strong world pressure, particularly because of the UN and the US attitudes.

After Kofi Annan took over the UN Secretary-General, Minurso was galvanised. Annan was determined to accelerate the process towards Saharawi's self-determination. In March 1997, Annan appointed James Baker, former United States Secretary of State, as his personal envoy to Western Sahara. Baker used his diplomatic skills and his international stature to make Morocco agree to a proposal on voter identification and a code of conduct guaranteeing the UN the authority to oversee a fair and free referendum. Since the Houston agreement brokered by Baker in 1997, the peace process has made significant progress. Most people who are eligible to vote in the referendum have been identified.

The UN Secretary-General has warned Morocco that if it continues its stalling tactics, he would ask the Security Council "to reassess the situation and the viability of the mandate of Minurso", The Saharawis have threatened that if Morocco reneges on its commitments again, they will re-ignite the war which forced King Hassan to deploy on a permanent basis tens of thousands of soldiers in the arid sands of the Sahara. Mohammad Abdelaziz, SADR President, has also stressed "that the Polisario Front would abide by the respect the Saharawi people's choice under the condition that the referendum is fair, free and democratic by allowing only Saharawis to vote".

As an inter-African conflict, the Western Sahara war has become a major challenge for the Organisation of African Unity (OAU). Indeed, in 1982, the Saharan conflict produced such acrimony within the OAU that the organisation was almost on the verge of collapse. Besides this, the success of Arab Maghreb Union (1989), according to some scholars, depends on the decolonisation and liberation of Western Sahara.

A permanent peace in Western Sahara is the need of the hour. It would provide socio-politico and economic stability not only to Morocco and Western Sahara region but to the whole Arab-Maghreb region. The ongoing occupation of Western Sahara and the prevailing conflict would only contribute to the impoverishment of the Moroccans and add to the sufferings of the Saharawi people by pushing them into refugee camps in neighbouring countries.

In addition to aggravating the tensions in the region, the delay in ending the conflict would further contribute to the waste of precious human, natural and economic resources which could be gainfully utilised for the socio-politico-economic development of the region as a whole. It is time the international community realised the centrality of the peace process in Western Sahara. We have stepped into a new century and also a new millennium. It is time we took stock of our actions. Is there something we can justly be proud of in the North African region? Can we say we have done everything possible to fulfil the region's aspirations? An independent Western Sahara would strengthen the aspirations of the neighbouring people and promote harmony in the Arab-Maghreb region.

It is also time for the Indian Government to contribute actively to the cause of a permanent peace in Western Sahara as this will only strengthen the forces of peace and progress everywhere. Peace is the only imperative in the Western Sahara region or else it could turn out to be the Balkans in Africa.

Commenting on the overall results of the voter identification process during a press conference in Algiers, the Saharawi Minister of Foreign Affairs warned recently that any delay in the referendum would force the Saharawis to resume armed struggle. It is hoped that the identification of the voters would be completed as per new schedule paving way for the people of the Western Sahara to decide their own political and economic future once and for all. The disagreement among the neighbours has to be resolved amicably.

50. Emerging African Nations

The then President Dr. S.D. Sharma described his visit to Namibia and Zimbabwe as a *pilgrimage to nations where freedom finally triumphed over the last colonial regimes*. He assured that India would firmly be committed as a partner in the process of their development as was the case at the time of their liberation struggle. He further emphasised that the bilateral ties between India, Namibia and Zimbabwe are in the best tradition of South-South Cooperation and an important element in bringing the continents of Asia and Africa closer.

The world has witnessed the countries of Africa awakening to freedom and independence in the aftermath of the changes brought about by World War II. The process is nearing completion. Namibia was one of the last few bastions of colonialism to become free through UN intervention.

South Africa is now on the threshold of freedom, a fact highlighted by the award of the Nobel peace prize to the African National Congress leader, Mr. Nelson Mandela, and the South African President, Mr. F.W. De Klark. But this process towards freedom was not easy.

The freedom movements in Africa, as in other parts of the world, were the consequence of the growth of nationalism and the increasing resentment against the exploitation and oppression by the colonial countries. The international situation further strengthened these movements. The Second World War had resulted in the general weakening of imperialism. It had also shattered the myth of the invincibility of some major colonial powers in Africa such as France and Belgium which had suffered defeat in Europe during the war.

The collapse of colonialism in Asia within a few years after the war also had a tremendous impact on freedom movements in Africa. The question of Africa's freedom gradually became one of the major issues in the world.

The first country in Black Africa to gain independence was

Ghana. The British had conquered a colony in this region to which they gave the name Gold Coast. The most prominent leader of the people of the Gold Coast colony was Kwame Krumah who, in 1949, had organised the Convention People's Party. A strong trade union movement also had emerged in Gold Coast. The Convention People's Party and the trade unions joined together to demand independence from Britain. However, most of their leaders were arrested and attempts were made to suppress the demand for freedom.

After 1950, the British Government started introducing certain constitutional reforms. Under pressure from the People's Party which had won a resounding victory in elections, the British Government agreed to the independence of Gold Coast. The new independent state which came into being on March 6, 1957, called itself Ghana, after the name of the old West African kingdom. The part of Togoland which had been under British control also joined Ghana.

The next country to achieve her independence was the French colony of Guinea in West Africa. In 1958, while embroiled in the war in Algeria, France held a referendum in her colonies which had been grouped together a French West Africa and French Equatorial Africa. The people of Guinea voted almost unanimously for complete independence and Guinea was proclaimed a republic on October 2, 1958.

The year 1960 is generally regarded as the Africa year. In that year, 17 countries in Africa gained their independence. These included all the French colonies in French West Africa and Equatorial Africa, and Nigeria and Congo (former Belgian Congo) now called Zaire.

Between 1961 and 1964 a number of countries in East and Central Africa became independent. These were Kenya, Uganda, Tanganyika, Zanzibar, Nyasaland, Northern Rhodesia and Ruanda-Urundi. Sierra Leone, Gambia, Basutoland and Bechunaland also gained their independence.

Before the end of the 1960s, almost all of Africa with the exception of Portuguese colonies of Angola, Mozambique and Guinea-Bissau and Cape Verde Island, and South Africa, South West Africa and Rhodesia had become free. Powerful freedom movements had arisen in the Portuguese colonies. They had organised their liberation forces and had secured the help of many countries in their struggle for freedom.

In April 1974, the Portuguese Army, much of which had been used to suppress the freedom struggles in the colonies, with the support of the people overthrew the 50-year old dictatorship in Portugal. The communists, socialists and other radical elements in the armed forces and the new Government of Portugal were opposed to the continuation of the Portuguese rule in Africa. They entered into negotiations with the freedom movements in the Portuguese colonies and by 1975 all the former Portuguese colonies in Africa became independent. Zimbabwe became independent in April 1980.

The last two major countries in Africa to achieve independence were the Republic of South Africa and South West Africa. Of these South Africa is militarily the most powerful. The Government of South Africa had the most oppressive regime in the world. The White minority in that country ruled over the vast majority of the African population. It practised the policy of apartheid, the separation of Black and White communities. This policy was used to maintain the rule of the White minority over the majority of the population which comprises Black and coloured people. It was really a policy of denial of human rights to the majority of the population.

The United Nations condemned the policies of South Africa. Many western countries maintained close economic and military relations with South Africa and had helped in sustaining the oppressive Government there. The main organisation of the South African people is the African National Congress (ANC) which for many years had been fighting for the liberation of South Africa.

South-West Africa of Namibia was a German colony before the First World War and was handed over to South Africa as a "mandate" after the defeat of Germany in that war. South Africa always treated South-West Africa as her colony and refused to withdraw from there in spite of the resolutions of the United Nations. The freedom movement in South-West Africa gained momentum in the recent years under the leadership of the South-West Africa People's Organisation (SWAPO). The governments and peoples of independent nations of Africa actively aided the freedom movements in these countries. They also played an important role in bringing about the end of the White minority rule in Zimbabwe.

Thus within the last two decades, most of Africa has become independent. Many African countries have changed their names. The colonial powers had given them names which had little to do with their past history and culture. Some countries and cities had been named after colonial adventures, for example Rhodesia, Leopoldville, Stanleyville, etc.

The African peoples are trying to overcome the damage caused to them during the colonial rule. Renaming their countries and cities after their original names is a part of their effort to establish and assert their independence and national identity. The need to unite in the face of common tasks and for the achievement of common aim has led to the emergence of unity amongst all African peoples. The most significant step taken in this direction was the formation of the Organisation of African Unity (OAU) in 1963.

The vestige of traditionalism and tribalism still persists in Africa. The lack of literacy among large sections of people and their loyalty to tribalism stands in the way of Africa's liberation and offers opportunity for outside intervention. There are among Africans some thoroughly westernised well-to-do leaders like Tshombe. They provide the disintegrating factors in African politics. The miseries of Congo is a classical example of the dangers from which the newly independent states of Africa are threatened.

The African States have inherited artificial boundaries. These boundaries were created by the imperialist powers in their scramble for Africa. Within Africa there is not a single border which has been drawn on the basis of dividing different races, tribes or peoples. Neither are there many borderlines which run along the natural geographical divisions of the land. The danger of such borderline existing between two states have been already demonstrated by several border conflicts including the clash between Morocco and Algeria, Kenya and Somalia.

Such conflicts did not arise before independence because boundaries then were unimportant: they were administrative divisions. The boundary disputes provide a stumbling block in the way of African unity and create the danger of neo-colonialism.

Africa is too valuable a price in the eyes of the imperialist powers to be given up without an attempt to retain the substance. No doubt the acceleration of National Liberation Movement has forced imperialism to strike a hasty retreat in the post-World War

II era, yet the colonial powers are on the lookout to re-enter Africa through the backdoor, taking advantage either of an internal or international dispute.

If an outside power is interested in selling armaments, destroying a government, diverting a particular economic policy or anything of this sort, then conflict or internal disunity would give the opportunity to intervene. Such an eventuality is fraught with much danger for African unity. Africa in that case may become involved in the global power conflict and cold war and African countries may find themselves in opposing camps.

Africa is, therefore eager to follow a policy on non-alignment. The problem of African unity is that each of the separate nations has the fear that a United Africa may become a backward and neglected area, exploited for the benefit of another part. There is also the problem of time and opportunity. The African people must be allowed to develop their national outlook and learn how to bring it in line with continental outlook before they are asked to take steps for African unity.

51. The Horn of Africa: An Arab-Maghreb Perspective

The Horn of Africa[1] is strategically, politically and economically important. It overlooks the point of convergence of the Red Sea, the Gulf of Aden and the Indian Ocean. In addition to dominating the Gulf of Aden and Bab-el-Mandeb, it commands the lines of communication running in the east, west, and south-west directions of the African continent. Its strategic location and the fragile and contentious regimes that have ruled the different countries in it expose it to the exploitative patronage of outside powers. The Horn of Africa has traditionally been a hotbed of intriguing politics. It first attracted the colonial powers—Britain, France and Italy—to the region and since the early 1960's has tempted the Super Powers to enter it. The colonial powers had their entry made easy by religious, ethnic and political rivalries and animosities among the peoples and nations of the region, which often weakened the central authority.

The Super Powers see in their intervention not only commercial advantages, as the colonial rulers did, but also the strategic and military importance of the area at the month of the Red Sea. Their interests were fuelled not only by the advantages that could accrue within Africa, but also by the more important leverage they could gain in the vital area of West Asian and North African affairs. This area is geo-strategically important for the Super Powers as it provides sea ports, bases and communications facilities of great importance. Italians and French in the past and Russians and Americans during the contemporary period have attempted to exercise strong influence on Ethiopian and Somali coasts. For example, France acquired a military base during the nineteenth century in the territory of Issas and Afars because of its geo-strategic importance. The Republic of Djibouti, as the territory of Issas and Afars came to be known since independence in 1977, has continued to receive substantial aid from France which still maintains its hold on the port.[2]

From a vantage point on the Horn, it is possible to command or interdict peaceful or military air and sea activity in Africa, West Asia and the Gulf region, the Indian Ocean, and the Near East. The possession of a military base anywhere in the Horn, for instance, can be used to influence the outcome of political and military struggles in its adjacent regions.[3] Arms transfers have been an important instrument for influencing elites of the region. Ethiopia and Somalia have received massive military assistance from both the USA and the former Soviet Union since the end of the World War II. In return, both the Super Powers at one time or the other gained a solid foothold and built military bases on the territories of the two host nations.

Economically, the Horn of Africa is the poorest region in the world with an average per capita GNP of only $205, well below the average of $330 for Sub-Saharan Africa as a whole. Ethiopia, with a per capita gross national product (GNP) of US $130 in 1987, is the poorest country for which figures were published by the World Bank.[4] In fact, the economies of the Horn comprise three distinct sectors viz.—the subsistence sector, the commercialised agricultural sector and the urban service sector, articulated to a varying degree with one another. Much of the subsistence economy, whether pastoral or agricultural, is vulnerable to drought and other natural disasters.

Areas of commercial agriculture are greatly restricted by the physical endowment of the Horn. In Somalia, until the recent ongoing clash resulting from civil war and foreign powers intervention (American, Pakistani and others), exports have depended heavily on livestock from the northern region. Ethiopia, like the other countries in the region, depends on a single crop for most of its export earnings, with coffee accounting for 63 per cent of the total in 1984.[5] The civil and territorial wars in the Horn of Africa are thus fought between governments whose economic base derives from their control of the cities and the zones of commercial agriculture, and insurgency movements which arise in economically peripheral or marginalised areas which lack viable commercial agriculture and access to the external market.[6] This is most strikingly true of Somalia, Ethiopia, and Eritrea. In Somalia, as per the *World Bank Annual Report (1990)*, weak stabilisation efforts and the private sector's lack of confidence, prompted by political unrest and the continued fighting in the north and elsewhere, continued to undermine economic performance. The picture of rural economic decay in Ethiopia stands in sharp contrast to the agricultural areas of Southern and Western Ethiopia, which unlike the northern highlands had been the victim of expropriation of land and the extreme exploitation of the indigenous population. The people of the South and West have, like those of Eritrea and Sudan, a radicalised intelligentsia willing and able to lead an insurgent movement against the central Ethiopian government. In the case of Somalia, both ethnic identity and access to political power are deeply affected by the ambivalence between a unifying Somali nationalism on the one hand, and the persistence of clan-based identities on the other.[7]

Thus, this part of Africa contains elements of practically all the major conflicts and tensions afflicting Africa today. Besides interstate wars and internal clashes, mounting external public debts, famines and droughts, and decline in agricultural and natural resources, and industrial production have combined with relative under-development of infra-structural facilities, poorly qualified manpower, low productivity techniques, increasing population, and demographic imbalances to produce disastrous consequences for the well-being of the people of the Horn.

This article looks at the very complexity of both intra-regional and external alignments in the Horn of Africa with special reference to Somalia. It also attempts to map the major features of this terrain in this area. Finally, it deals with the structure of relations between this area and the Arab Maghreb states.

The Genesis of the Socio-Economic and Political Crisis in Somalia

Although the Somalian crisis stems from domestic socio-economic, and political factors, the involvement of outside actors like those of the United States, the former Soviet Union, European States, the UN Peace Keeping Force, Pakistan, Egyptian and other forces, has often prolonged the crisis, as elsewhere in the Horn, and injected additional uncertainty in regard to the future. Recently, nearly 16 months after storming Somalian shore (right in front of television cameras) American forces pulled out leaving behind an apprehensive 20-nation African-Asian UN force of about 20,000 men, the bulk of which come from Pakistan, Egypt and

India. The Americans did take credit in helping save the lives of hundreds of thousands of Somalis who might have starved to death. But they also left behind more than 2,000 dead Somalis and very little in the way of improvements. The UN is spending $1.6 billion in Somalia and the United States has spent much more. But for the Somalis the tragedy is that 90 per cent of the cash has been wasted on the military operation, which has made the streets dangerous and insecure[8] not only for the foreigners but also for the Somalis themselves.

There is visible manifestation of great strain among the Somali people either in the rural areas or in urban conglomerations that have come up. Part of the explanation for this phenomenon appears to be the pattern of colonial and neo-colonial or post-colonial experience which Somalia underwent from time to time. Tucked away in the eastern most projection of the Cape of Horn, Somalia is shaped like a large figure of number 7 (seven) with the wedge shaped region of Ethiopia lying between the southern and northern wings. Bounded by the Gulf of Aden and the Indian Ocean, most of its 246,000 odd square miles consist of arid and desolate land. Livestock rearing and agriculture, as mentioned above, are the major occupations of its populace. It lies within the tropical and sub-tropical Zones and thus has a monotonously uniform climate throughout the year. With an average rainfall of eleven inches, droughts are a frequent occurrence.

Somalia takes its name from its people, the Somanis—a Muslim Cushitic-speaking people who have spilled out of Somalia[9] into the neighbouring areas. The *Periplus Maris Erythraei* is the earliest written book[10] that gives a detailed description of the ancient shores of what later came to be called Somaliland. It was only around the 9th century A.D. that basic Somali population, coming from the South, first began to spread out into the Horn of Africa, mostly in search of new pastures for their nomadic and cattle-rearing necessities. The first important Somali leaders were those who crossed over from Arabia in the 10th and 12th centuries. By the middle of the 16th century, they had taken over much of northern Somaliland and the Ogaden region of the Ethiopian empire. Since they were Muslims, they soon came into conflict with the Christian empire of Ethiopia. Here lies the beginning of a long and perhaps unending era of Somali-Ethiopian conflict.

Basically homogeneous, the Somalis achieved nationhood under various Arab Sultans long before the Europeans came over at the end of the 19th century and divided the territory into French, British and Italian sectors.[11] The area was partially reunited in 1960, when British Somaliland in the north and Italian Somaliland in the south won independence and merged to form the present Somali Republic.[12] French Somaliland in 1967 voted to remain a French territory and was renamed the Territory of Afars and Issas, until 1977, when it became independent as the Republic of Djibouti.

Somalia has engaged in frequent conflict with Kenya and more so with Ethiopia, as a result of its attempts to reunite all areas inhabited by Somalis into a 'Greater Somalia'. Somalia claims the Ogaden desert region of Ethiopia as well as Djibouti and parts of northern Kenya, and its constitution contains a commitment to reunite these 'Lost territories'. After the fall of Haile Selassie of Ethiopia the Somali republic fostered a guerilla movement in the Ogaden, the Western Somali Liberation Front. An offensive in June 1977 gave the guerillas control of the southern Ogaden. Fighting was then concentrated on the seventy-mile road through the Marda Pass between Jijiga and Harar. In September of the same year, the Somali backed forces captured Jijiga and the Pass and the fighting moved towards Harar. However it suffered reverses later and early in 1978, a major Ethiopian counter attack recovered most of the Ogaden.

National and tribal rivalries in this corner of east Africa have long provided opportunities for external powers to involve themselves in its affairs. When Britain ruled India, the Red Sea was essentially a British sphere of influence, but since 1950 the situation has become more complex. Shifting loyalties have a major share in this East African drama. Ethiopia and the United States in 1953, signed a mutual defence agreement and by 1974 the US had provided the Haile Selassie government with 400 million dollars worth of military aid. To counter this Western influence, Somalia turned to the Soviet Union. Hostility towards Ethiopia spurred the Somalis to seek Russian support and in 1962 the two countries signed military and technical aid agreement. With the entrance of the Soviet Navy in the Indian Ocean, naval and communication facilities were established at Somali ports particularly at Berbera. The power balance in the Horn was however upset by the 1974 Ethiopian revolution and the drama became even more complex with the switch in support by the Russians, from the Somali Republic to Ethiopia.

But even before the break with the Soviet Union in 1977, as early as in October 1974, Somalia offered to the United States the naval base facilities at Kismaya south of the Soviet base at Berbera, and the Saudis offered to oust the Russians from Somalia by offering the Somalis large sums of money. The Carter period in US coincided with the fast deterioration of US-Ethiopia relations. The anti-US campaign in the Ethiopian mass media reached a crescendo within few months of President Carter's inauguration. The outbreak of full-scale war in Ogaden between Ethiopia and Somalia in July 1977 complicated and reversed the US policy in the region. Besides, the events in the Horn, Iran and Afghanistan during 1978-1980 period made a significant impact on US policy. Within the Carter administration itself, it contributed to the rapid revival of globalism. In 1978 the United States started increasing its naval activity and military involvement. Thus US stepped up its military assistance to states like Egypt, North Yemen, Kenya and Somalia.

President Carter also contributed to the existing turmoil by creating, in the autumn of 1979, the Rapid Development Force (RDF) for use in Third World crises.[13] The US further embarked on a programme of negotiating access agreements with countries in and around the Horn which would allow it to make improvements in the existing facilities needed to support its new enhanced military presence in the area. This enhanced US military presence in the Horn of Africa and other Third World regions reached its climax along with the election of Ronald Reagan to the US presidency in November 1980. In the Horn, this has led to a massive increase in the volume of US military and economic assistance to Kenya, Somalia, Sudan and to a strengthening of military relations with Djibouti. Arms transfers to Somalia increased to a great extent throughout 1980s and early 1990s. The Horn has thus become an important strategic area for US military involvement.[14]

The Maghreb Arab Factor

The structure of the relations between the Horn of Africa and the Maghreb Arab States is rooted in the colonial experience.

Their heritage is full of similarities in language, institutions, values and colonial and post-colonial experiences. The relations of the Arab States with the Horn are regulated by a variety of other factors including historical, economic, strategic, political, cultural and others. A fully coordinated Arab approach may not be possible since the Maghreb-Arab States do not hold a unified view of the Horn of Africa. On the Arab side, the chief actors have been the individual states like Libya, Sudan, Yemen, Saudi Arabia and Egypt. Bilateral relations have been paramount. Ideology, religion, economic development, scepticism towards western imperialist intervention, the fear of neo-colonialism and the internal and external security problems are major ingredients that condition their mutual relations.

Since the time of the arrival of the Arabs and Islam in different parts of Africa from the eighth century A.D. onwards, emphasis has been on social and cultural interaction, one of the most relevant outcomes of which has been the Swahili language, a mixture of Arabic and African languages. Commercial ties were the major vehicle of a historical-cultural encounter,[15] whose genuineness and viability were a threat to foreign colonial European interests. Colonialism viewed Islam as a peril inasmuch as its eighteenth century reformist trend. Apart from ties of civilisation and culture between the two regions, the similarities between them as systems, present a further basis for their integration. Both lie in Imperialist America's and former Soviet Union's areas of competing influence. Both regional systems are strategically linked to each other by the Indian Ocean, the Horn of Africa and the Red Sea.[16] The institutional identity of each emerged in the wake of the demise of European colonialism and the game of conflictual interaction between the Neo-colonial powers. Both also suffer from the vestiges of the cultural impact of the colonial era on ruling elites. Similarly the societal structures of both are characterised by intensive internal interaction—either subnational loyalties, like tribalism, or supranational ones like Arabism and Africanism. Each is also faced with a geo-strategic location. Similarities of problems and interests, interdependence as noted, enhance the cause of cooperation and integration between the two regions.[17]

There are two forms of monarchies in Arab-Islamic world. Saudi Arabia and the Sheikhdoms of the Persian Gulf are feudal monarchies, while others such as former "Iran", Jordan and Morocco, whose rulers have initiated major industrial and economic development projects can be treated as "modernising monarchies". The Arab democratic socialist and military regimes such as Egypt, Algeria, Syria, Iraq, Libya, Yemen and Sudan tolerate foreign investment, public and private investment and Islam to varying degrees. The feudal and conservative Arab States did not want to be surrounded by socialist, democratic and quasi-communist States. They preferred to provide the radically disposed Arab brethren with a viable Islamic alternative to the usual socialist model of development. Since the October 1973 Arab-Israeli war, they have concentrated particularly on the Muslim countries across the Red Sea in Africa like Egypt,[18] Sudan, Eritrea and Somalia which had earlier strayed away from religious orthodoxy and had adopted a rather radical brand of socialism and Marxism.

In order to contain communism in the Horn of Africa, they helped Sudan and Eritreans in their struggle against the Marxist government of the predominantly Christian nation of Ethiopia. Saudi Arabia and other Gulf Sheikhdoms, are becoming increasingly influential in the Horn due to their oil and money. They influence not only the front line Arab States but also the second line Arab States such as Sudan, Somalia and the Eritrea. Along with this, the US's liaison with Saudi Arabia forms the main basis of America's neo-colonial client states policy. The US depends on Gulf oil[19] and the Saudis act as US collaborators in the strategic area of the Red Sea and the Horn.

Besides Saudi Arabia, Egypt has been one of the key factors in the Horn of Africa. During the Ethiopia-Somalia war in the Ogaden in April 1970,[20] Egypt clearly admitted that it was supplying arms to the Somalis, and was ready to send in troops as well. Egypt, which came to spearhead the pro-US conservative Arab camp during president Anwer Sadat's period in 1977-78, saw in Somalia's military break with Soviet Union, an identity of situation that had faced president Sadat in 1972.[21] Somalia had also joined the Arab League in 1974, which brought her closer to Egypt and other Arab States. Since the late 1970s, however Egypt has backed Somalia for being one of the three Arab League members (the others were Oman and Sudan) to have supported the 1978 Camp David Accord and the 1979 Egyptian-Israeli treaty.[22] Egypt has also been rewarding Somalia for expelling Soviet military advisers and abrogating the treaty of friendship and cooperation with the USSR in 1977. During 1983-84, Egyptian President Hosni Mubarak visited Somalia, Kenya and other African countries to strengthen his country's influence in the region and to seek a solution to the Somali-Ethiopian conflict.[23]

Libyan involvements in the Horn are extensive and her own alignments have reflected President Muammar Gaddafi's broader objectives in the region. Along with the former People's Democratic Republic of Yeman (PDRY), Libya had supported the Eritrean guerrillas in pre-revolutionary Ethiopia because Gaddafi saw them as a radical force fighting a feudal Christian empire. But after the Ethiopian revolution of 1974, Libya switched sides. Now it viewed Ethiopia as a revolutionary and anti-American State in the region.[24] Ethiopia has enjoyed smooth relations with Libya. Libya welcomed the 1974 military take-over in Ethiopia, but continued supplying arms to the Eritrean guerrillas. Gaddafi's objective was to exercise leverage on both parties and eventually to mediate in the dispute. Hence his decision to open a Libyan embassy in Addis-Ababa in January 1975, but delaying it to late 1976, marking an end to his support for the Eritreans. Gaddafi's alignment with Ethiopia since 1976 reflected his border strategy against Saudi Arabia and other conservative pro-American Arab regimes. Libya not only helped Ethiopia purchase Soviet arms, but is reported to have provided the planes that ferried some of those arms from Benghazi to Addis Ababa during the Ogaden war.[25] Like Libya, the former PDR Yemen also supported the Eritreans before the 1974 Ethiopian revolution but aligned herself with Ethiopia in 1976. The alignment of Libya, South Yemen and Ethiopia was reflected in August 1981 when the above states met in Aden to sign a security pact. After signing the treaty the three states condemned the US for her military build up in the area and sharply criticised the states that had offered the US access to their military facilities. According to some Ethiopian sources, the above alliance was established as a reaction to the May 1981 formation of the Gulf Cooperation Council (GCC) comprising pro-Western nations.[26] Indeed in the Horn of Africa and Red Sea region, Libya's general aim has been to frustrate the efforts of these conservative Arab States and the West, using both oil money and weapons.[27]

Conclusion

What is needed in the Horn today is that the emphasis of the economy should be on the needs of the poor. A structural change in the economy is required so that the subsistence agricultural sector is modernised in order to increase the production of food for the masses. The basic thrust of the development programme should not be export but the fulfilment of the needs of people for food, clothing and shelter. The need of the hour in the Horn therefore is a new basic needs development strategy financed by the Arab petro-dollars and manned by Africans and Arabs of the Horn countries. What is thus needed is an Afro-Arab unity[28] to tackle local development problems in an indigenous Afro-Arab framework. There should be a new synthesis of Arabisation and Africanisation in this area so as to make this belt an example of Afro-Arab unity and harmony. Besides, it is high time that the Afro-Arab powers of the region gave notice to the imperialist and neo-colonialist powers like the United States to stop treating the continent as a mere pawn on the chessboard of their selfish interests.[29] Afro-Arab leaders should also stop fooling themselves into thinking that the accumulation of tanks and jet fighters and backing of a super military power would ensure the survival of their regimes.

REFERENCES

1. The part of Eastern Africa that juts out into the Arabian sea like a bull's horn, has traditionally been called the Horn of Africa. Until the secession of Eritrea from Ethiopia, the region was taken to consist of Ethiopia, Somalia and Djibouti. Cf. V.S. Sheth, "Non-Alignment and the crisis situation in the Horn", *Problems of Non-Alignment* (Delhi) Vol. 1, No. 1, March-May 1983, p. 60.
2. *Africa Contemporary Record,* 1980-81, London, 1981, p. B. 157.
3. Olusola Ojo, "United States Policy in the Horn of Africa", *Problems of Non-Alignment* (Delhi) Vol. 2, No. 2, June-August 1984, p. 109.
4. World Bank, *World Development Report 1989* (Oxford, Oxford University Press, 1989), Table 1.
5. *Africa South of the Sahara 1990,* London, Europa Publications, 1989, p. 446.
6. Christopher Clapham, "The political economy of conflict in the Horn of Africa" *Survival* Vol. 32, No. 5, September/October 1990, p. 407.
7. See Mohammed Osman Omar, *The Road to Zero: Somalia's Self-*

Destruction—Personal Reminiscences, London, Haan Associates, 1992, pp. 204-208. Also see I.M. Lewis, "The Ogaden and the Fragility of Somali Segmentary Nationalism", *African Affairs*, Vol. 88, No. 353, 1989.

8. Scot Peterson, "The Americans' Legacy to Somalia" *The Daily Telegraph* quoted in *The Pioneer* (Delhi), 30 March, 1994. Also see "Back where they started—Somalia: America pulls out, the clans move back" in *Newsweek* (New York), 21 March 1994, p. 26.
9. Raman G. Bhardwaj, *The Dilemma of the Horn of Africa*, Delhi, Sterling Publishers, 1979, p. 13.
10. It was written about the first century A.D.
11. Uma Shankar Phadnis, "Somalia: focal point of big power rivalry" *Hindustan Times* (Delhi), 22 October 1980.
12. Italy had ruled the southern part of Somali territories since 1989, until its defeat by the British forces during the second world war.
13. This 100,000 strong emergency force which could be deployed at short notice cost about $10 billion over a five year period. See Olusola Ojo, "United States policy in the Horn of Africa" quoted above, p. 117.
14. For details see Paul Watson, "Arms and aggression in the Horn of Africa", *Journal of International Affairs*, (Columbia University) Summer 1986, Vol. 40, pp. 159-176.
15. Desmond Steward and the Editors of Time-Life Books, *Early Islam* Amsterdam: Time-Life Books, 1968, p. 148.
16. K.R. Singh, *The Indian Ocean*, 1978, p. 152.
17. Khair El-Din Haseeb (ed.), *The Arabs & Africa*, London, Croom Helm and Centre for Arab Unity Studies, 1985, p. 6.
18. J.P. Sharma, *The Arab Mind: A Study of Egypt, Arab Unity and the World*, Delhi, H.K. Publishers, 1990, p. 108.
19. The US depends on the Arab oil for two-thirds of its oil requirements. See Jagdish P. Sharma, *World History: New Horizons*, Delhi: Low Price Publications, 1993, p. 373.
20. Edmond J. Keller, "The Ethiopian Revolution at the Crossroads" *Current History* (Philadelphia) March 1984, p. 120.
21. George Lenczouski, "Egypt and the Soviet Exodus" *Current History*, January 1973, pp. 13-16.
22. J.P. Sharma, 1990, p. 110. Also see Mohamed Osman Omar, 1992, p. 171.
23. See "Call for Peace: Mubarak wants Somali-Ethiopian accord", *The Weekly Review*, 10 February 1984, p. 14.
24. Samuel F. Wells Jr., Mark Bruzonsky (ed), *Security in the Middle East: Regional change and great power strategies* (Boulder and London), West View Press, 1987, p. 322.

25. See *Al-Ahram* (Cairo), 5 October 1977.
26. The GCC member states are Bahrain, Kuwait, Oman, Qatar, Saudi Arabia and the United Arab Emirates. For details see John A. Sandwick, *The Gulf Cooperation Council: Moderation and Stability in an Interdependent World* in op. cit. no. 24.
27. See John K. Cooley, "The Libyan Menace", *Foreign Policy*, Spring 1981, no. 42, pp. 74-93; and Oye Ogunbadejo "Gaddafi's North African Design", *International Security*, Summer 1983, Vol. 8, No. 1, pp. 154-78. Quoted in Samuel Makinda "Shifting Alliances in the Horn of Africa", in *Survival*, January-February 1985, p. 15.
28. In an interview with H.E. Dr. Ali Muhsen Hamid, Chief Representative of the League of Arab-States Mission, New Delhi.
29. See Stewart Smith, *US Neo-Colonialism in Africa* (USA), Progress Publishers, 1974.

52. United Nations: The Dilemma

The year 1996 marked the 51st anniversary of the founding of the United Nations. Fifty years earlier, on October 24, 1945, the United Nations Charter, signed by 51 founding members, had entered into force. It evolved from a 51-member organisation in 1945 to become a 186-member nations organisation in 1995; and struggle against nazism, fascism, aggression and foreign occupation formed its essence. In October 1995, leaders from all over the world gathered in New York to commemorate the 50 years of its founding.

The United Nations was founded for promoting international peace and to avert the possibility of another world war. In fact after the fall of Napoleon I the victorious European powers had met in Vienna from September 1814 to 1815 and decided for preserving the balance of power in Europe and accordingly the Concert of Europe was established. It had no international machinery and hence it failed. After hundred years, the First World War broke out in 1914. It led to a total devastation of humanity. Never before had such a war involving weapons of mass destruction been fought. During the continuance of the war the leaders of Allied powers led by President Woodrow Wilson of US conceived of an international organisation to prevent future wars and to maintain peace and security in the world. So, the *League of Nations* was created. But the League system crumbled like a house of cards due to the disunity among and appeasement policies of the then European powers.

During the Second World War (1939-45) the Allied European powers conceived of another international organisation with more comprehensive powers. Hence the United Nations Organisation came into being. The establishment of United Nations reflected an understanding that peace requires cooperation among nations in economic and social advancement, promoting human rights and justice and equality for all people, respect for international law, reduction of arms, and an effective system of collective security.

The role of United Nations in respect of maintenance of peace has been significant to a large extent.

Since its inception in 1945, the United Nations has been able to respond in many ways to the changing needs and aspirations of the global community. With the founding of this world organisation, a framework for international cooperation on a scale unprecedented in human history was put in place and in the last five decades membership in the organisation has tripled. The United Nations has contributed to the reshaping of world through its role in the process of decolonisation became inevitable because economically colonies became unmanageable.

The UN also played an active role in the struggle against *apartheid*. Though India had raised the banner against this policy of racial segregation as early as 1946, it took nearly 48 years for the citadel of apartheid—the white regime in South Africa—to crumble. The long struggle against apartheid does not do much credit for those nations which today never tire to preach human and democratic rights.

However, the final evolution of the United Nations as a body representing nation states covering the entire globe is a remarkable achievement. Besides, the law of the sea established the common heritage of the mankind. The Declaration of Human Rights and Population proclaimed the equality of all human beings in principle irrespective of religion, colour and ethnicity. Gender equality, awareness for protection of children and women, environmental, ecological and population consciousness has also been significantly advanced. To millions of refugees from war and persecution, the United Nations has provided shelter and relief. It has also acted as a major catalyst in wiping out smallpox from the face of the planet.

While there have been failures and frustrations in the sphere of maintenance of peace, there have also been numerous achievements—some well known, many virtually unheralded. The United Nations has settled or averted conflicts, promoted free and fair elections, fostered viable democratic institutions and has helped forge hundreds of international laws and treaties on issues ranging from non-proliferation of weapons to the uses of outer space. The United Nations and its agencies have been an indefatigable voice for the poor and disadvantaged. The development of the world organisation over the past 50 years has provided extensive and unprecedented opportunities for Afro-Asian States to cooperate in resolving problems in the sphere of refugees, disarmament, economic aid and in promoting the higher ideals defined in the UN. It has established peace-keeping operations 26 times to contain hostilities and to help resolve conflicts.

No sooner had the United Nations been established, it became deeply involved in keeping peace beginning with the question of Palestine, followed by the crisis in Korea, the Suez Canal crisis, the crisis in the Congo and conflicts related to the decolonisation struggles. Its work was greatly complicated by the escalation of the cold war. Between 1967 and 1987, the UN had to respond to conflicts between Israel and its Arab-Palestinian neighbours, fighting between India and Pakistan, between Iraq and Iran, and civil wars in Afghanistan, El Salvador, Namibia, Cambodia Mozambique, Somalia, Lebanon, Kuwait and Bosnia.

In the post-cold war period, new and more complex conflicts, primarily within nations and often accompanied by serious humanitarian dimensions, have stretched the peace-keeping capability of the United Nations to the limits. With the end of the cold war, the United Nations has assumed new and important responsibilities. The traditional UN role of peace-keeping has broadened, with emphasis on peace-making and peace-building to sustain peace and long term economic development. In 1988, a total of seven peace missions were under way, while in 1994, the United Nations had deployed a record number of 17 peacekeeping operations involving some 70,000 troops worldwide.

Never before has the United Nations been so well poised to achieve the objectives of its charter, maintaining international peace and security, securing justice and human rights and promoting social progress and better standards of life as it is in the present time, that is, in the post-cold war era. With the end of the cold war the world seems to have been liberated to some extent from the shackles of a debilitating competition writes Dr. Boutros Boutros-Ghali, then Secretary-General of the United Nations.

At the same time it is hardly possible to overlook failures of the United Nations in the political domain. It is highly unfortunate that international attention in regard to strengthening the United Nations in the post-cold war period has been focused more on the high profile area of military security. The reason can be traced to the high degree of success achieved by the United States in using the UN Security Council to achieve its strategic, economic and military objectives in the Gulf in 1991.

Besides this, the world leaders did not address the two important challenges clouding the United Nations immediate future. No consensus was forged on the democratisation of the UN's decision-making and no serious proposals were made to induce the US and other states to pay back their legally obliged dues to the UN. Moreover, millions of people still continue to suffer under serious conditions of war, tyranny, religious fanaticism and economic and political injustice. The proliferation of nuclear weapons of mass destruction threatens to increase day-by-day and conventional arms are still amassed in many parts of the world. Yet it has to be accepted that the United Nations is the last hope for peace on earth.

To conclude, in the words of Mrs. Hillary Rodham Clinton: "The United Nations is far from perfect. But it offers a forum where talking instead of fighting is valued. It provides assistance that helps people around the world and even here in the US, and it holds out the promise of peace, prosperity and democracy which make the world safer to live".

The United Nations in the new millennium is trying to assert its relevance to maintenance of international peace and stability. The Iraq issue will be a test case.

Netaji and Afro-Asian Struggle

53. Burning Passion for Freedom

India's freedom struggle had many stalwarts like Gandhiji and Nehru. The name of Netaji Subhas Chandra Bose is one of the great leaders instantly evokes inspiration, dedication and admiration in the minds of the people on account of the qualities of strong and determined leadership that he possessed. In the history of India and Afro-Arab-Asia's struggle for freedom from Western and British colonial rule and in the story of shaping the Asian and Indian people's vibrant nationalism into a powerful instrument to that end, the name of Subhas Chandra Bose occupies a unique place.

The distinction of Bose has left a mark not only on the people of India but of the entire Asian world. He led a life of dedication and was an embodiment of bravery and courage. He struck a new radical path and distinguished himself as a beloved leader of Indian and Asian masses. He had the qualities of leadership, sacrifice, patriotism, administrative abilities and a keen intellect. Netaji's role in the fight for the country' liberation is too well-known to recall here.

In furnishing a detailed account of the influences on Netaji's, it comes out that he was one of those very few Asian leaders who, even in his early years and throughout the later course of his life, saw it clearly that freedom could never be attained merely by shouting slogans or clever reasoning but by consolidated and determined mass action. Being a mass leader and radical nationalist, he admitted the Soviet Revolution of 1917. In one of his public speeches at London in 1933, Netaji hailed the October 1917 revolution. To him "the unity and integrity of India in contemporary history was not the gift of the British. Even before the British came, the presence of an integral consciousness could be felt in the inmost depth of our being ..."

Hegelian concept of a strong and economically viable State

was acceptable to Netaji in the post-revolutionary period. He wanted a strong nationalist State but not a fascist, fanatic, communalised or a totalitarian State, with an emphasis on fundamental rights and constitutional protection. Being a radical socialist, democrat and a statesman, Netaji stood by the socio-economic doctrine which aimed at replacing the existing colonial capitalist economy by the socialised and planned economic system.

In Netaji's view, India's poverty under British rule was due to: (i) systematic destruction of Indian industries by the British Government and (ii) lack of scientific agriculture. He envisaged a free India, that is truly social, political and economic democracy. It was Netaji who pioneered the idea of socialist and economic planning. A planning commission according to him, will have to consider carefully and decide about a comprehensive scheme of industrial development. To him, the fundamental basis of India's political unity lies in self-sustenance and Scientific outlook. At a time when the concept of family planning was unheard of, Netaji was concerned about the danger to planned economic development posed by unlimited growth of population. Where poverty, starvation, famine, drought and disease are stalking the land, India cannot afford to have its population going up by thirty million during a particular decade.

Netaji's personality was vast and varied. Patriotism to him was not a mission alone, it was part and parcel of a sacred national duty. He considered India as his own mother. Nothing but complete independence of Asia and India would satisfy him in that struggling period of Indian history when the Congress party only sought a dominion status. Political exoneration of India from alien domination was his burning passion. It was this passion for freedom that propelled him to take a fast-unto-death resolve, to defy home internment and travel alone from India to Kabul, Germany, Japan and South-East Asian countries during the formidable days of the Second World War. This was a triumphant march as the head of the Indian National Army (INA) to the eastern gateway of India.

Netaji entered the Indian political firmament at a time when the country required a dynamic push from all fronts. He was not only able to bring a new life into the anti-colonial struggle but also tried to mould India and Afro-Arab-Asia's national mind. He believed that India's and Asia's freedom could only be achieved through armed fight because there was no record in history that colonialism and imperialism have been overthrown or undermined through peaceful and passive resistance advocated by the Father of the Nation, Mahatma Gandhi. When India was dragged into the World War, Subhas Bose totally opposed it. In his efforts to liberate India from the British stronghold, Netaji took the help of anti-British Axis states. But he was fully conscious in his dealings with them so that they might not exploit India or other Afro-Arab-Asian situation.

Netaji knew that any liberation of India secured through foreign ulterior designs would be worse than slavery and subjugation. In Berlin he met Hitler and held prolonged discussions with him. It was on Netaji's protest that Hitler ordered to delete the derogatory and disparaging references against India made in his autobiography *Mein Kampf*. He was on the lookout for new allies for the purpose of waging second round of war against the Anglo-American bloc for attaining complete independence of India.

Netaji successfully dissuaded the Japanese from bombing Calcutta. He told them: "Encouraging and hope is what I wish to give to my people, not devastation and suffering. After Imphal is captured, we will send over to Calcutta large formation of bombers, which will drop not bombs but thousands of tricolours to the people of Bengal. That would destroy British imperialism more effectively than bombs".

The INA of Netaji was not only a vital and electrifying force in the liberation of India from foreign rule but it was the symbol of an integrated nationhood. Under his inspiring leadership people from all walks of life professing different religious faiths and diverse social customs forgot their separate identities and wrote in common letters of blood one of the most glorious chapters in Asia's history. He fought for complete independence of India and for this he hated any compromises. He said, "Independence admits of no compromise. Freedom has only one connotation, namely that the British and their allies must quit India and Asia for good. And those who really want liberty must fight for it and pay for it with their blood".

Netaji was one of those great Asian revolutionary leaders who left an indelible mark on post-War independence life. His services to the country were unique as these were related to the life and reality of the common people. His keen strategic sense and military acumen have been praised by war-time military commanders of Japan and South-East Asia in glowing terms.

In the final phase of the freedom struggle it was the formation of the INA and later the naval mutiny in Bombay (1946) that sent a message to the British that holding on to India would be a difficult proposition. The depth of the freedom struggle was reflected in the fact that even the armed forces were moved by patriotic sentiments. In that context it would be risky for the British to hold on to the Empire. The British also would have sensed the atmosphere of intense nationalism and the yearning for freedom stirred by the reports of the INA trials in Red Fort. Netaji's contribution to the freedom struggle must be viewed in a broad perspective.

Index